Dog Economics

Archaeologists, anthropologists, and evolutionary biologists study the origins of our relationship with dogs and how it has evolved over time. Sociologists and legal scholars study the roles of dogs in the modern family. Veterinarian researchers address the relationship in the context of professional practice, yet economists have produced scant scholarship on the relationship between humans and dogs. *Dog Economics* applies economic concepts to relationships between people and dogs to inform our understanding of their domestication. It interprets their contemporary role as both property and family members and explores factors that affect the demand for dogs as well as market failures in the American puppy market. Offering economic perspectives on our varied relationships with dogs, this book assesses mortality risks and addresses end-of-life issues that commonly arise. It develops a framework for classifying canine occupations, considers the impact of pet insurance on euthanasia, and assesses the social value of guide dogs.

David L. Weimer is Fellow of the National Academy of Public Administration. His contributions to public policy scholarship have been widely recognized as he has received the Policy Field Distinguished Contribution Award from the Association for Public Policy Analysis and Management and the Outstanding Achievement Award from the Society for Benefit-Cost Analysis.

Aidan R. Vining is Emeritus CNABS Professor of Business and Government Relations, Simon Fraser University. He is a winner of the John Vanderkamp Prize (Canadian Economics Association) and the J. E. Hodgetts Award (Institute of Public Administration of Canada). He has published widely. His family fosters candidate dogs for guide training.

Dog Economics

Perspectives on Our Canine Relationships

DAVID L. WEIMER
University of Wisconsin–Madison

AIDAN R. VINING
Simon Fraser University

Shaftesbury Road, Cambridge CB2 8EA, United Kingdom

One Liberty Plaza, 20th Floor, New York, NY 10006, USA

477 Williamstown Road, Port Melbourne, VIC 3207, Australia

314–321, 3rd Floor, Plot 3, Splendor Forum, Jasola District Centre,
New Delhi – 110025, India

103 Penang Road, #05–06/07, Visioncrest Commercial, Singapore 238467

Cambridge University Press is part of Cambridge University Press & Assessment,
a department of the University of Cambridge.

We share the University's mission to contribute to society through the pursuit of
education, learning and research at the highest international levels of excellence.

www.cambridge.org
Information on this title: www.cambridge.org/9781009445559

DOI: 10.1017/9781009445504

© David L. Weimer and Aidan R. Vining 2024

First published 2024

A catalogue record for this publication is available from the British Library

Library of Congress Cataloging-in-Publication Data
NAMES: Weimer, David L., author. | Vining, Aidan R., author.
TITLE: Dog economics : perspectives on our canine relationships / David L.
Weimer, University of Wisconsin–Madison, Aidan R. Vining, Simon Fraser
University.
DESCRIPTION: Cambridge, United Kingdom ; New York, NY : Cambridge
University Press, 2024. | Includes bibliographical references and index.
IDENTIFIERS: LCCN 2023031358 | ISBN 9781009445559 (hardback) |
ISBN 9781009445535 (paperback) | ISBN 9781009445504 (ebook)
SUBJECTS: LCSH: Dogs – Economic aspects. | Dogs – Social aspects. |
Economics – Psychological aspects. | Dog owners. | Human-animal
relationships – Economic aspects.
CLASSIFICATION: LCC SF426.2 .W34 2024 | DDC 636.7–dc23/eng/20231026
LC record available at https://lccn.loc.gov/2023031358

ISBN 978-1-009-44555-9 Hardback
ISBN 978-1-009-44553-5 Paperback

To all the dogs who enrich our lives and to all the humans who do their best for them.

Clockwise from top left: Ming, Taz, Luis and Tilly

Contents

Figures

Tables

Preface

We like dogs. One of your authors grew up in a family with a dog but then went dogless until the COVID pandemic. Your other author has had many dogs in his family over the years, usually a couple of permanent residents as well as many fostered dogs, both in preparation for training as guide or assistance dogs and as rescues from unfortunate circumstances. We rarely pass up an opportunity to pet (or spoil) someone else's dog.

For nearly forty years, we have collaborated on public policy scholarship and continue to do so. Most of this work involves applying economic concepts to help inform policy analysis or to address emerging issues in organizational design. We invariably find economic concepts to be useful in helping to frame public policy issues and in predicting the consequences of alternative policies. These concepts are almost always valuable in getting started though rarely sufficient for completing public policy analyses. We aspire to bring this same approach to dogonomics: that is, to showing how economic perspectives help us better understand the place of dogs in contemporary American society. Of course, economics does not provide anything like the full story. Consequently, although we set ourselves the task of applying economic concepts throughout the book, we try to take full advantage of the research done by numerous other disciplines and perspectives on all aspects of interactions between our species.

The story of the origin of this book begins with an aside from an economist at the Food and Drug Administration who was responsible for organizing a cost–benefit analysis to support new rules that sought to make pet food safer. He mentioned to one of us that although estimates of the value of a (human) statistical life are widely available to monetize changes in human mortality risk, no comparable value was then available for dogs. One of your authors eventually organized a team of former students to estimate the value of statistical life for pet dogs using a type of survey experiment developed by environmental economists called contingent valuation. Not only was the project very enjoyable for the team, but, at least by academic standards, the resulting publication attracted considerable public attention. Chad Zimmerman also thought the economics of dogs might attract an audience. He suggested that we write a book about it. As we had not previously thought of writing such a book, this is that rare case for which the assertion that "this book would not have been written without you" is literally true. Thank you, Chad.

Our aim was to write this book to be accessible to noneconomists, so we sought to explain economic concepts as clearly as possible. We use only a small number of straightforward diagrams to convey concepts, and we present empirical results without dragging readers through complicated statistical analyses. Anyone who has taken an introductory course in economics should find all the material immediately accessible. The glossary of key terms should enable those readers without prior exposure to economics also to navigate through with only occasional detours. Thus, readers who are fond of dogs should find this book accessible, as well as interesting.

We also see some potential use of this book for instructional purposes. About half of U.S. households now have dogs. If economists are like the general population, probably an heroic assumption, then perhaps half of the instructors of introductory and intermediate economics courses own dogs. They and many of their students would find this to be a fun supplementary text – dogs are more interesting than widgets! We also hope that economists with dogs might decide that it would be both useful and fun to contribute to the field of dogonomics.

Our application of economics to understanding the human–dog relationship draws on research from biologists, psychologists, legal scholars, philosophers, historians, and veterinary medicine researchers from around the world, but especially in the United States, United Kingdom, Australia, and Canada. We hope that scholars who work in these areas will find our references helpful for putting their own work in broader context. We think that this book would be especially interesting and useful for veterinary students and others whose research involves dogs.

A number of people have contributed to this project in various ways. Carol Silva, Hank Jenkins-Smith, Deven Carlson, Simon Haeder, and

Joseph Ripberger collaborated on the research project to estimate the value of statistical dog life that served as what turned out to be the initial step toward this book. Levi Bankston helped us identify relevant surveys. We also thank W. Kip Viscusi, Glenn Blomquist, Mariel Barnes, Stéphane Lavertu, Melanie Manion, Jerry Mitchell, and Ulrike Radermacher for their comments and encouragement. Robert Dreesen was encouraging and suggested a valuable expansion. Sable Gravesandy, Claire Sissen and Swati Kumari helped move the project smoothly to publication. As always, we bear responsibility for any errors and all interpretations in this book.

Dogonomics

Homo Economicus versus Canem Amans

Suddenly Angus knew what he must do. The decision was made without any real thought, without any consideration of counter-arguments, or even practicalities. And Angus rationalized this to himself, thinking that if everybody thought too much about whether or not to have a dog, then nobody would ever have one. There were good reasons to have a dog, but there were so many equally good reasons not to have one, and if people ever engaged in any calculation of benefit and convenience there would be no place for dogs in our lives. But that was not the way it was; people took on dogs out of love, without questioning whether it was the right time or the right place for love. Love simply took over and prompted one to act there and then. That was how dogs were taken into our lives; in that spirit of spontaneous affection, and not because we had considered and approved their case. Their case was messy and inconvenient and demanding and yet we did it; we took on dogs, as Angus now did with this puppy on its lead and its two unrealistic young owners.

– Alexander McCall Smith, *The Peppermint Tea Chronicles*
(New York: Anchor Books, 2019), p. 294.

Angus, whose dog Cyril sports a gold tooth and dreams of biting ankles, recognizes the affection and attachment the two boys already have for the puppy that they have been hiding from their parents. His musing raises the big question of why people choose to own dogs despite the substantial costs of doing so.[1] The costs of owning dogs accrue directly as expenditures for food and necessary veterinary care, but also in terms of what economists

---

[1] Throughout this book, we use the terminology of ownership, which is consistent with both law and economic convention. We recognize, however, that some people object to the idea of owning another sentient being, an objection that we address in Chapter 6.

call *opportunity costs*.[2] These opportunity costs include such things as the value of time spent providing care and the loss of flexibility in schedules, travel, where one can live, and even romantic partners. Angus, as do many of us, sees this love of dogs as swamping consideration of these costs.

What would economists make of Angus's calculus? Before answering this question, we note that two schools of economics, once antagonistic but now fairly well integrated, dominate contemporary economics. *Neoclassical economics* assumes individual rationality in the sense that people make the best possible choices to promote their own interests. Neoclassical economics considers behavior to be rational if it promotes the wellbeing of the individual. It is more precisely labeled instrumental rationality in that it deals only with the means people follow and not the ends they seek. Neoclassical economics is agnostic about the rationality of ends, requiring only that they be based on *coherent preferences*.

Behavioral economics, however, recognizes that people sometimes make decisions that neoclassicists would simply consider to be mistakes. Rather than assuming perfect rationality, behavioral economists consider a range of ways that people fail to make value-maximizing decisions. Behavioral economics generally considers failures of instrumental rationality but also considers situations in which preferences may not be coherent. For purposes of understanding peoples' relationships with dogs, neoclassical economics requires a fully rational assessment of costs and benefits in decisions about dog ownership while behavioral economics allows for decisions made with misperceptions of these costs and benefits.

Many neoclassical economists might respond to Angus by explaining the choice to adopt or keep a dog as being based on a rational calculation in which the anticipated benefits of doing so, somehow, exceed the costs. Thus, rather than labeling these benefits as love, they would frame them in terms of the various services that dogs provide, such as companionship or protection. In contrast, rather than assuming perfect rationality, behavioral economists would consider a range of ways that people fail to make value-maximizing decisions about dog ownership. For example, in adoption decisions, people may well underestimate the costs and risks of owning a dog, overestimate the benefits of ownership, or simply be distracted by the ancillary cuteness of puppies. An important contribution to the theory of behavioral economics sees ancillary factors, such as cuteness during puppyhood, as influencing decisions (adopting) but not relevant to the utility (satisfaction) that will actually be realized (living

---

[2] The Glossary provides definitions or explanations of italicized economic terms.

with the adult dog).[3] Once we have dogs, a behavioral consequence – the *endowment effect* – may well stop us from rationally assessing the benefits and costs of continued ownership: once one has a dog, one perceives costs and benefits of ownership differently than one would before one has the dog. Despite their other differences, however, both neo-classicists and behaviorists would probably relegate love to the error term in their models along with any unmeasured or putatively unmeasurable services provided by dogs. That is, if one were to statistically model the decision to own a dog as a function of observable costs and benefits for individuals, there would be some errors attributable to the exclusion of any relevant cost or benefit from the model. As economists do not have a way of measuring love, its effect would be realized as error. In other words, as Tina Turner sang, "What's love got to do with it."

In this book, we consider, and assess as best we can, how much of human behaviors involving dogs can be explained by economic theory writ large. That is, we seek to determine how much of our love for dogs can be understood as economically rational behavior, whether neoclassically perfect or behaviorally imperfect. So, we characterize decisions about dogs as choices involving trade-offs as in most other choices we make in our lives. We take the liberty of calling this project dogonomics.

One might ask why we focus particularly on the relationship between people and dogs? Well, for a start, the large scale of the market for pet-related goods and services means it is economically important, in terms of expenditures of both money and time.[4] In 2021, U.S. consumers spent $123.6 billion on pet products. The approximately half of households that own dogs are responsible for much of this spending. Dogs are the most frequently kept pet. Some people face substantial upfront costs when they purchase dogs from breeders. In terms of ongoing expenditures, annual averages for dogs in the United States include $458 for surgical veterinary visits, $242 for routine veterinary visits, $287 for food, $81 for food treats, $228 for kennel boarding, $81 for vitamins, $47 for grooming aids, and $56 for toys for a total of $1,480.[5] Beyond this recurring spending, some dog caregivers are willing to make exceptionally

---

[3] On ancillary factors, see B. Douglas Bernheim and Antonio Rangel. "Toward Choice-Theoretic Foundations for Behavioral Welfare Economics." *American Economic Review* 97, no. 2 (2007): 464–470.

[4] Andrew Van Dam and Alyssa Fowers. "Who Spends the Most Time (and Money) on Pets?" Data Department, *Washington Post*, December 30 (2022).

[5] 2021–2022 APPA National Pet Owners Survey as reported by the APPA. www .americanpetproducts.org/press_industrytrends.asp. The comparable total amount for cats is $902. Accessed November 4, 2022.

large expenditures for veterinary care for very ill or injured dogs.[6] In addition to direct expenditures, many owners now purchase insurance to reduce the risk of having to pay for costly veterinary services. Beyond costs borne directly by dog owners, municipalities also bear costs, usually passing along the costs of licensing to owners through fees but increasingly passing along the costs of dog parks to taxpayers.[7] Further, the care and feeding of dogs increases our carbon footprint.[8] Thus, dog ownership, and related activities, such as the training of guide and therapy dogs, involve considerable economic activity.

In modern societies, morality and law prohibit the commodification of children or parents or other persons in a dependent position. However, dogs (and we probably must admit cats)[9] often have an unusual dual status as both commodities and what can best be described as family members.[10] That is, many people make economic decisions about obtaining and owning dogs as if they were members of the family. Indeed, some experimental evidence suggests that, similar to parental spending on children, spending on pets makes people happier than spending on themselves.[11] However, our canine household members can be legally bought, sold, and disposed of subject to only minimal restrictions.[12] The economics of the family has been a vibrant area of economic and policy scholarship. This field encompasses many important subjects, such as the allocation of time by parents and the degree of *utility* interdependence

[6] For example, a survey experiment found that, on average people would be willing to pay over $4 thousand for life-saving surgery for their dog, with some willing to pay much larger amounts. Colleen P. Kirk, "Dogs Have Masters, Cats Have Staff: Consumers' Psychological Ownership and Their Economic Valuation of Pets." *Journal of Business Research* 99, June (2019): 306–318.

[7] Edwin Gómez and Ron Malega. "Dog Park Use: Perceived Benefits, Park Proximity, and Individual and Neighborhood Effects." *Journal of Leisure Research* 51, no. 3 (2020): 287–307.

[8] Nives Dolsak and Aseem Prakash. "Dogs Are Humans' Best Friends: Could We Reduce Their Carbon Footprint?" *Forbes*, April 9, 2023.

[9] For an engaging discussion of both cats and dogs as more than commodities, see David Grimm. *Citizen Canine: Our Evolving Relationship with Cats and Dogs* (New York, NY: PublicAffairs, 2014).

[10] On the factors that have led an increasingly high percentage of U.S. families viewing pets as family members, see Anrea Laurent-Simpson. *Just Like Family: How Companion Animals Joined the Household* (New York, NY: New York University Press, 2021).

[11] Michael W. White, Nazia Khan, Jennifer S. Deren, Jessica J. Sim, and Elizabeth A. Majka. "Give a Dog a Bone: Spending Money on Pets Promotes Happiness." *Journal of Positive Psychology* 17, no. 4 (2022): 589–595.

[12] One of our teachers in graduate school, a neoclassical economist with missionary zeal, finally touched off a revolt in our policy analysis course when he proposed modeling children as consumer durables without allowable disposal.

among family members.[13] How does the role of dogs within the family fit within the economic models of the family? Or does it require some other, or at least expanded, framework? The perspective we present in this book is that, regardless of whether dog owners embrace their dogs as members of the family, almost all owners would consider them to be unlike any other commodity.

Beyond their economic significance and unique status as both commodity and family member, a growing body of research documents the impacts of dogs on human health. These impacts, collectively referred to as zooeyia, include a range of health benefits and health risks that dogs bestow on their owners. They give dogs' relevance to public health.

Zooeyiatic impacts manifest through a variety of mechanisms.[14] Petting and grooming dogs provides tactile simulation, increasingly seen as important for human wellbeing,[15] Dogs' demands for walks almost certainly increase the frequency and quality of their owners' outdoor exercise. Dogs out and about on walks and runs often attract the attention of other dog owners or people who would like to be dog owners. As we are prone to do so, we can elevate this to a social science insight by noting that walking a dog may increase the owner's stock of social capital by prompting contact with neighbors and fellow dog park users that would otherwise not occur. The evidence suggests that the companionship provided by dogs may also have psychological benefits beyond the enjoyment of shared time; contact with dogs may even contribute to the development of the immune system in the children of their owners. Of course, there may also be health risks to being around dogs, such as bites,[16] allergic reactions, injuries from rambunctious dogs pulling on their leash, and the negative psychological effects on owners of dogs suffering injuries, illnesses, or death.

Aside from scholarly motives for seeking to understand the economics of owning dogs, we have a personal motivation: we are quite fond of

[13] Gary S. Becker. "On the Relevance of the New Economics of the Family." *American Economic Review* 64, no. 2 (1974): 317–319.

[14] Kate Hodgson, Luisa Barton, Marcia Darling, Viola Antao, Florence A. Kim, and Alan Monavvari. "Pets' Impact on Your Patients' Health: Leveraging Benefits and Mitigating Risk." *Journal of the American Board of Family Medicine* 28, no. 4 (2015): 526–534.

[15] Nancy R. Gee, Kerri E. Rodriguez, Aubrey H. Fine, and Janet P. Trammell. "Dogs Supporting Human Health and Well-Being: A Biopsychosocial Approach." *Frontiers in Veterinary Science* 8, March (2021): 1–11.

[16] The Insurance Information Institute estimates that in 2021 U.S. insurers paid out $882 million in damage claims from dog bites. www.iii.org/article/spotlight-on-dog-bite-liability. Accessed November 3, 2022.

dogs. We are fond of our current dogs and have happy memories of our departed dogs that we brought into our families (as well as those that managed to wheedle their way in).[17] We are also sympathetic to most of the dogs we encounter on the street or in dog parks. We even sometimes fall victim to click bait that is dog-themed. Thus, beyond the professorial satisfaction of contributing to what we hope will be considered scholarship, we enjoy studying the essential ingredient of dogonomics – dogs!

Our effort to develop the field of dogonomics gives us considerable leeway as to the choice of topics. We selected six topics that we think will be substantively interesting to dog owners, intellectually interesting to applied economists, pedagogically valuable for economics students, and perhaps useful for policy makers. We do not seek to break new theoretical ground, but rather to explore how some familiar, and some less familiar, economic models help us understand the relationship between humans and dogs. We write for a general audience, so we seek to explain economic concepts clearly and avoid unnecessary jargon. As public policy researchers, we find economic theories and concepts to be very useful, indeed crucial, to our understanding of policy-relevant problems. However, in view of the novelty of dogonomics, we approach our topics with a somewhat open mind about the usefulness of economic theory for understanding the relationship between people and dogs.

Most broadly, we seek to use economic concepts to place the role of dogs as human companions and coproducers of goods and services in a larger social, and indeed cultural, context. To do so we draw on the most fundamental microeconomic idea, the market for dogs, which involves interesting heterogeneity in both supply and demand. The dog market – more accurately the various markets for dogs – has myriad impacts that spill over to the rest of society, or what economists refer to as external effects. We also seek to place the human–dog interaction in an even broader context of the economics of the evolution of both species in geologic time and individual relationships in dog-life time. This requires exploring some topics that many readers may not realize now fall within the imperialistic grasp of economists, such as the evolution of species (the domain of evolutionary biologists) and the meaning of property and personhood (the domain of philosophers, ethicists, and legal scholars).

---

[17] In the interests of full disclosure, Ming (a parti standard poodle) resides with the family of one of your authors. Tazzy (Labrador retriever who produces puppies to be candidate guide dogs), Matilda (a mini dachshund) and Luis (a Palm Desert rescue of some kind) resides with the other author's family.

We note three limitations inherent in our current pursuit of dogonomics. First, economics considers only human behavior and human welfare. This speciesism is unproblematic for our primary task of understanding how people interact with dogs. However, it has relevance for how we assess the welfare of alternative public policies affecting dogs. The normative contribution of economics is its protocols for assessing the relative efficiency of alternative policies in terms of their net benefit, the difference between their aggregate benefits and costs to people. The welfare of dogs only comes into play in the assessment of economic efficiency through the values people place on it. Contributions to humane societies clearly show a willingness of people to sacrifice consumption of goods for better treatment of animals. However, these contributions grossly underestimate the total value people place on better treatment because of the incentive to "free ride" on the contributions of others.

Maximizing economic efficiency does not necessarily correspond to the utilitarian principle of promoting the greatest happiness for the greatest number of people, not just because it ignores the distribution of consumption, but also because other values beyond consumption may be relevant to choosing good public policies. So, for example, some people may perversely get pleasure from treating dogs cruelly, but a large majority of people now recognize dogs as sentient beings deserving of respect. Thus, even without embracing the argument that the utilitarian principle requires us to consider the happiness of dogs in all our decisions,[18] most people now see preventing cruelty to dogs as good public policy. Thus, as is generally the case, good policy analysis requires the consideration of a full range of values, usually including economic efficiency, but rarely limited to it.[19]

Second, we focus almost exclusively on U.S. public policies relevant to the welfare of dogs. We do so not because of a lack of policy-relevant research from other countries – much relevant research originates in the United Kingdom, Australia, and many other countries. We also do not believe that "American exceptionalism" requires us to consider the United States as a special case. Rather, we believe that understanding

---

[18] The seminal argument for including animals in application of the utilitarian principle, is Peter Singer. *Animal Liberation* (New York, NY: Avon Books, 1975). For an overview of competing philosophical frameworks for considering the welfare of animals, see Matthew Calarco. *Thinking Through Animals: Identity, Difference, Indistinction* (Stanford, CA: Stanford University Press, 2015).

[19] David L. Weimer and Aidan R. Vining. *Policy Analysis: Concepts and Practice*, 6th ed. (New York, NY: Routledge, 2017).

public policy requires familiarity with the formal and informal organizations that shape it.

Third, we do plead guilty to "dog exceptionalism," a belief that the human relationship with dogs is qualitatively different than the human relationship with other animals. As the first domesticated animal, they have the longest shared history with humans. In addition to being the most common American pet, they perform both ancient functions, like guarding and herding, and contemporary ones, like assisting the disabled. Certainly, people can establish emotional bonds with other animals, most often cats and horses. However, the integration of these animals into our contemporary lives falls short of that of our dogs. Note that our dog exceptionalism differs from claims of exceptional intelligence, so-called canine exceptionalism, but rather on their ubiquitous presence in the lives of so many Americans. We would welcome economic interpretation of human relationships with other animals – catonomics anyone?

As biologists, archaeologists, and anthropologists are teaching us, people and dogs share a long history. A convergence of evidence from the Bonn-Oberkassel site in Germany shows domestication occurred at least 14 thousand years ago, and based on older fossil evidence, perhaps longer than 30 thousand years ago.[20] Explanations for domestication vary, ranging from the role of dogs as hunting partners and camp guards to dogs as a reserve food source.

Chapter 2 overviews the wide-ranging scientific research on the origins of the domestication of dogs and considers the extent to which economic perspectives, specifically classical and evolutionary game theories, contribute to an understanding of domestication as mutualistic symbiosis. In this context, economics becomes relevant through the lenses of an interspecies division of labor.[21] A hypothesis of mutual symbiosis inevitably raises a more provocative question: To what extent did dogs domesticate us? Moving beyond the initiation of domestication, we explore the idea that the economic model of goods that have both consumption and

---

[20] Olaf Thalmann, Beth Shapiro, Pin Cui, Verena J. Schuenemann, Susanna K. Sawyer, D. L. Greenfield, Mietje B. Germonpré, M. V. Sablin, F. López-Giráldez, X. Domingo-Roura, and H. Napierala. "Complete Mitochondrial Genomes of Ancient Canids Suggest a European Origin of Domestic Dogs." *Science* 342, no. 6160 (2013): 871–874. For a broad overview of the field, see Darcy F. Morey. *Dogs: Domestication and the Development of a Social Bond* (New York, NY: Cambridge University Press, 2010).

[21] Yu Uchiumi and Akira Sasaki. "Evolution of Division of Labour in Mutualistic Symbiosis." *Proceedings of the Royal Society B* 287, no. 1930 (2020): 1–10.

production values helps us understand the forces that propelled it in early human societies.

Subsequent chapters shift our focus from the natural history of the interspecies relationship between humans and dogs that developed over the thousands of years during which dogs emerged as a separate species from wolves to the contemporary relationship. In Chapter 3, we turn to the many decisions that people make about the acquisition and owning of dogs. We do so primarily in the context of dogs' roles in contemporary American families. Some dogs have tasks, such as participating in hunting, herding, guiding, competitive showing, law enforcement, and guarding – dogs also increasingly contribute to disease detection.[22] But the overwhelming majority of dogs in the United States primarily provide companionship for the families that adopt them. Indeed, most families state that they consider their dogs to be family members. Do economic models of the family shed any light on dog ownership, such as the distribution of dog-care tasks among household members? Chapter 3 also considers why some people decide to become dog owners and the factors that affect their choice of breeds and specific dogs. Both behavioral economics and models of fads shed some light on these questions. We conclude our discussion of the demand for dogs by illustrating how simple market analysis can help us understand the jump in dog ownership that emerged during the COVID pandemic.

Chapter 4 focuses on the supply side of the market. We recognize the diversity of suppliers of puppies to the market, so we characterize different types of suppliers, ranging from high-quality breeders to socalled puppy mills. From an economic perspective, each of these types of supply exhibit different levels of two *market failures* that result in the puppy market not being allocatively efficient. One of the market failures, *information asymmetry*, occurs because buyers of puppies have less information about their "quality" than do those raising them, resulting in buyers purchasing too many or the wrong puppies. The other market failure, *negative externality*, occurs because some puppy suppliers do not bear the full costs of producing puppies, resulting in overproduction of puppies that eventually contributes to the hundreds of thousand dogs euthanized each year in shelters.

Public policies that are intended to improve the lot of humans sometimes affect dogs as well. For example, Congress has given the Food and

---

[22] Biagio D'Aniello, Claudia Pinelli, Mario Varcamonti, Marcello Rendine, Pietro Lombardi, and Anna Scandurra. "COVID Sniffer Dogs: Technical and Ethical Concerns." *Frontiers in Veterinary Science* 8, June (2021): 662–667.

Drug Administration quite extensive authority to regulate the content of pet food. As we explain in Chapter 5, this authority followed on the deaths of dogs and cats from imported ingredients adulterated with melamine.[23] We consider how to value – and *shadow price* – reductions in mortality risk for dogs that are expected to result from proposed regulations. Federal regulators routinely use empirically based estimates of the *value of statistical life* in assessing the benefits to people of proposed health and safety regulations. These estimates are inferred from trade-offs people make between money and mortality risk, either as revealed by their actions or elicited through surveys. We present the results of a survey experiment that allows estimation of the monetary value owners implicitly place on their dogs when they assess trade-offs between money and changes in their dogs' mortality risk. In other words, it provides an estimate of the *value of statistical dog life* that can be used like the value of statistical life in estimating the net benefits of proposed policies and perhaps to help courts more fairly compensate owners for the wrongful deaths of their dogs.

Sadly, our longer lifespan often requires us to confront the death of our dogs. Chapter 6 sets out a property rights framework that helps elucidate how decisions about human and canine end-of-life decisions differ. People often express a preference for palliative over heroic invasive care, whether as death threatens or earlier, through health care directives. Owners must make decisions for their dogs without being able to converse with them, although we all know they can usually communicate with us when something is going on that they do not like. Owners also have the option of choosing euthanasia to end suffering – or even anticipated suffering, as was the case during the mass euthanasia of dogs and cats in London at the start of World War II.[24]

Financial considerations, both veterinary fees and the opportunity cost of providing care to injured or ill dogs, often play a role in decisions about euthanasia, raising challenging ethical issues for both owners and veterinarians. Although pet insurance that helps defray veterinary fees currently serves less than 5 percent of dog owners, its prevalence is growing fast. Pet insurance enables owners to avoid unnecessary euthanasia but it also creates an incentive for veterinary care that may not be in the best interests of the dog.

---

[23] Marion Nestle. *Pet Food Politics: The Chihuahua in the Coal Mine* (Berkeley, CA: University of California Press, 2008).

[24] Hilda Kean. *The Great Cat and Dog Massacre: The Real Story of World War Two's Unknown Tragedy* (Chicago, IL: University of Chicago Press, 2017).

Chapter 6 also considers the use of dogs in medical research. Many of the almost 60 thousand dogs used in medical research each year in the United States suffer from some form of experimental intervention and usually from the stress of being isolated in laboratories; further, many dogs are subsequently euthanized either as part of the experimental protocol or because they are no longer useful to researchers. As recently brought to public attention by the rescued Virginia beagles, the sources of supply of dogs for medical research also raise concerns about humane treatment.[25] We consider what an economic perspective can offer in thinking about the trade-offs between generating valuable knowledge through medical research and treating dogs humanely.

Although pet dogs receive most of our attention, Chapter 7 considers working dogs. We draw on the theory of comparative advantage to help us categorize these occupations. Along with the traditional roles of working dogs in hunting, herding, and guarding, we assess their contemporary roles in helping people who are visually or hearing impaired, physically or mentally disabled, or subject to seizures. We also discuss how dogs' olfactory superiority enables them to contribute to public safety in the location of people and substances as well as detect people's diseases and warn them of imminent adverse health events.

Chapter 7 also presents two cases that apply economics to canine occupations. One case discusses the supply of guide dogs for the blind and reviews estimates of the direct economic costs and benefits of their use. A second case addresses the controversy surrounding federal rules that removed the requirement that airlines accommodate emotional support dogs as service dogs. It also summarizes the economic analysis conducted by the Department of Transportation to support its change in the rules governing emotional support animals.

We conclude in Chapter 8 with some speculation about how the human relationship with dogs will develop in the future. We expect property rights to continue to evolve to increase the effective protection humans provide to dogs. These changes will play out within a political system that changes policy through multiple mechanisms in response to changes in the distribution of interests. We also expect that the growth in genomic knowledge will accelerate the impact of "designer dogs," not just on the roles dogs play, but also on the genetic makeup of the canine population.

---

[25] Jesus Jiménez and April Rubin. "4,000 Beagles Are Being Rescued from a Virginia Facility. Now They Need New Homes." *New York Times*, July 12 (2022).

* * *

Angus sees our welcoming of dogs into our lives as an expression of love that goes beyond economic rationality. Our introductory tour of dogonomics shows that many aspects of our relationship with dogs can be understood as rational behavior, whether perfectly so or tempered by the cognitive limitations and biases of our species. We explore these differing perspectives on rationality in the following chapters. Yet, the two somewhat differing economic perspectives we provide cannot fully account for the strong desire of many people to have dogs in their lives. People willingly take on the responsibility for caring for members of this other species. Perhaps embracing dogs is a legacy of the symbiosis between our species. From an economic perspective, this is just an innate preference. From the perspective of many dog owners, it is indeed love.

2

Chasing the Tale

Origins of the Human–Dog Relationship

Dogs evolved from wolves.[1] This evolutionary transformation occurred in the company of humans through a process of interspecies symbiosis. The numerous breeds purposely developed by humans, as well as human individual and collective actions that are less organized, suggest that the decisions and actions of *Homo sapiens* now largely determine dog evolution. Quite possibly, our millennia of close association with dogs have also affected our own evolution, perhaps predisposing us toward valuing their presence in our lives. But when did the transformation of wolf into dog get started, and how has it evolved over time? What specific economic concepts and models help us understand how and why the symbiosis developed? And what biological and sociocultural forces have sustained it across both time and space? We address these questions as a prelude to our treatment of the economics of dogs in our modern lives.

2.1 SNIFFING OUT THE BEGINNING: THE ARCHAEOLOGICAL (AND NOW GENETIC) EVIDENCE

The genetic and archaeological evidence suggests that the close human-canine association emerged more than 20 thousand years ago, somewhere in Eurasia. We advisedly use the broad and somewhat vague term "close association," at least at this point. The word association allows

---

[1] Genetic evidence suggests that after an initial flow of genes from wolves to dogs, what further flow occurred tended to be from dogs back to wolves. Anders Bergström, Laurent Frantz, Ryan Schmidt, Erik Ersmark, Ophelie Lebrasseur, Linus Girdland-Flink, Audrey T. Lin et al. "Origins and Genetic Legacy of Prehistoric Dogs." *Science* 370, no. 6516 (2020): 557–564.

us to sidestep somewhat both the evolutionary processes by which the association arose and its exact nature within an evolutionary perspective. Biologists usually divide symbiosis – any close relationship between two species where at least one of the species benefits – into three forms: mutualism, commensalism, and parasitism.[2] With mutualism, both species benefit from the relationship; with commensalism, one species benefits and the other species neither benefits nor is harmed (i.e., it bears no evolutionary relevant cost); and with parasitism, one species benefits and the other species is harmed (e.g., as in the interaction between dogs and roundworms). Evolutionary biologists have empirically shown that the form of symbiosis can evolve over time, at least at the bacterial level.[3]

To the extent that economics, and especially the applied economics that is of most relevance to dog-related policies, regulation, and markets, primarily concerns itself with contemporary and expected future margins of human behavior, we could largely ignore the evolutionary and biological causal factors that underlie our cross-species association. Thus, the primary focus of this chapter is on what we consider to be the basic economics of the human–canine interaction. Although we do not dive deeply into the genesis of how the association arose, we do dangle our toes. We do so because economic concepts and methods – most specifically ideas from game theory – have played an important role in structuring theory and empirical research around basic evolutionary, and related, questions. We also do so because causal factors, however far back in time they arose, help us think about human and dog interactional behaviors in the present.

Genetic evidence suggests that the domestic dog (*Canis lupus familiaris*) diverged from the gray wolf (*Canis lupus*) as long ago as 100 thousand years somewhere in East Asia.[4] However, the earliest archeological evidence of domesticated canids (beyond just association) is found further west and only around 14 thousand years ago.[5] Even then, the relationship was complex and multidimensional; Luc Janssens and his

[2] Aparajita Das and Ajit Varma. "Symbiosis: The Art of Living." In Ajit Varma and Amit C. Kharkwal, eds., *Symbiotic Fungi, Soil Biology 18* (Berlin, DE: Springer-Verlag, 2009), 1–28.

[3] Paul Herrera, Lisa Schuster, Cecilia Wentrup, Lena König, Thomas Kempinger, Hyunsoo Na, Jasmin Schwarz et al. "Molecular Causes of an Evolutionary Shift along the Parasitism–Mutualism Continuum in a Bacterial Symbiont." *Proceedings of the National Academy of Sciences* 117, no. 35 (2020): 21658–21666.

[4] Xiaoming Wang and Richard H. Tedford. "Evolutionary History of Canids." In Per Jensen, ed., *The Behavioural Biology of Dogs* (Cambridge, MA: CABI, 2007), 3–20.

[5] Darcy F. Morey. *Dogs: Domestication and the Development of a Social Bond* (New York, NY: Cambridge University Press, 2010).

colleagues present poignant evidence of early humans caring for a very sick young dog that had almost no chance of survival without their care.[6]

2.2 HOW DID WE DOMESTICATE DOGS … OR HOW DID WE DOMESTICATE EACH OTHER?

How might the close association have evolved? Kayla Stoy and her colleagues point out that "Despite the ubiquity and importance of mutualistic interactions, we know little about the evolutionary genetics underlying their long-term persistence."[7] Biologists do have some suggestive evidence about how genetic temporal processes work from bacterial symbiosis; but that is very far from symbiosis between more complex organisms. Thus, behavioralists of all stripes have considered a wide range of other kinds of evidence, including indirect evidence of biological processes by observing the results of selective breeding of dogs, of the closely related fox, and of other domesticated animals, as well as contemporary interactions between species. After reviewing these interesting questions and some of the alternative hypothesizes about the genesis of the human–dog association, we focus on economic theory, and related evidence, that might help explain, or at least interpret, interspecies symbiosis. We should keep in mind that we are not claiming or describing genetic comingling between species, so while we think this terminology is informative, it is to some extent metaphorical. In that vein, Edward O. Wilson uses the term "social symbiosis."[8] However, as we discuss in the next section, while there is no interspecies gene mixing, humans have clearly and repeatedly influenced the canine genetic makeup.

Biologists have documented many examples of symbiosis between species ranging from aphids and ants to honey guides and humans. Charles Darwin described the convincing evidence of the ubiquity of symbiosis as one of the most serious challenges to the theory of evolution.[9]

---

[6] Luc Janssens, Liane Giemsch, Ralf Schmitz, Martin Street, Stefan Van Dongen, and Philippe Crombé. "A New Look at an Old Dog: Bonn-Oberkassel Reconsidered." *Journal of Archaeological Science* 92, April (2018): 126–138.

[7] Kayla S. Stoy, Amanda K. Gibson, Nicole M. Gerardo, and Levi T. Morran. "A Need to Consider the Evolutionary Genetics of Host–Symbiont Mutualisms." *Journal of Evolutionary Biology* 33, no. 12 (2020): 1656–1668 at 1656.

[8] Edward O. Wilson. *Sociobiology: The New Synthesis* (Cambridge, MA: Harvard University Press, 2000).

[9] There is some disagreement among evolutionary biologists on whether symbiosis still represents a serious challenge to the neo-Darwinism synthesis (the standard contemporary version of Darwinism incorporating modern genetics, as represented by John

To help understand the evolution of interspecies symbiosis, biologists after Darwin's era have drawn on game theory, a basic tool of economics, and the other social sciences.[10] The resulting framework, evolutionary game theory, is now a widely used approach to studying intraspecies evolution, interspecies symbiosis, and even the prevalence of social norms among humans.[11] Although it would take us too far afield to provide more than a cursory discussion of evolutionary game theory, we think brief introductions to classical and evolutionary game theories are useful in understanding how cooperation between people and wolves might have originally arisen and been sustained. Before considering game theory models related to the emergence of mutualistic symbiosis (the relationship in which we assume *Homo sapiens* and dogs now coexist), we briefly review the explanations that have been offered for the origin of domestication.

2.3 POSSIBLE EXPLANATIONS FOR THE EARLY STAGES OF DOMESTICATION

What use is a dog? To man, that is. To consider this difficult and contentious question, we draw on two studies that summarize most of the alternative hypothesizes. In discussing these hypothesizes, some biologists distinguish between what they call utilitarian motivation hypotheses and others they describe as nonutilitarian motives;[12] this is something we

Maynard Smith and Richard Dawkins). For the case that it does, see Lynn Margulis and David Bermudes. "Symbiosis as a Mechanism of Evolution: Status of Cell Symbiosis Theory." *Symbiosis* 1, no. 2 (1985): 101–124. For an accessible discussion of the importance of the idea that symbiosis is different, see Bradford Harris. "Evolution's Other Narrative." *American Scientist* 101, no. 6 (2013): 410. For a very balanced assessment, see Maureen A. O'Malley. "Endosymbiosis and Its Implications for Evolutionary Theory." *Proceedings of the National Academy of Sciences* 112, no. 33 (2015): 10270–10277.

[10] Seminal works include John Maynard Smith and George R. Price. "The Logic of Animal Conflict." *Nature* 246, no. 5427 (1973): 15–18; John Maynard Smith. "The Theory of Games and the Evolution of Animal Conflicts." *Journal of Theoretical Biology* 47, no. 1 (1974): 209–221 and John Maynard Smith. *Evolution and the Theory of Games* (New York, NY: Cambridge University Press, 1982).

[11] H. Peyton Young. "The Evolution of Social Norms." *Annual Review of Economics* 7, no. 1 (2015): 359–387.

[12] Luc A. A. Janssens and Dennis F. Lawler. "The Earliest Domesticated Wolves: On Creating Dogs." In Sabine Gaudzinski-Windheuser and Olaf Jöris, eds., *The Beef Behind All Possible Pasts the Tandem-Festschrift in Honour of Elaine Turner and Martin Street, Volume 2* (Mainz, DE: Verlag des Römisch-Germanischen Zentralmuseums, 2021), 485–504.

return to later in this chapter (and in a later chapter) but using different terminology for reasons we explain. C. Clyde Manwell and C. M. Ann Baker summarize ten possible canine domestication scenarios (partly in the context of Australian indigenous populations and dingoes).[13] Because these domestication scenarios do not exclusively assume the domestication of wolf puppies (but rather dingoes and other potential hybrid proto-canids), here we use the broader label "canid domestication." These scenarios are not mutually exclusive explanations.

Manwell and Baker pose what we identify as the following ten scenarios. First, canids could have provided value to humans as auxiliary hunters. Their value as hunting partners rests on both a similarity and difference. Dogs and humans have comparable endurance, which allows them to cooperate over long distances. However, canids have a much better sense of smell than humans, a useful complement to hunting. We can expect canids to share the same functions in hunting that archaeologists have identified for dogs. These include locating and encountering prey, indicating specific locations of prey, restricting the movement of prey, and pursuing and recovering prey.[14]

Second, canids could have come into contact with humans by being either big or small game "kill thieves." When humans made large game kills, especially during the "Pleistocene Overkill," which hypothesized that humans hunted megafauna to extinction,[15] they often had a temporary abundance of food that could not always be guarded against canid larceny. Canids would also have been able to outrace humans to small game killed with primitive missile weapons. (Readers who have had dogs know that many still have some larceny in their hearts: your authors have witnessed otherwise well-behaved dogs give in to the temptation to grab blocks of cheese, and once even a whole ham, from tables!) The possibility of opportunities for such larceny would have conditioned some canids to seek to be near humans.

Third, canids could have served as guards or sentinels for the clan because of sensory complementarities with humans. Although humans

---

[13] C. Clyde Manwell and C. M. Ann Baker. "Domestication of the Dog: Hunter, Food, Bed-warmer, or Emotional Object?" *Zeitschrift für Tierzüchtung und Züchtungsbiologie* 101, no. 1–5 (1984): 241–256.

[14] See Angela R. Perri. "Prehistoric Dogs as Hunting Tools: The Advent of Animal Biotechnology." In Brandi Bethke and Amanda Burtt, eds., *Dogs: Archaeology Beyond Domestication* (Gainsville, FL: University Press of Florida, 2020), 7–44.

[15] Todd A. Surovell, Spencer R. Pelton, Richard Anderson-Sprecher, and Adam D. Myers. "Test of Martin's Overkill Hypothesis Using Radiocarbon Dates on Extinct Megafauna." *Proceedings of the National Academy of Sciences* 113, no. 4 (2016): 886–891.

generally have better day and night vision, canids tend to have better vision at dawn and twilight. More importantly, canids have keener senses of smell and hearing than humans, enabling them to detect the presence of animals that humans cannot see. Along with better senses of smell and hearing, shorter spells of REM sleep would have made canids especially valuable sentinels at night. They also would have had the capability to directly interdict smaller intruders.

Fourth, canids could have acted as auxiliary fighters in early intrahuman conflicts or possibly *Homo sapiens'* conflicts with Neanderthals or Denisovans. Beyond the especially valuable role of sentinel in conflict situations, canids could directly attack enemies with teeth and claws or intimidate them with growls. History offers many descriptions of dogs engaging in this function – and even as recently as the sixteenth-century conquistadors deployed war dogs against the native peoples of the New World.[16]

Fifth, the canid could have served as a human food source (the "edible dog" in Manwell and Baker's terminology). Stationary clans might very well have captured or raised canids as a regular food source, just as dogs are a food source today in some Asian countries. However, canids might have been more valuable as a reserve food source. Sharing kills with canids may have been done explicitly as a means of storing food. It also may have been just an expedient strategy in times of scarcity. Relatedly, it is known that the indigenous peoples of the north-west coast of North America kept dogs for the use of their hair in clothing.

Sixth, women could have engaged in heterospecific suckling of canids. It is reasonable to assume that women in early human clans experienced high rates of infant mortality so that there would often be lactating women who had no infants to feed. Consequently, it is possible that abandoned or orphaned canid pubs might be introduced to the clan and then adopted by women who had lost infants. The sucking would likely have created a bond between the pup and the women that could have resulted in the canid staying with the clan into adulthood. The heterospecific suckling of dogs and pigs has been documented in a geographically wide range of contemporary societies, consistent with the possibility of its role in canid domestication.[17]

---

[16] For an account of the gruesome use of war dogs by the conquistadors, as well as dogs as more benign characters in historical events, see Stanley Coren. *The Pawprints of History: Dogs and the Course of Human Events* (New York, NY: Free Press, 2002).

[17] Frederick J. Simoons and James A. Baldwin. "Breast-Feeding of Animals by Women: Its Socio-Cultural Context and Geographic Occurrence." *Anthropos* 77, no. 3/4 (1982): 421–448.

Seventh, the canid could have served as a bed warmer, or more generally, participate in interspecies huddling in the presence of extreme cold. Participants in huddling effectively reduce their ratios of surface area to volume, reducing their losses of body heat. The huddling is mutually beneficial for both the canids and the humans. One can imagine that reliance on huddling may have reduced the amount of bedding required, which would have been valuable to clans that changed locations frequently: canids were effectively self-propelled bedding. Manwell and Baker speculate that bed warming might have been the earliest source of domestication.

Eighth, canids could have contributed to cleansing campsites by serving as scavengers. Rather than thieving game, canids may have been invited to eat food remains, especially those unpalatable for humans, to help avoid rodent and insect infestations. (In contrast to this indirect rodent control through sanitation, it is likely that cats began associating with humans after agriculture permitted the storage of grain that attracted rodents.[18])

Ninth, canids could have played an important role in transportation. Although their capacity for directly carrying loads is relatively small, they would have effectively pulled sleds in regions with substantial snow or ice. Dogs still pull sleds for some northern clans today. One reason that they have maintained this role despite the domestication of draft animals is that they can share food with humans. We might speculate that Ernest Shackleton's South Pole expedition would have fared much better if it employed more dogs than ponies.

Tenth, canids could have become emotional objects for humans. The emotional link may have arisen from human engagement with young animals, whether as a consequence of heterospecific suckling or through other contact. Or it may have been a byproduct of associating with canids preforming other functions. Manwell and Baker write: "The presence of an animal strongly integrated with cultural traditions of a people, succoured at considerable cost, yet seemingly devoid of economic implications, has resulted in speculations over a variety of aesthetic, religious, ceremonial or psychological functions for animals."[19]

Luc A. A. Janssens and Dennis F. Lawler posit a number of motivational reasons that are very similar to those presented by Manwell and

---

[18] Carlos A. Driscoll, Juliet Clutton-Brock, Andrew C. Kitchener, and Stephen J. O'Brien. "The Taming of the Cat." *Scientific American* 300, no. 6 (2009): 68–75.
[19] Manwell and Baker, p. 250.

Baker and so we see no need to repeat them, but they also distinguish between two underlying mechanisms; either collection of (very young) wolves or some other canid pups or through self-domestication.[20] From a game-theoretic (and evolutionary) perspective, the distinction between pup collection and self-domestication is potentially important because self-domestication-related hypothesizes lend themselves more readily to a transition to mutualistic symbiosis, while puppy collection is more akin to parasitism or commensalism (the latter being the case where wolf puppies suffer from abandonment unrelated to humans).

2.4 INSIGHTS FROM CLASSICAL GAME THEORY

Game theory is widely utilized in the social sciences, especially in economics, where it has now become one of the primary frameworks for graduate training. Although it has evolved considerably since its introduction in the 1940s, we refer to its contemporary use in the social sciences as classical game theory. This distinguishes it from evolutionary game theory, which shifts focus from the strategic behavior of individuals to competition among strategies inherent in individuals, such as through genetics in the case of studies of the evolution of species or social norms in the case of human interaction. Each of these game-theoretic frameworks offers some insights that are useful for thinking about canine domestication.

In classical game theory, a game specifies players, their strategies, payoffs jointly conditional on selected strategies, and their knowledge of the strategies and payoffs. Here, we focus our attention on what are called non-cooperative games, which assume that the players cannot make binding commitments about the strategies they will play. Social scientists, mathematicians, and (as we will see) biologists have developed a wide range of games, as well as various ways of classifying them. The strategies are then tested against each other, mostly in controlled experimental (laboratory) settings. This allows for systemic variation in the parameters of the game, such as the payoffs and available information. This is very convenient and potentially informative! However, we have to keep the limitations of such games in mind when extrapolating their results to actual human and animal behaviors and especially to the interaction between humans and other species.

[20] Janssens and Lawler, pp. 491–492.

Stage Game: Played One Time

Pack Strategies

Clan		Share (S)	Hoard (H)
Clan	Share (S)	2,2	−1,3
Strategies	Hoard (H)	3,−1	0,0

Equilibrium: (H,H)

Repeated Game: Stage Game Repeated with Probability p

Some possible equilibria in repeated game:

1. Clan and Pack always hoard.

(H,H)(H,H)(H,H)...

2. Clan and Pack share in first round and then continue sharing as long as the other player shared on the last round. If either player hoards, the other never shares again. This strategy in the repeated game is an equilibrium if and only if the probability of playing another round of the stage game is sufficiently large ($p > 1/3$):

(S,S)(S,S)(S,S)...

FIGURE 2.1 Hunting Game (prisoner's dilemma): Single round and repeated

The situation most relevant to our current interest is the game displayed in Figure 2.1. It considers a game that can be played either once or multiple times – following conventional usage, we refer to the basic structure of the game played one time as the *stage game* and the multiple rounds of play of the stage game as the *repeated game*. The table within Figure 2.1 displays the players, strategies, and payoffs for the stage game. For our initial purposes, we label it as the Hunting Game, although, as our earlier discussion indicated, hunting is only one of a number of equally plausible, or perhaps even more plausible, other explanations. Readers familiar with game theory will recognize the Hunting Game as a particular example of the Prisoner's Dilemma game, which famously illustrates how individuals rationally seeking to maximize their own payoffs can lead to social inefficiency.

In our version of the Prisoner's Dilemma game, we label one player the "Clan," and the other, the "Pack," for *Homo sapiens* and wolves, respectively. The Clan and the Pack each has two possible (mutually exclusive) strategies, "Share" or "Hoard." Share means that the Clan or the Pack cooperates in hunting big prey and sharing the resulting food (protein and fat). Hoard means that a player does not cooperate.

The payoffs to the players are given in the cells of the two-by-two table of strategies with the first number showing the payoff to the Clan and the second number showing the payoff to the Pack. So, for example, if the Clan hoards and the Pack shares, the Clan gets a positive payoff of 3 units of food and the Pack gets none of the kill and loses the equivalent of 1 unit of food from uncompensated effort. To predict the outcome of the Hunting Game, we identify combinations of strategies of the players that are *Nash equilibria* in the sense that neither player could increase its payoff by unilaterally changing its strategy.

We first assume that the stage game will only be played once. When the game is played only once, an inspection of the table of payoffs displayed in Figure 2.1 should make it clear why both players decide to engage in hoarding (H,H). This is an equilibrium because, if the other player is hoarding, unilaterally moving to sharing would reduce food payoffs from 0 to −1. Indeed, it turns out that (H,H) is the only equilibrium – which one can verify by identifying desirable changes in strategies for one or both players for any of the other strategy combinations. We can see why other strategies when the game is played only once are not equilibria. For example, one player sharing and the other hoarding, that is, either (S,H) or (H,S), is not an equilibrium because the sharing player could unilaterally increase its payoff from −1 to 0 units of food by changing strategies to hoarding. Both players sharing (S,S) is also not an equilibrium because either player could increase its payoff from 2 to 3 units of food by switching to hoarding. Thus, even though (S,S) would potentially give each player a higher payoff than (H,H), it is not an equilibrium and therefore unlikely to occur. It is this divergence between the equilibrium of mutual hoarding and the more desirable outcome that would result from mutual sharing that makes this game structure so interesting to social scientists. Although a Clan and a Pack randomly encountering each other would benefit from sharing in a big game hunt (S,S) and so maximize their food gains, their individual incentives would be to hoard so that the predicted outcome would be the equilibrium (H,H).

Next assume that there is repeated interaction rather than one-time play of the stage game. This repeated interaction might occur because of some degree of colocation; this becomes more likely as the number of clans, or wolf packs, or both, increase over time. If some clans and packs do settle near each other to permit repeated interaction, then the possibility for a cooperative equilibrium arises. The model of repeated cooperation shown in Figure 2.1 assumes that the stage game is repeated in successive rounds with a probability of p. That is, after playing the stage game, the probability of playing it again is p. Strategies in this repeated game are defined as choices of stage game strategies conditional on what has occurred in previous rounds of play. Equilibrium strategies in the repeated game involving sharing by a clan and a pack are possible if the probability of playing another round of the stage game is sufficiently high.

For example, consider the following strategy in a repeated game: share in the first round and continue sharing if the other player shared in the previous round. If the other player hoards, then hoard in all future rounds. Both players following this strategy will be an equilibrium if the expected payoff to each player of following the strategy is greater than ever hoarding. If the Clan and the Pack each follow this strategy, then the expected payoffs are $2(1 + p + p^2 + p^3 + ...)$, which equals an expected $2 / (1 - p)$ units of food. Hoarding in the first round would earn a payoff of 3 units of food, but o unit in all future rounds. The sharing strategy will be an equilibrium if $2 / (1 - p) > 3$, or $p > 1 / 3$. This illustrates that, if the probability of repeated interaction is sufficiently high, then mutual sharing (S,S) in each round is an equilibrium in the repeated game and therefore a plausible prediction of strategy choices and outcomes.

This strategy, however, is only one of the possible equilibria in this repeated game. Other sharing equilibria could also exist in the presence of large enough values of p. For example, one famous and highly intuitive strategy is known as "tit for tat."[21] In this strategy one player starts off by sharing in the first round and then copying what the other player did on the previous round. A tit-for-tat strategy should result in sharing if p is sufficiently large.[22] Indeed, unlike an unforgiving strategy of punishing a case of hoarding by responding with hoarding ever after, tit for tat opens up the possibility of strategies that embody forgiveness: that is, returning to sharing if one of the players hoarded, whether deliberately or inadvertently. In moving from repeated games

---

[21] The somewhat surprising success of the tit-for-tat strategy was made famous in a tournament of different strategies pitted against each other in the repeated prisoner's dilemma game. See Robert Axelrod, *The Evolution of Cooperation* (New York, NY: Basic Books, 1984).

[22] The so-called Folk Theorem indicates that repeated games usually have an infinite number of "cooperative" equilibria. See Drew Fudenberg and Eric Maskin. "The Folk Theorem in Repeated Games with Discounting or Incomplete Information." *Econometrica* 54, no. 3 (1986): 533–554.

with two players to multiplayer games, tit for tat may provide some degree of robustness of sharing even in the presence of hoarding by a single player.

Note that in a game with only a single equilibrium like the Hunting Game, if players know the number of repeated interactions with certainty, then a cooperative equilibrium of mutual sharing is not possible. We deduce this by backward induction, through which each player would have an incentive to switch to hoard in the last round. Anticipating hoarding in the last round, the players would have an incentive to hoard in the penultimate round. This process would unravel mutual sharing. To sustain the equilibrium of mutual sharing, there must always be a positive probability of playing the stage game at least one more time. It may be possible to support cooperative equilibria in stage games repeated a fixed number of times if there are more than one equilibrium.

How plausible is it that such sharing could evolve? For it to occur, a clan and pack must first interact in some way. One can imagine a number of reasons why clans and packs might tend to colocate as a precursor to interaction. Many reasons would relate to the attraction of locations with reliable supplies of water and adequate tree cover; this is a strong driver of species colocation in spatial environments with uneven resource endowments. More related to associational behavior, wolves are effective (and often apex) scavengers in colder climates. The Pack would find it beneficial to eat parts of kills that clans do not consume in situations when food is plentiful (and not storable); the Clan may benefit from fewer rodents if the wolves clean up – a source of canid and human association we have already noted.

It is also possible that sharing arose through some more idiosyncratic circumstances such as a clan and pack cornering the same mastodon and sharing in the abundance that a very large carcass provides. This could provide a context for a first round of sharing that might then be repeated to mutual benefit.[23] These scenarios imply that sharing could somehow continue. Assuming foresight and memory by clans, one way of getting to repetition is to assume foresight and memory by particular packs; some research does suggest that wolves as well as dogs may have an

---

[23] On the limitations of explaining mutual animal behavior with such games, see Nichola J. Raihani and R. Bshary. "Resolving the Iterated Prisoner's Dilemma: Theory and Reality." *Journal of Evolutionary Biology* 24, no. 8 (2011): 1628–1639.

aversion to inequality, suggesting a social awareness potentially relevant to reciprocity.[24]

More generally, how plausible are games as models of either animal or interspecies interaction? Although not directly relevant to the evolution of cooperation between humans and canines, a detour to the question of what we know about whether, and if so how, animals play games may help us assess the plausibility of game-theoretic explanations of animal behavior. We are specifically interested here in these questions from the perspective of the findings from experimental game theory, which have been conducted in two different contexts. The first context is whether some animals appear to play games with humans. The second context is intraspecies interaction between individual members of some nonhuman species. In both contexts, most of this research has been conducted with various primate species.

Both contexts raise a fascinating underlying question: are interactions (and so games) between members of nonhuman species different from the same kinds of interactions between humans? A starting point for thinking about capacity to play games is the cognitive trade-off hypothesis.[25] This hypothesis conjectures that the brains of different species specialize in different capabilities – which economists would frame as different species having different absolute and comparative advantages.[26] In humans, cortical growth has evolved around language and categorization. Both are extremely valuable to humans, at the expense of other capacities that are better retained by other species, such as detailed perception and pattern recognition. These capacities are critical for many species in their intraspecies social

---

[24] See Jennifer L. Essler, Sarah Marshall-Pescini, and Friederike Range. "Domestication Does Not Explain the Presence of Inequity Aversion in Dogs." *Current Biology* 27, no. 12 (2017): 1861–1865. For an overview of the research on inequality aversion in dogs, see Jim McGetrick and Friederike Range. "Inequity Aversion in Dogs: A Review." *Learning & Behavior* 46, no. 4 (2018): 479–500.

[25] Elsa Adessi and her colleagues discuss how nonhuman animals "think" about economics given their cognitive abilities and limitations. Elsa Addessi, Michael J. Beran, Sacha Bourgeois-Gironde, Sarah F. Brosnan, and Jean-Baptiste Leca. "Are the Roots of Human Economic Systems Shared with Non-human Primates?" *Neuroscience & Biobehavioral Reviews* 109 (2020): 1–15.

[26] A comparison of similarly raised wolf and dog pups shows the genetic basis for cognitive differences between these species. Eniko Kubinyi, Zxofia Viranyi, and Ádám Miklósi. "Comparative Social Cognition: From Wolf and Dog to Humans." *Comparative Cognition & Behavior Reviews* 2 (2007): 26–46.

interaction in the absence of language or for competitive activities such as hunting.[27] In intraspecies games, the evidence shows that a range of primates can play cooperatively.[28] Regarding primate games against humans, the experimental evidence shows that in some games chimpanzees do as well as humans, and, in some pattern recognition games, they do better.[29]

2.5 INSIGHTS FROM EVOLUTIONARY GAME THEORY

A framing of interspecies interaction that is clearly more consistent with the requirements of evolutionary theory, however, would be that some wolves had a genetic trait that predisposed them to share. Rather than modeling individual rationality in the choice of strategies, from this perspective one models the success of strategies. John M. Smith was one of the pioneers of this approach to modeling evolution, now called evolutionary game theory.[30] Rather than individual players choosing strategies, the players have genetically endowed strategies. Some strategies will mutate and replicate in some circumstances. The primary focus is on identifying *evolutionarily stable strategies* (ESS). ESSs are such that if they are present in the whole population, they cannot be successfully invaded by a mutant strategy that then persists in the population.

Biologists typically model evolutionary change with dynamic versions of evolutionary game theory that simulate genetic changes over time (and sometimes space). The most common approach models interactions among members of the population such that those who gain relatively more resources from their interactions with other members have more offspring.[31] Computer simulation methods, such as agent-based models, allow researchers to assess the dynamics of evolutionary change in more

[27] Christopher F. Martin, Rahul Bhui, Peter Bossaerts, Tetsuro Matsuzawa, and Colin Camerer. "Chimpanzee Choice Rates in Competitive Games Match Equilibrium Game Theory Predictions." *Scientific Reports* 4, no. 1 (2014): 1–6.

[28] Gillian L. Vale, Lawrence E. Williams, Steven J. Schapiro, Susan P. Lambeth, and Sarah F. Brosnan. "Responses to Economic Games of Cooperation and Conflict in Squirrel Monkeys (*Saimiri boliviensis*)." *Animal Behavior and Cognition* 6, no. 1 (2019): 32–47.

[29] Martin et al.

[30] John M. Smith. *Evolution and the Theory of Games* (New York, NY: Cambridge University Press, 1982).

[31] Carlos P. Roca, José A. Cuesta, and Angel Sánchez. "Evolutionary Game Theory: Temporal and Spatial Effects beyond Replicator Dynamics." *Physics of Life Reviews* 6, no. 4 (2009): 208–249.

		Player 2 Strategies	
		Hawk (H)	Dove (D)
Player 1	Hawk (H)	$(V–C)/2, (V–C)/2$	$V,0$
Strategies	Dove (D)	$0,V$	$V/2,V/2$

Pure Strategy Stage Game Equilibria: (H,D) and (D,H)
Mixed Strategy Stage Game Equilibrium: Play H with probability V/C

Neither pure strategy is an ESS; mixed strategy is an ESS.

FIGURE 2.2 Hawk–dove game with high costs of fighting ($C > V$)

complex models than can be solved mathematically.[32] However, for our purposes, the simple static version of evolutionary game theory provides an adequate introduction to the basic approach.

In the Hunting Game example shown in Figure 2.1, mutual hoarding is also an ESS because if all individuals are genetically predisposed to hoard, it will be impossible for an individual with the sharing mutation to successfully invade the hoarder population. A sharing invader would consistently lose, both absolutely and relative to the incumbent hoarding population. The possibility of an ESS that allows multiple genetic strategies (called "mixed strategies") requires a game with multiple equilibria.

A canonical example in evolutionary game theory that features equilibria resulting in the survival of a diversity of genetic strategies is the Hawk–Dove game in which the players are seeking some resource and bear a cost in competing or fighting for it. In the Hawk–Dove game, the possible strategies are to be either a Hawk – threatening and fighting if resisted – or a Dove – backing down when threatened (in Monty Python parlance "run away"). The relevant features of the Hawk–Dove game are shown in Figure 2.2 for the case in which the cost of fighting (C) exceeds the value of the resource (V) – if V were greater than C, then the game would be similar to the Hunting Game in which there is only one equilibrium, which would be (H,H) in this case. We can interpret the Hawk–Dove game from the perspective of classical game theory. Doing so, there are three equilibria. Two of these equilibria, (H,D) and (D,H), are pure strategies like the equilibrium as in the Hunting Game, while the third is a mixed equilibrium that involves the players randomizing their strategies such that there

---

[32] For an overview of the use of agent-based simulation models for investigating more complex evolutionary processes, see Christoph Adami, Jory Schossau, and Arend Hintze. "Evolutionary Game Theory Using Agent-Based Methods." *Physics of Life Reviews* 19 (2016): 1–26.

is a probability of V/C of playing H and a probability of $(1 - V/C)$ of playing D.[33]

Now we switch from classical game theory back to an evolutionary game perspective in which individual players are not making purposive switches in strategies, but instead mutate from an initial strategy to a new one. In doing so, we can show why neither of the two pure strategies would be ESS. To see why, imagine that everyone in the population is an H. It would be possible for a D to invade and replicate by gaining a higher payoff. However, if the entire population became D, then an H could invade and replicate. This same logic applies when the population includes some mix of H and D individuals. Assume that the proportion of H individuals in the population is q and therefore the proportion of C individuals is $1-q$. A mutation of an H to a D would replicate or survive if it increased the mutant's expected payoff. The expected payoff to being an H is $q\big[(V-C)/2\big]+(1-q)V$. The expected payoff from mutating to a D is $q(0)+(1-q)V/2$. But some algebra shows that $q\big[(V-C)/2\big]+(1-q)V < q(0)+(1-q)V/2$ only if $q > V/C$. A similar calculation shows that mutating from C to H increases the expected payoff only if $q < V/C$. Only when the genetic endowment of H and C in the population corresponds to the mixed strategy would there be no opportunity to survive and successfully replicate – an ESS only results when the likelihood of an H meeting a D is equal to V/C.

We can think of a game of this sort as representing the genetic "strategy" of some individual wolves in a wolf pack "deciding" whether to associate with humans, such that associating and not associating have payoffs as in the Hawk–Dove game: it is better to not associate if food can simply be taken from those humans who do acquire it. The mixed strategy equilibrium corresponds to an ESS that requires the existence of both associating and nonassociating types of wolves within the wolf population. Wolves who do associate are those that are more genetically susceptible to domestication and becoming dogs, while those who do not are predisposed to remain wolves.

2.6 INDUCED MUTATION

It is common to think of genetic change for mammals as occurring over relatively long periods of time. One might therefore expect that any

---

[33] The mixed strategy assigns probabilities to the pure strategies for each player such that the other player has the same expected payoff from either of its strategies.

genetic mutations in wolves that would be significant enough to affect the propensity to be domesticated would be very slow to accumulate and require numerous generations of wolves or proto-dogs. However, recent experience with intensive selective breeding suggests that this is not necessarily the case. Experiments in Russia with captive foxes that have little associative behavior with humans have shown that it can be induced through selective breeding.[34] "Starting from what amounted to a population of wild foxes, within six generations (6 years for these foxes, as they reproduce annually), selection for tameness, and tameness alone, produced a subset of foxes that licked the hand of experimenters, could be picked up and petted, whined when humans departed, and wagged their tails when humans approached. An astonishingly fast transformation."[35] Furthermore, any resulting genetic and epigenetic changes in the foxes are driven by human (mainly economic) motivational forces rather than by neo-Darwinian replication forces.[36] These results from the selective breeding of foxes make fairly rapid genetic changes that moved wolves toward dogs plausible: humans may have adopted relatively associative wolves and bred them to produce even more associative wolves that noticeably evolved toward dogs within human lifetimes.

From the human perspective, devoting resources for the care of dogs might have been evolutionarily costly. One explanation for the human attachment to dogs is that dogs take advantage of human responses that evolved to facilitate interaction with other humans. Evolving an appearance more like human babies and evolving behaviors that encouraged humans to impute familiar mental processes to dogs enabled the dogs to secure resources from humans.[37] As the functional value of dogs developed, humans who evolved to be more accepting of dogs would have gained an advantage. From this perspective, dogs evolved from parasite to mutualists. We next turn to the economics of clans keeping dogs.

[34] Lee A. Dugatkin, Lyudmila Trut, and Liudmila N. Trut. *How to Tame a Fox (and Build a Dog): Visionary Scientists and a Siberian Tale of Jump-started Evolution* (Chicago, IL: University of Chicago Press, 2017). Also see Lyudrnila N. Trut. "Early Canid Domestication: The Farm-Fox Experiment." *Scientifur* 24, no. 2 (2000): 124.

[35] Lee A. Dugatkin. "The Silver Fox Domestication Experiment." *Evolution: Education and Outreach* 11, no. 1 (2018): 1–5 at 2.

[36] Dean Lueck and Gustavo Torrens. "Property Rights and Domestication." *Journal of Institutional Economics* 16, no. 2 (2020): 199–215.

[37] John Archer. "Why Do People Love Their Pets?" *Evolution and Human Behavior* 18, no. 4 (1997): 237–259.

2.7 DOGS ONCE IN THE CLAN: THE
ECONOMICS OF DOG COPRODUCTION

Early human clans most likely viewed dogs both as companions and productive resources.[38] (In economic terminology, the companionship would
be considered a consumption value and therefore dogs would be considered
to be consumption goods.) Figures 2.3 and 2.4 illustrate the implications
of dogs having some value in production of goods as well. As a starting
point, Figure 2.3 displays the unlikely situation in which dogs have only
companionship value – perhaps adopted cute puppies that become simply
companions. The vertical axis indicates the quantity of goods, other than
dogs, such as food, clothing, and leisure that the clan consumes, whereas
the horizontal axis represents the number of dogs that the clan keeps.

Consuming either dog companionship or other goods involves a cost.
Leisure must be given up to secure other goods (an *opportunity cost*) and
consuming the companionship of dogs involves a cost in terms of sharing
food with them and spending time caring for them beyond the value of the
companionship from interaction. For illustrative purposes, imagine that
all other goods and dogs each have a constant per unit "price" in terms
of time needed to secure them. The clan has a fixed amount of total available time. If the clan spends all of its time on acquiring other goods, then
it could consume G_m, but it must do so without any dogs. Alternatively,
although this is obviously not advisable if the clan hopes to survive, the

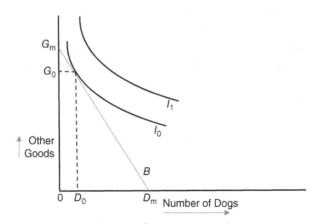

FIGURE 2.3 Dogs as companions

---

[38] On goods that contribute to both consumption and production, see Wing Suen and Pak
H. Mo. "Simple Analytics of Productive Consumption." *Journal of Political Economy*
102, no. 2 (1994): 372–383.

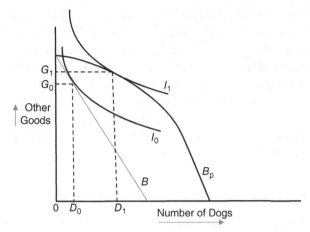

FIGURE 2.4 Dogs as companions and productive resources
Source: Adapted from Wing Suen and Pak H. Mo. "Simple Analytics of Productive Consumption." *Journal of Political Economy* 102, no. 2 (1994): 372–383, Figure 1.

clan could spend all of its time on acquiring dogs, and so consuming the companionship of D_m dogs. The line connecting these points, labeled B, represents a budget constraint that indicates the possible combinations of companion of dogs and other goods that the clan could consume.

The various combinations of dogs and other goods each give the clan some levels of utility, or satisfaction. All possible combinations allow us to construct an index of satisfaction. The higher the index value, the greater is the level of satisfaction. As the clan would like more of all goods including dogs, points in the space further to the northeast in Figure 2.3 give higher levels of satisfaction. Different combinations of companion dogs and other goods can provide the same level of satisfaction. The curves labeled I_0 and I_1 are *indifference curves* that show such combinations. If the clan has coherent preferences, then a family of indifference curves like I_0 and I_1 exists; they do not intersect, and they lie either closer or further from the origin marked o. I_0 is drawn to be just tangent to the budget constraint and is the indifference curve offering the highest level of satisfaction that the clan can achieve with budget constraint B; it results in consumption of D_0 companion dogs and G_0 other goods.

Figure 2.4 illustrates the consequences of dogs also having productive value for the clan. For example, assume that the clan uses dogs in hunting or guarding the camp at night. Or perhaps the dogs contribute directly to consumption by providing warmth on cold nights that makes sleep more pleasant (hence a very cold "three dog night"). These contributions to production thus shift the budget constraint further to the northeast as more dogs join the clan, increasing consumption possibilities. Now the clan can reach indifference curve I_1, an indifference curve that offers a higher level of clan satisfaction than was possible if dogs offer just companionship. With the added production of dogs, the clan can consume dog companionship D_1, a greater amount than the D_0 consumed if dogs were not productive. It can also consume more of other goods as well: G_1 is greater than G_0.

2.8 INCENTIVES FOR THE CREATION OF BREEDS

Economic models explain species mutualism in terms of "biological markets" in which the species can trade resources.[39] As in economic models of international trade in which comparative advantage enables both countries to gain from specialization in production, comparative advantage may facilitate specialization that expands the resources available to the species through mutualism. We have already considered various ways that canid and humans can benefit from exchange. However, once domestication transformed wolves into dogs, humans had the opportunity to engage in economic selection, a form of artificial selection rather than natural selection.[40] How can we explain the human motivation to invest resources in creating more productive breeds?

Consider the situation in which dogs are only production inputs (perish the thought!) Figure 2.5, for example, illustrates the role of dogs in sheep herding. The curve labeled B shows benefits as a function of the size of the flock. The curve labeled C_{nd} is the cost a shepherd bears in herding different flock sizes without the assistance of dogs. The point on the horizontal axis labeled Q_{nd} indicates the number of sheep that maximizes the excess of benefits over costs for the shepherd; this difference, or "profit," is represented by the length of the arrow labeled N_{nd}. The curve labeled C_d is the cost the shepherd bears from working with dogs. For very small flock sizes, working with dogs may actually involve higher

---

[39] Mark W. Schwartz and Jason D. Hoeksema. "Specialization and Resource Trade: Biological Markets as a Model of Mutualisms." *Ecology* 79, no. 3 (1998): 1029–1038; Peter Hammerstein and Ronald Noë. "Biological Trade and Markets." *Philosophical Transactions of the Royal Society B: Biological Sciences* 371, no. 1687 (2016): 1–12.

[40] Carlos A. Driscoll, David W. Macdonald, and Stephen J. O'Brien. "From Wild Animals to Domestic Pets, an Evolutionary View of Domestication." *Proceedings of the National Academy of Sciences* 106, no. Suppl 1 (2009): 9971–9978.

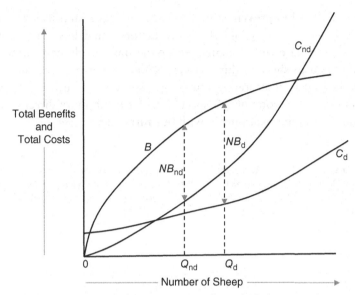

FIGURE 2.5 Human–dog cooperation from the human perspective

cost. However, at some incrementally larger flock size, the increase in the cost of herding with the assistance of dogs falls below that of doing it without dogs. The result is that a larger flock size, labeled Q_d now maximizes the excess of benefits over costs for the shepherd; this difference is represented by the length of the arrow labeled N_d.

The curve labeled C_d assumes the availability of dogs with some level of skill in herding. When dogs first began being used in herding, C_d was likely very close to C_{nd} because of relatively low levels of herding instinct. However, economic selection likely resulted as shepherds kept and bred dogs that were more helpful in herding (and perhaps less prone to eat lamb on their own, which in turn might favor sheep that are less afraid of dogs). This selective breeding would lower C_d, enabling the shepherd to increase "profits" by increasing flock size. Similar economic selection likely operated to create breeds particularly skillful in other productive activities such as hunting and guarding. Indirect economic selection eventually became common as specialists in breeding dogs selected for physical characteristics potential customers found attractive.

2.9 CONCLUSION

Dogs were the first domesticated animal species – our association with domesticated dogs has been so long and widespread that tracing genetic changes in dogs has proven valuable to archaeologists in tracing the prehistoric migrations of people.[41] Many factors could have encouraged wolves to associate with humans, setting the stage for domestication. As we have tried to show in this chapter, economic perspectives and tools can be helpful in interpreting our long association with dogs. In subsequent chapters, economic perspectives offer much more direct insight into our continuing relationship with our furry friends.

[41] Angela R. Perri, Tatiana R. Feuerborn, Laurent A. F. Frantz, Greger Larson, Ripan S. Malhi, David J. Meltzer, and Kelsey E. Witt. "Dog Domestication and the Dual Dispersal of People and Dogs into the Americas." *Proceedings of the National Academy of Sciences* 118, no. 6 (2021): 1–8.

3

Love Me, Love My Dog

The Demand for Dogs

Whatever the evolutionary forces that over the millennia have led to the unique relationship between *Homo sapiens* and *Canis lupus familiaris*, human beings now make mostly explicit choices about whether to acquire dogs and the particular dogs that they will own. On the one hand, the legal status of dogs as property in most countries – at least until the last 20 years – suggests that the demand for them is like that for other *consumer durables*. On the other hand, their changing legal status in some states and their increasingly common social status as "family members" suggest that many owners consider their dogs to be much more than just another commodity. There is a similar trend in other parts of the world, especially in Europe, to accord some animals a legal status beyond that of nonsentient property, although not a status equal to that of human dependents. Legal scholars variously label this changing status of dogs using terms that range from "quasi-property" to "quasi-personhood."[1]

In this chapter, we consider some of the implications of this tension between dogs as property as against dogs as something beyond inanimate property – in essence, their dual nature. In the chapter, we focus on decisions people make about dog ownership using a number of economic concepts and perspectives. However, where dogs are placed within a property rights regime pervades every important question about the nature and treatment of dogs; consequently, we return to the dual status of dogs in a number of later chapters. In Chapter 6, we do so in

[1] Angela Fernandez. "Not Quite Property, Not Quite Persons: A Quasi Approach for Non-human Animals." *Canadian Journal of Comparative and Contemporary Law* 5, no. 1 (2019): 155–231.

the context of their end-of-life treatment and use in medical research. In Chapter 8, we consider the role of public, and possibly, private, regulation of the markets for dogs (we use the plural deliberately). This is inextricably intertwined with the (dual) nature of dogs.

We begin by reporting on the prevalence of dogs in U.S. households and the evidence that a large majority of households consider dogs to be family members. We then turn to the factors that affect demand for dogs in general, especially the demand for specific types or breeds of dogs, which, to some extent, we think can be explained at least somewhat by the theory of fads. Finally, we consider dog ownership in two unusual circumstances, dog ownership by the homeless and the increase in dog ownership during the COVID pandemic. We demonstrate how simple microeconomic analysis of markets can help us understand the surge in dog ownership induced by COVID and predict its long-term impacts.

3.1 DOGS AT HOME: THE SURVEY EVIDENCE

Estimating the fraction of households that include dogs requires surveying, with all its imperfections. Although quantitative estimates vary, we can be confident in making two generalizations. First, the fraction of U.S. households with dogs has been increasing over the last 70 years. Second, approximately half of all households now have at least one dog. We briefly review the survey evidence that supports these claims.

In 1947, a Gallop Poll estimated that 32 percent of U.S. households owned at least one dog.[2] More recently, two organizations now regularly conduct proprietary surveys that ask questions about dog ownership. The surveys conducted by the American Pet Products Association (APPA) emphasize questions that are of particular interest to the producers of pet-related products. The surveys by the American Veterinary Medical Association (AVMA) emphasize questions that are related to the demand for veterinary services. Surveys by both of these organizations and other sources show an upward trend in the percentage of pet, and particularly dog, ownership. For instance, the APPA estimated that the percentage of U.S. households with pets increased from 56 percent in 1988 to 70 percent in 2022, with increases in dog ownership rates increasing from 37 to 54

---

[2] Gallup Organization, *Gallup Poll # 1947-0390: Middle East/Government/Congress, Gallup Organization* (Ithaca, NY: Roper Center for Public Opinion Research, Cornell University, 1947).

percent.[3] The AVMA reports dog ownership rates of 37 percent in 2007 and 45 percent in 2020.[4] Jennifer Applebaum and colleagues compared the 2018 APPA and AVMA dog ownership estimates with an estimate from the General Social Survey (GSS), which provides a well-regarded survey with both a transparent methodology and public access to its data.[5] The GSS estimate of dog ownership for 2018 is 46 percent, which falls between the APPA estimate of 48 percent and the AVMA estimate of 38 percent. These results suggest that the most recent APPA estimate of 54 percent is probably too high, but that it is nonetheless reasonable to assume that the actual percentage of ownership is now over 50 percent.

The GSS researchers also took advantage of the opportunity to use their 2018 survey to assess a number of interesting sociodemographic differences in dog ownership rates.[6] Several differences stand out. Households headed by White or Hispanic Americans are much more likely to own dogs than other groups, with rates of 54 and 44 percent, respectively. Households headed by Black Americans, in contrast, were considerably less likely to do so, with an ownership rate of 23 percent. With respect to income differences, the survey finds that ownership rates peak in the third quartile of family income. Ownership is highest in the 50–59 years of age group. As might be expected, city households are less likely to own a dog (40 percent) than are small-town/rural households (55 percent). With respect to marital status, married couples without children are most likely to own dogs (53 percent) and single adults are the least likely (26 percent). In terms of dwelling type, households living in trailers have the highest ownership rate (62 percent) followed by households living in detached single-family houses (54 percent) and households in multi-family units (22 percent). It is still unclear if these 2018 estimates, based on pre-COVID demographics, will substantially change post-pandemic. As we discuss later in this chapter, COVID has elevated dog ownership rates, but this could be a temporary phenomenon.

[3] For estimates of the percentage of households with dogs from 1988 through 2016, see Andrew N. Rowan, "Companion Animal Statistics in the USA" (2018). Demography and Statistics for Companion Animal Populations Collection, 7. www.wellbeingintlstudiesrepository.org/demscapop/7. The most recent estimate for 2022 is based on 69 million U.S. households with dogs as reported by the APPA and 127.7 million households. Accessed November 6, 2022.

[4] R. Scott Nolan. "Pet Ownership Rate Stabilizes as Spending Increases." *AVMA News*, October 26, 2022. www.avma.org/news/pet-ownership-rate-stabilizes-spending-increases. Accessed August 23, 2023.

[5] Jennifer W. Applebaum, Chuck W. Peek, and Barbara A. Zsembik. "Examining US Pet Ownership Using the General Social Survey." *Social Science Journal* (2020): 1–10.

[6] Ibid., Table 2, p. 5.

TABLE 3.1 *Multiple dog roles reported by owners*
n = 4,973

Role	Percent	Percent pet
Pet	93	100
Guide	4	83
Companion	51	92
Guard	25	92
Agriculture	1	69
Breeder	1	85

Source: PVL Survey, May 18 to 23, 2018. See Deven Carlson, Simon Haeder, Hank Jenkins-Smith, Joseph Ripberger, Carol Silva, and David Weimer. "Monetizing Bowser: A Contingent Valuation of the Statistical Value of Dog Life." *Journal of Benefit-Cost Analysis* 11, no. 1 (2019): 131–149.

3.2 THE REASONS FOR ACQUIRING DOGS

Why do households say they acquire dogs? To address this important question, we use data collected in a nationally representative 2018 survey of almost 5,000 U.S. dog owners.[7] As we discuss in more detail in Chapter 6, the primary purpose of the survey was to provide data for estimating people's willingness to pay to reduce the mortality risk faced by their dogs. That survey did so to facilitate an estimate of the average implicit value people place on the lives of their dogs. Fortunately, the survey, which we henceforth refer to as the PVL Survey, also collected data that is very useful for answering questions about why people acquire dogs.

Table 3.1 reports the percentages of respondents who indicated that their dogs played a specific role in their household. Respondents were also given the opportunity to specify more than one role if they wished to do so. The potential roles are listed in the first data column of Table 3.1. The second column shows the percentage of respondents who indicated a specific role or roles. A large majority of respondents, 93 percent, viewed their dogs as pets. Over half of respondents considered them to be companions, and about a quarter considered them to be guards. Other roles were much less common. Beyond guard duty, 4 percent of dogs served as guides for the disabled, 1 percent worked in agriculture, and 1 percent

---

[7] The PVL Survey was conducted from May 18 to 23, 2018. For a description of the survey, see Deven Carlson, Simon Haeder, Hank Jenkins-Smith, Joseph Ripberger, Carol Silva, and David Weimer. "Monetizing Bowser: A Contingent Valuation of the Statistical Value of Dog Life." *Journal of Benefit-Cost Analysis* 11, no. 1 (2019): 131–149.

TABLE 3.2 *Positive aspects of pet ownership*

	Positive aspects	
Response	Improves quality of life in home (percent) $n = 4,589$	Important for kids to learn responsibility (percent) $n = 4,586$
Strongly disagree	1	1
Disagree	0	0
Somewhat disagree	1	1
Neither agree nor disagree	4	8
Somewhat agree	8	13
Agree	21	29
Strongly agree	66	47

Source: PVL Survey, May 18 to 23, 2018.

were used for breeding purposes. As we would expect, the roles overlapped. We return to discuss the roles of dogs in more detail in Chapter 7. As indicated in the last column, most dogs that are seen as companions or guards were also considered pets (92 percent each). Most of the nonguard working dogs were also viewed as pets: 83 percent, 85 percent, and 69 percent with guide, breeding, and agricultural roles, respectively.

The PVL Survey asked respondents if they agreed with a number of statements presented to them about the value of pets. As all the respondents were dog owners, it is reasonable to interpret their responses as primarily applying specifically to dogs. Table 3.2 summarizes the statements and the responses on a seven-point scale that ranges from "strongly disagree" to "strongly agree." The first statement was, "Pets improve the quality of life in my home." As the first data column of Table 3.2 shows, 87 percent of respondents agreed or strongly agreed. The second statement was, "It is important for kids to learn responsibility by taking care of pets." As the second column of Table 3.2 shows, 76 percent of respondents agreed or strongly agreed.[8] A large majority of respondents clearly see their dogs as contributing to their quality of life. A majority of respondents regard caring for dogs as also offering an opportunity for children to learn responsibility.

---

[8] The percentages agreeing or strongly agreeing were 80 percent and 73 percent, respectively, for respondents with and without children living at home.

3.3 ALL IN THE FAMILY

Many Americans state that they view their dogs as family members. Table 3.3 shows the frequency of responses to the statement "I consider my pets to be part of the family" among those who view their dogs as pets. Because all respondents were dog owners, we again interpret these answers as applying specifically to dogs, as well as to pets in general. As shown in the first data column of Table 3.3, 95 percent of respondents at least somewhat agreed with this statement about family inclusion. Both men and women showed a similar level of overall agreement, as shown in data columns two and three. Respondents who agreed or strongly agreed accounted for 89 percent, with strongly agree being the modal response. Clearly, a large majority of dog owners say they consider their dogs to be members of their families.

The sociologist Andrea Laurent-Simpson reviews a number of factors that have contributed to what she labels the "multispecies family," often one that includes dogs.[9] She argues that an early factor in the emergence (although obviously not from an evolutionary perspective!) was the development of an urban middle class that regarded pets as a residual connection to their rural roots and as a way of instilling in children a responsibility of care toward animals – urbanization may also have contributed to the move of dogs from the yard to the house, making their inclusion in the family seem more natural. Further, as their roles shifted from participating in tasks like hunting, herding, and guarding to becoming sources of

TABLE 3.3　*Pet dogs as family members*

	"I consider my pets to be part of the family"		
Response	All (percent) *n* = 4,591	Female (percent) *n* = 2,314	Male (percent) *n* = 2,277
Strongly disagree	1	1	1
Disagree	0	0	1
Somewhat disagree	1	1	1
Neither agree nor disagree	3	4	4
Somewhat agree	6	5	8
Agree	16	12	20
Strongly agree	73	78	66

Source: PVL Survey, May 18 to 23, 2018.

[9] Andrea Laurent-Simpson. *Just Like Family: How Companion Animals Joined the Household* (New York, NY: New York University Press, 2021).

entertainment and companionship, many family members came to perceive dogs as being more like persons. She also argues that, more recently, the broadening of the perceived meaning of the family itself has opened the doors to thinking of dogs as family members.[10] In sum, the family is primarily a social, rather than biological, construct.

How are views on dogs as family members changing over time? The earliest relevant national U.S. survey question we are able to find is from 2001. A CBS News Poll asked dog owners, "Do you consider your dog to be a member of your family, or not?"[11] Similar to the 2018 PVL responses, 90 percent of the respondents answered that they considered their dogs to be family members. Another survey in 2005 found that 85 percent of respondents viewed dogs as family members.[12] These findings suggest that the change toward viewing dogs as family members in North America is not that recent. We certainly can recall from our youth households in which dogs seemed to be viewed as family members. We also note John Steinbeck's, *Travels with Charley: In Search for America*,[13] which suggests he viewed his poodle Charley as a family member, perhaps even the one he chose as his companion as he faced his terminal illness.

3.4 CHANGING SOCIAL AND LEGAL CONSTRUCTS OF THE FAMILY

Laurent-Simpson notes the changes that have occurred in family structure over the last two centuries. In North America, families are no longer thought of as being composed of heterosexual parents with children. Blended families, same-sex marriages, unmarried couples, and childless couples are now common and are socially, and usually legally, regarded as family demographic units. This broader and more fluid social and legal construction of the family provides a framework that facilitates the shift of dogs (and cats)

---

[10] Lundy Langston. "Political and Social Construction of Families Through Pedagogy in Family Law Classrooms." *Denver University Law Review* 73, no. 1 (1995): 179–200.
  Janet Halley and Kerry Rittich. "Critical Directions in Comparative Family Law: Genealogies and Contemporary Studies of Family Law Exceptionalism." *The American Journal of Comparative Law* 58, no. 4 (2010): 753–775.
[11] CBS News. CBS News Poll: Taxes/Economy/Energy/China, *CBS News* (Ithaca, NY: Roper Center for Public Opinion Research, Cornell University, 2001).
[12] Pew Research Center for the People & the Press/Pew Social & Demographic Trends, Pew Research Center Poll # 2005-SDT01: Pew Social Trends: Family Bonds. Princeton Survey Research Associates International (Ithaca, NY: Roper Center for Public Opinion Research, Cornell University, 2005).
[13] John Steinbeck. *Travels with Charley: In Search for America* (New York, NY: Viking Press, 1962).

from just pets to some status more akin to family members. Adults in families now often see and refer to themselves as dogs' parents. Their parents may even see and refer to themselves as the dogs' grandparents.

Changing social and legal constructs of the family affects the nature and extent of supervision for both children and dogs. One of your authors grew up in a small U.S. town in the 1950s. Both children and dogs largely roamed free. Many parents sent their children out to play with no more instructions than "to return home in time for dinner." Many dogs roamed almost at will as well; approximately a quarter of all dogs in the United States were free to roam in the 1960s.[14] They were undoubtedly happy to have such freedom! But they certainly produced their share of negative effects, including excrement underfoot, dead baby rabbits, chased cars, undesired puppies, and the residue of unpleasant encounters with skunks.[15] Today, parents of small children who let them roam would likely get a visit from the family service department, and those who let their dogs roam would likely end up with a fine, or even dreaded impoundment.

How has the change in roles from village roamer to household companion affected the welfare of dogs? It has certainly involved trade-offs. With the constraints of household companionship come safety, greater food security, and access to veterinary care. However, it also brings "unrealistic social demands that can lead to anxiety, depression, and aggression" and it results in some dogs sharing the risk of obesity with their human companions.[16] One may be tempted to draw parallels with the changing welfare of children as their lives have become more programmed with less opportunity to roam.

3.5 THE ALLOCATION OF HOUSEHOLD CARE RESPONSIBILITIES

Turning to the necessary care of dogs, how does the care of dogs reflect the well-documented unequal division of household labor between genders? Although there is some evidence of movement toward greater

---

[14] Andrew N. Rowan and Tamara Kartal. "Dog Population & Dog Sheltering Trends in the United States of America." *Animals (Basel)* 8, no. 5 (2018): 68–88.

[15] Your author's free-roaming dog needed tomato-juice baths after several encounters with skunks.

[16] Iben Meyer, Björn Forkman, Merete Fredholm, Carmen Glanville, Bernt Guldbrandt-sen, Eliza R. Izaguirre, Clare Palmer, and Peter Sandøe. "Pampered Pets or Poor Bastards? The Welfare of Dogs Kept as Companion Animals." *Applied Animal Behaviour Science* 251, June (2022): 1–6 at 1.

TABLE 3.4 *Gendered roles in dog care in households with two or more adults*

	Based on respondents answering that they are primarily responsible	
	Women (percent)	Men (percent)
Feeding	83	81
Grooming	69	60
Walking	78	82
Taking to vet	76	75

Source: PVL Survey, May 18 to 23, 2018.

gender equality in the division of childcare and household labor over time, a gap remains.[17] The PVL Survey asked respondents about their roles in the care of their dogs. Table 3.4 shows the responses of pet owners to questions about care for dogs in households with two or more adults. The percentages of women and men who report being primarily responsible for feeding and taking their dogs to the veterinarian are quite similar. However, women are 9 percentage points more likely than men to report that they are the primary dog groomer, and men are 4 percentage points more likely than women to report that they are the primary dog walker.[18]

We believe that these particular reported percentages are somewhat suspect. With a random selection of the respondents in multi-adult households, we would expect to find aggregate reports of being primarily responsible for each particular type of care averaging out to about 50 percent – perhaps somewhat more if adults equally share responsibility, so that an ambiguity might reasonably allow each to report being primarily responsible. The data in Table 3.4 suggest that there is overreporting of care, perhaps based on wishful thinking! A study that compares data from time diaries with survey responses suggests overreporting in surveys of time spent on household tasks by both genders. But the study found greater overreporting of care by males following the addition of a child to

[17] For example, see Suzanne M. Bianchi, Liana C. Sayer, Melissa A. Milkie, and John P. Robinson. "Housework: Who Did, Does or Will Do It, and How Much Does It Matter?" *Social Forces* 91, no. 1 (2012): 55–63. For an overview, see Oriel Sullivan. "The Gendered Division of Household Labor." In Barbara J. Risman, Carissa M. Froyum, William J. Scarborough, eds., *Handbook of the Sociology of Gender*, 2nd ed. (Cham, Switzerland: Springer, 2018), pp. 377–392.

[18] Controlling for full-time employment out of the house does not substantially alter these gender differences.

the family.[19] A comparison of responses by women and men in the same couple about their own and their partner's time spent on household labor also suggests more overreporting by males.[20] The overreporting of care and the evidence that men are more prone to engage in it suggest that we should be cautious in interpreting Table 3.4 as a reliable indication that men and women share dog-care responsibilities roughly equally.

Families make decisions about what is to be produced within the household and what is to be imported into it. When all adults in the family work outside the home, constraints of time and schedule flexibility may make importing, such as for meals and cleaning services, more attractive. Higher household income may facilitate such imports. In the case of dog care, families may turn to professional dog walkers, groomers, and daycare providers. Indeed, inflexibility in work schedules may make the purchase of dog services more pressing than *substitutes* for other household labor – especially puppies and elderly dogs usually need to do their business more often than just before and after their keepers' work hours. The size of the pet services industry has been growing with increased dog ownership and increasing household income, and financial analysts predict that the industry will continue to grow at a fast rate over the decade.[21]

3.6 DOGS AS HOUSEHOLD CO-CONSUMERS

Most introductory textbook treatments of consumption focus on the individual as the appropriate unit of analysis. However, as we discuss in more detail in the next section, the theory of the family treats households as making consumption choices. In practice, most households collectively make the major consumption decisions, so it is a more useful unit of analysis. Allowances to children (or spouses or partners) may delegate some consumption decisions, but most important purchases result from some discussion or even negotiation among family members.

---

[19] Jill E. Yavorsky, Claire M. Kamp Dush, and Sarah J. Schoppe-Sullivan. "The Production of Inequality: The Gender Division of Labor Across the Transition to Parenthood." *Journal of Marriage and the Family* 77, no. 3 (2015): 662–679.

[20] Yoshinori Kamo. "'He Said, She Said': Assessing Discrepancies in Husbands' and Wives' Reports on the Division of Household Labor." *Social Science Research* 29, no. 4 (2000): 459–476.

[21] For example, Morgan Stanley predicts that the pet services industry in the United States will grow at the substantial annual rate of 8 percent through 2030. Morgan Stanley "Research Report: Puppy Love Boosts Pet Care Industry," November 2 (2022). www.morganstanley.com/ideas/pet-care-industry-outlook-2030. Accessed February 3, 2023.

Within families, children are sometimes involved in important consumption decisions. This could certainly include the decision about whether to add a dog to the family. Once a dog does join a family, it may also be involved in co-consumption in several ways.[22] First, as a part of everyday life, the dog may serve an intermediary role in connecting an owner to services that would not otherwise be purchased, such as veterinary care, grooming services, and visits to dog parks. The presence of a dog can affect individual and family consumption decisions more generally. For example, the presence of the dog may affect choices ranging from meeting (and so the choice) of spouses to car purchases. Second, as a "princess" or "prince" in the household, an owner may attempt to interpret the dog's experience in consumption, anticipating the dog's preferences and needs. Third, as a "pawed therapist" for an owner, the dog can augment experiences of well-being for the owner. For example, the dog may induce exercise and social interactions (the dog magnet) that would otherwise not occur. Thus, like children, dogs affect household consumption decisions even without having a vote at the family kitchen table!

3.7 SOME FACTORS THAT AFFECT THE DEMAND FOR DOGS AS FAMILY MEMBERS

In comparison to the 50 percent of U.S. households that own dogs, only about 40 percent of all families now include children under the age of 18 years.[23] Indeed, as the fraction of households with dogs has increased over time, the fraction of households with children has declined. If dogs as well as children are considered part of the family, then the economist instinctively asks if these trends are occurring because adults view dogs as substitutes for children – as the cost of producing quality children increases, demand for pets and pet quality go up. Of course, these correlations by themselves are only suggestive because other factors that are relevant to the demand for children and pets are also changing over time. Indeed, as suggested by the responses in Table 3.2 to the question about the role of pets in children-learning responsibility, it is quite possible that children and pets are *complements* rather than substitutes – as the cost of producing quality children decreases, demand for pets increases.

[22] Eliisa Kylkilahti, Henna Syrjälä, Jaakko Autio, Ari Kuismin, and Minna Autio. "Understanding Co-consumption between Consumers and Their Pets." *International Journal of Consumer Studies* 40, no. 1 (2016): 125–131.
[23] United States Census Bureau. "Census Bureau Releases New Estimates on America's Families and Living Arrangements," November 29, 2021.

Economist Gary Becker pioneered the study of the family from the perspective of the allocation of resources within households.[24] Within that framework, reciprocal *altruism* among family members underlies the assumption of the existence of a joint household utility function that translates the consumption of goods into an index of satisfaction. (This assumption allows us to show indifference curves for the clan in Figures 2.3 and 2.4.) We assume that households maximize their collective utility by making choices about the allocation of time among market and household labor in a way that facilitates the consumption of goods to maximize satisfaction. Among these goods are the number and "quality" of children, where household investment in children determines their quality.

3.8 ARE PETS SUBSTITUTES OR COMPLEMENTS?

One approach to answering the question of whether pets are substitutes for children involves adding the number and quality of pets to the household utility function and deriving the relationships of interest. Peter M. Schwarz and colleagues take this approach.[25] They do so by framing their analysis in terms of a Becker-like model in which the quantity and quality of pets, as well as the quantity and quality of children, affect household utility. They use data from the Consumer Expenditure Survey, which surveys families for five successive quarters.[26] The researchers used data from the first quarter of 1980 through the first quarter of 2003. After eliminating farm and military households and cases with missing data, they had over 47 thousand observations of single-adult households, of which 23 percent had pets. Among the over 66 thousand observations of married-couple households, 46 percent of households had pets. For both sets of observations, the complete data set allowed them to estimate the probability of having a pet. The data on expenditures on pets by pet owners was quite comprehensive and supported their estimation of models of pet expenditures (purchases of pets, pet supplies, medicine for

[24] See, for example, Gary S. Becker. "An Economic Analysis of Fertility." In *National Bureau of Economic Research, Demographic and Economic Change in Developed Countries* (Princeton, NJ: Princeton University Press, 1960), 209–231; Gary S. Becker. "On the Relevance of the New Economics of the Family." *American Economic Review* 64, no. 2 (1974): 317–319; and Gary S. Becker. *Treatise on the Economics of the Family* (Cambridge, MA: Harvard University Press, 1981).

[25] Peter M. Schwarz, Jennifer L. Troyer, and Jennifer Beck Walker. "Animal House: Economics of Pets and the Household." *The BE Journal of Economic Analysis & Policy* 7, no. 1 (2007): 1–25.

[26] Bureau of Labor Statistics. www.bls.gov/cex/. Accessed November 6, 2022.

pets, pet services, and veterinary expenses for pets). These data provided information that allowed them to address the difficult empirical question of whether children and pets are *substitutes* or *complements*.

The statistical approach involved two sets of equations estimated separately for the samples of single-adult and married-couple households. The first set of models predicted the probability that a household has a pet as a function of explanatory variables, including the number and ages of children, that may affect pet ownership. The second set of models estimated the relationship between expenditures on pets and a similar set of explanatory variables for those households with pets.[27]

The researchers found that, across both single-adult and married-couple households, having children younger than 2 years old did decrease the probability of having a pet. However, the presence of children between 2 and 17 years old in the household increased the probability of having a pet. This age dichotomy suggests that pets are not substitutes for very young children but are complements for older children! However, that is not quite the end of the story. Across both samples, the presence of children 2–17 years old in the household reduced pet expenditures; in married-couple households, having more children also reduced pet expenditures. These effects on pet expenditures suggest that pets can also be substitutes for older children as well in some specific situations. The researchers were also able to estimate income *elasticities* for pet expenditures that indicate by what percentage pet expenditures increase for a 1-percent increase in income. Their estimates indicate a very inelastic relationship: pets are viewed more as necessities than as luxuries. Interestingly, the income elasticities are similar for single-adult households (whether male or female headed), for married-couple households, and for separated male and female earnings within married-couple households. That is, pet owners in different family situations and with different income levels tend to make similar expenditures on their pets.

3.9 DOG EXPOSURE MATTERS

Underlying most empirical research into consumer behavior like that employed by Schwarz and his colleagues is the assumption that consumers share similar utility functions that differ only by commonly observed

---

[27] Readers may recognize that the researchers had to take account of selection into pet ownership to derive consistent statistical estimates of the factors affecting expenditure on pets. The authors used a maximum likelihood approach that is an alternative to the widely known Heckman Two-Step Procedure. Home ownership served as an instrument for identifying the probability of pet ownership.

demographic characteristics, such as age, educational attainment, and gender. However, other differences that are often not measured are almost always relevant to demand – their omission contributes to the (residual) error terms in statistical models. With respect to household demand for dogs, for instance, one can easily hypothesize that adults who fear dogs, perhaps because of unpleasant encounters when they were children, would not want to own dogs. Adults with favorable prior experiences with dogs would be more likely to own dogs. In other words, prior socialization may affect attitudes, as with political socialization, where mothers' political views strongly influence children.[28] Evidence from a cohort study in the United Kingdom shows that mothers who had a dog when they were children contribute to positive attitudes toward dog ownership by their adult children: mothers with pets as children were more likely to own dogs irrespective of education level.[29] Aspects of employment may also affect dog ownership behavior: uncertain work schedules and required travel for work may make it difficult to care for a dog, especially for adults living alone.

Family composition may not always reflect careful choice. A child may only join a family because of an unexpected pregnancy. Although dogs mostly join families through explicit choices, some acquisitions are unplanned and occur without any preparation. Evidence from the United Kingdom shows that about a fifth of dogs serendipitously join their families without them performing any research.[30] Along the same lines, a study of U.S. adopters distinguishes between "planners," who analyze desired characteristics before selecting a dog, and "impartials," who do not; the latter include some people who can be described as being "smitten" by a particular dog.[31] (Luis, you lucky dog!) Planners can potentially do research to help match desired characteristics to breeds.

[28] Richard G. Niemi and Barbara I. Sobieszek. "Political Socialization." *Annual Review of Sociology* 3 (1977): 209–233.

[29] Carri Westgarth, Jon Heron, Andy R. Ness, Peter Bundred, Rosalind M. Gaskell, Karen P. Coyne, Alexander J. German, Sandra McCune, and Susan Dawson. "Family Pet Ownership During Childhood: Findings from a UK Birth Cohort and Implications for Public Health Research." *International Journal of Environmental Research and Public Health* 7, no. 10 (2010): 3704–3729.

[30] Katrina E. Holland, Rebecca Mead, Rachel A. Casey, Melissa M. Upjohn, and Robert M. Christley. "'Don't Bring Me a Dog … I'll Just Keep It': Understanding Unplanned Dog Acquisitions amongst a Sample of Dog Owners Attending Canine Health and Welfare Community Events in the United Kingdom." *Animals (Basel)* 11, no. 3 (2021): 605–620.

[31] Leslie Irvine. *If You Tame Me: Understanding Our Connection with Animals* (Philadelphia, PA: Temple University Press, 2004), 94.

3.10 MYOPIA AND OPTIMISM BIAS

As do children, dogs have innate characteristics that can influence their life course. Unlike the parents of children, prospective dog owners can influence the characteristics of their dogs through the choice of breeds, the type and reliability of sources (see Chapter 4), or even the choice of specific parents for puppies. (The emergence of gender screening and sperm selection may be eroding this distinction!) Perhaps, like many new parents, first-time dog owners could easily underestimate the time, expense, and required changes in lifestyle that will result from their decision to bring a dog into the family. Unlike the parents of children, dog owners can relinquish their dogs to shelters, and many do. However, despite behavioral problems and unexpected costs, most dogs remain in the family.[32]

The unforeseen costs that surprise many new dog owners may result from a failure to gather information about dog ownership. It may also result from *optimism bias*, in which people overestimate the probability of favorable events and underestimate the probability of unfavorable events.[33] More generally, prospective dog owners may make decisions based on the perceived utility that they will receive (choice utility), which differs from the utility that they actually experience.[34]

Economists Bernheim B. Douglas and Antonio Rangel posit that choice utility may be affected by ancillary factors that affect decisions but not experienced utility.[35] In the dog acquisition context, the irresistible cuteness of puppies may be one such ancillary factor. Some people acquiring

---

[32] Common methodological practices, such as the lumping of behavioral issues into a single category, have likely led to an overemphasis on behavioral problems of dogs in relinquishment. See Gary J. Patronek, Janis Bradley, and Elizabeth Arps. "Saving Normal: A New Look at Behavioral Incompatibilities and Dog Relinquishment to Shelters." *Journal of Veterinary Behavior* 49, March (2022): 36–45. Also see Kim Lambert, Jason Coe, Lee Niel, Cate Dewey, and Jan M. Sargeant. "A Systematic Review and Meta-analysis of the Proportion of Dogs Surrendered for Dog-related and Owner-related Reasons." *Preventive Veterinary Medicine* 118, no. 1 (2015): 148–160.

[33] For example, see Neil D. Weinstein. "Unrealistic Optimism about Future Life Events." *Journal of Personality and Social Psychology* 39, no. 5 (1980): 806–820. The concept has been explored extensively in the context of project management. For an overview, see James Prater, Konstantinos Kirytopoulos, and Tony Ma. "Optimism Bias within the Project Management Context: A Systematic Quantitative Literature Review." *International Journal of Managing Projects in Business* 10, no. 2 (2017): 370–385.

[34] Daniel Kahneman and Richard H. Thaler. "Economic Analysis and the Psychology of Utility: Applications to Compensation Policy." *American Economic Review* 81, no. 2 (1991): 341–346.

[35] Bernheim B. Douglas and Antonio Rangel. "Toward Choice-Theoretic Foundations for Behavioral Welfare Economics." *American Economic Review* 97, no. 2 (2007): 464–470.

puppies are myopic and do not think about the long-term relationship between owner and dog, especially for larger breeds that may become difficult to manage as adults. Nonetheless, the fact that most people do keep their dogs suggests an emotional bond of some sort usually forms. It might very well be based on altruism, either toward other family members, especially children, who become attached to the dog, or toward the dog itself. It might also be a manifestation of an *endowment effect* in which the costs of losing the desired aspects of the dog's membership in the family receive more weight than the benefits of avoiding the undesirable behaviors.[36]

3.11 FACTORS THAT AFFECT THE CHOICE OF DOGS: LOOKS MATTER

The long association of dogs with humans has resulted in a great variety of the kinds of dogs. They range in size from tiny "teacup" dogs to large mastiffs. They vary considerably in color and facial features, and whether they have fur, hair, or both. Their temperaments and aptitudes differ by breed, as well as by the personalities of individual dogs. Their expected longevity and morbidity risks vary across sizes and breeds. As puppies are usually adopted months after birth, their socialization to people and other dogs, as well as their physical condition, also vary. Although some dogs enter families in somewhat unusual circumstances that do not require explicit choices about their characteristics, such as by taking in a dog that a relative or friend can no longer keep, purposeful selection does require it.

Research by behaviorists who study animals demonstrates the importance of the physical appearance of dogs to many prospective owners.[37] Anthropomorphic selection has clearly shaped the evolution of dogs. One of these selection pressures favors "physical and behavioral traits that facilitate the attribution of human mental states to nonhumans."[38] Anthropomorphic selection helps explain the high demand for brachycephalic breeds like French bulldogs, whose wide faces and short snouts

---

[36] The endowment effect has been an important concept in the development of behavioral economics. See, for example, Daniel Kahneman, Jack L. Knetsch, and Richard H. Thaler. "Anomalies: The Endowment Effect, Loss Aversion, and Status Quo Bias." *Journal of Economic Perspectives* 5, no. 1 (1991): 193–206.

[37] This section benefits greatly from Katrina E. Holland. "Acquiring a Pet Dog: A Review of Factors Affecting the Decision-Making of Prospective Dog Owners." *Animals (Basel)* 9, no. 4 (2019): 124–142.

[38] James Serpell. "Anthropomorphism and Anthropomorphic selection – Beyond the 'Cute Response'." *Society & Animals* 11, no. 1 (2003): 83–100 at p. 446.

make them resemble human babies more than most other breeds.[39] This demand for brachycephalic dogs exists despite the widely known increased health risks they face. A survey of U.S. residents found that over a quarter of respondents did not consider genetic health to be an important factor in the choice of their dog.[40]

A study of U.S. breed popularity over the period 1926–2005 examined the influence of breed characteristics, such as behavioral traits, longevity, and inherited disorders.[41] The only breed characteristic that was consistently significantly positively correlated with breed popularity was risk of an inherited disorder. This correlation held not only for the entire period but also for the most recent year of data, 2005. This correlation, however, almost certainly does not indicate a causal relationship, but rather suggests that dog purchasers tend to ignore inherited disorders. Although less consistently, correlations observed over time of popularity with behavioral traits nonetheless do suggest that breeds are popular despite negative traits, such as aggression toward owner, or lack of positive traits, such as trainability. These results suggest that breed popularity reflects fashion rather than function.

3.12 THE ROLE OF FASHION AND FADS

An early instance of the influence of fashion involves American's perception of the desirability of German shepherds as pets. During World War I, Germany purposely promoted the German shepherd as a national symbol. In response, its popularity fell in the United States. However, the 1918 film *Rin Tin Tin* and its sequels, starring a German shepherd rescued by an American GI in France, rehabilitated the breed to make it one of the most popular in the United States in the late 1920s.[42]

---

[39] Rowena M. A. Packer, Dan G. O'Neill, Francesca Fletcher, and Mark J. Farnworth. "Come for the Looks, Stay for the Personality? A Mixed Methods Investigation of Reacquisition and Owner Recommendation of Bulldogs, French Bulldogs and Pugs." *PLoS One* 15, no. 8 (2020): 1–21. See also Julie Hecht and Alexandra Horowitz. "Seeing Dogs: Human Preferences for Dog Physical Attributes." *Anthrozoös* 28, no. 1 (2015): 153–163.

[40] Courtney Bir, Nicole J. Olynk Widmar, and Candace C. Croney. "Stated Preferences for Dog Characteristics and Sources of Acquisition." *Animals (Basel)* 7, no. 8 (2017): 59–78.

[41] Stefano Ghirlanda, Alberto Acerbi, Harold Herzog, and James A. Serpell. "Fashion vs. Function in Cultural Evolution: The Case of Dog Breed Popularity." *PLoS One* 8, no. 9 (2013): 1–6.

[42] "Paws for Thought: A Dog Is Man's Best Friend but People Are Fickle." *The Economist*, December 24 (2022): 16–17.

Harold Herzog provides detailed evidence about the importance of fashion over function in an analysis of almost 48.6 million puppy registrations with the American Kennel Club from 1946 through 2003.[43] Some breeds, like affenpincers, show a constant low level of registrations, others, like Labrador retrievers, show a steady increase, and some, like Cocker spaniels, show repeated cycling. However, nine breeds, Afghan hounds, chow chows, Dalmatians, Doberman pinschers, Great Danes, Irish setters, Old English sheep dogs, Rottweilers, and Saint Bernards, show a striking pattern of growth followed by decline. Increases (booms) occurred over periods ranging from 10 to 18 years and decreases (busts) occurred over periods ranging from 10 to 16 years. The percentage increase from the initiation of increase to its peak ranges from 716 percent for Dalmatians to 10,772 percent for Old English sheep dogs!

Herzog examined in detail the Dalmatian boom that followed the 1985 rerelease of the film *101 Dalmatians* and found that it was followed by an especially dramatic bust. Herzog also notes that the Old English Sheep Dog boom followed the release of the 1959 film, *The Shaggy Dog*. (The 2006 remake of *The Shaggy Dog* featured a Bearded Collie, which then rose in the American Kennel Club's Most Popular Dog Breed Ranking from 101 in 2005 to 32 in 2020.)[44] A more recent analysis that looked at the impact of the release of 29 films featuring 36 breeds on American Kennel Club registration trends found statistically significant increases lasting up to 10 years following release of the films.[45] Interestingly, a similar analysis of the effects of the breed of the winner of the Westminster Kennel Club Dog Show on breed popularity failed to find an effect,[46] "suggesting that reaching a small specialized audience may not be as effective as reaching the general public" in creating a fashion.[47]

[43] Harold A. Herzog. "Forty-two Thousand and One Dalmatians: Fads, Social Contagion, and Dog Breed Popularity." *Society & Animals* 14, no. 4 (2006): 383–397.

[44] Jan Reisen. "The Most Popular Dog Breeds of 2020." *American Kennel Club*, March 16 (2021); and American Kennel Club, Dog Registration Statistics, www.akc.org/press-releases/labrador-retriever-leads-the-pack-according-to-akcs-2005-registration/. Accessed August 23, 2023.

[45] Stefano Ghirlanda, Alberto Acerbi, and Harold Herzog. "Dog Movie Stars and Dog Breed Popularity: A Case Study in Media Influence on Choice." *PLoS One* 9, no. 9 (2014): 1–5. The authors also find positive registration trends prior to release of films suggesting that filmmakers may have purposely chosen trendy breeds.

[46] Harold A. Herzog and Steven M. Elias. "Effects of Winning the Westminster Kennel Club Dog Show on Breed Popularity." *Journal of the American Veterinary Medical Association* 225, no. 3 (2004): 365–367.

[47] Ghirlanda et al., p. 4.

3.13 THE UNDERLYING ECONOMICS OF FADS

The economic theory of fads and fashion attributes their occurrence to "information cascades" that emerge "when it is optimal for an individual, having observed the actions of those ahead of him, to follow the behavior of the preceding individual without regard to his own information."[48] Cascades can either go up to apply upward momentum (a series of early adoptions results in subsequent adoptions) or down to apply downward momentum (a series of early rejections results in subsequent rejections). If everyone receives signals with the same accuracy, then the cascade develops when the observed actions of those earlier in the cascade incorporate more information than an individual signal, so that the optimal decision simply becomes a mimicking of the action rather than applying one's own information to the decision. Fads tend to be broad but brittle, in the sense that they are widely followed but that a relatively small amount of new information can break their momentum. A boom-and-bust pattern of breed popularity is consistent with the presence of information cascades. So too are increases in breed popularity that follow films starring dogs that begin a cascade for the featured breed. But breeds do differ substantively in terms of traits and characteristics of relevance to potential owners, so that fads are likely to follow preferences to some extent. Public information about these traits and characteristics is readily available as an alternative to observed actions. Further, wider adoption of a breed increases the chances of encountering it, creating a greater opportunity to observe the traits and characteristics as well as the popularity of the breed reflected in the up cascade.

3.14 ARE BREED CHOICES RATIONAL?

The focus of prospective owners on appearance or popular breeds, even when it involves trade-offs with health risks, does not necessarily conflict with neoclassical demand theory. Neoclassical theory tends to treat preferences as exogenous, or put more bluntly, "there is no accounting for tastes." Yet, many behavioral economists would argue that such decisions reflect irrational time preferences: the person making the decision places too much weight on immediate gains (adorability) or losses relative to future gains or losses (down-the-road medical expenses and forgone dog-years of life).

[48] Sushil Bikhchandani, David Hirshleifer, and Ivo Welch. "A Theory of Fads, Fashion, Custom, and Cultural Change as Informational Cascades." *Journal of Political Economy* 100, no. 5 (1992): 992–1026 at p. 994.

Neoclassical economics usually assumes that people employ constant *exponential discounting* over the time horizon; consequently, the percentage lower value of receiving a dollar today relative to receiving a dollar next year is the same as, say, the lower value of receiving a dollar 10 years from now relative to receiving a dollar 11 years from now. Only the use of exponential discounting, that applies the same percentage discount over time, can guarantee what economists call "time consistency." Using exponential discounting, and assuming no changes in circumstances, a decision made about future consumption today will not change when the future time period is actually reached. Richard Thaler provides a clear illustration of how time inconsistency works: someone who is unwilling to trade one apple today to receive two apples tomorrow, but would be willing today to agree to trade one apple a year from now for two apples a year and a day from now.[49] Time inconsistency arises because, although the person would agree to a binding contract today to wait the extra day for another apple a year from now, he or she would still choose one apple if free to actually make the choice 1 year from now.

One way to explain the prevalence of time inconsistency is to assume that people use nonexponential discounting that applies a larger percentage penalty for delay the closer it is to the present.[50] An alternative model recognizes that immediate impatience is a response to a temptation.[51] In the case of dog acquisition, the temptation may be to select an especially cute puppy or a breed that is perceived to confer social status despite awareness of higher health or behavioral risks.

3.15 HOUSEHOLDS WITHOUT HOUSES

Providing adequate care for dogs can be demanding, even for those with stable housing and a decent income. Dog ownership is obviously much more challenging for the homeless. Nonetheless, the estimates that about 10 percent of the homeless have service animals, emotional support animals, or companion animals.[52] Consistent with this estimate,

---

[49] Richard Thaler. "Some Experimental Evidence on Dynamic Inconsistency." *Economic Letters* 8, no. 3 (1981): 201–207.

[50] For an overview, see David L. Weimer. *Behavioral Economics for Cost-Benefit Analysis: Benefit Validity When Sovereign Consumers Seem to Make Mistakes* (New York, NY: Cambridge University Press, 2017).

[51] Faruk Gul and Wolfgang Pesendorfer. "Self-control, Revealed Preference and Consumption Choice." *Review of Economic Dynamics* 7, no. 2 (2004), 243–264.

[52] Estimate based on reports from Continuum of Care (CoC) Programs. National Alliance to End Homelessness and PetSmart Charities. *Improving Outcomes in Homelessness: Keeping*

a large-sample study of the unsheltered homeless in Los Angeles found pre-COVID rates of pet ownership ranging between 9 and 12 percent.[53] Although we do not have quantitative data on the type of pet accompanying the homeless, our observations on the street and of photos on advocacy web pages suggest that dogs predominate.

A review of relevant research identifies a number of adverse effects of pet ownership for the homeless.[54] Pet ownership may contribute to becoming or remaining unsheltered in the first place.[55] Many landlords do not allow pets, reducing the possibilities for moving into housing; not all shelters accommodate pets, so that some homeless who otherwise would be at least temporarily sheltered are not. Pet ownership may also reduce the feasibility of employment for the homeless, enrollment in training programs, and access to other support services when potential participants cannot provide safe care for their pets when they are not with them. Providing food for pets stresses already very limited financial resources, and paid veterinary care is beyond reach.

Many homeless people decide to keep pets despite these disadvantages. This will not surprise many of our readers. Pets provide companionship and comfort in stressful circumstances. Research suggests that pet companionship improves the mental health of the homeless and reduces stress, depression, and possibly the rate of suicide.[56] Pets may be especially beneficial for homeless youth.[57] As with others, pets may increase social interaction

People and Pets Together (n.d.), www.endhomelessness.org/wp-content/uploads/2020/03/ Keeping-People-and-Pets-Together-031220.pdf. Accessed November 6, 2022.

[53] Benjamin Henwood, Eldin Dzubur, Harmony Rhoades, Patricia St. Clair, and Robynn Cox. "Pet Ownership in the Unsheltered Homeless Population in Los Angeles." *Journal of Social Distress and Homelessness* 30, no. 2 (2021): 191–194.

[54] Nick Kerman, Sophia Gran-Ruaz, and Michelle Lem. "Pet Ownership and Homelessness: A Scoping Review." *Journal of Social Distress and the Homeless* 28, no. 2 (2019): 106–114.

[55] A U.S. study found that 18 percent of homeless pet owners in its sample refused housing because of their pets. Courtney Cronley, Elizabeth B. Strand, David A. Patterson, and Sarah Gwaltney. "Homeless People Who Are Animal Caretakers: A Comparative Study." *Psychological Reports* 105, no. 2 (2009): 481–499.

[56] Michelle Cleary, Denis Visentin, Deependra Kaji Thapa, Sancia West, Toby Raeburn, and Rachel Kornhaber. "The Homeless and their Animal Companions: An Integrative Review." *Administration and Policy in Mental Health and Mental Health Services Research* 47, no. 1 (2020): 47–59.

[57] Harmony Rhoades, Hailey Winetrobe, and Eric Rice. "Pet Ownership among Homeless Youth: Associations with Mental Health, Service Utilization and Housing Status." *Child Psychiatry & Human Development* 46, no. 2 (2015): 237–244; Michelle Lem, Jason B. Coe, Derek B. Haley, Elizabeth Stone, and William O'Grady. "The Protective Association between Pet Ownership and Depression among Street-Involved Youth: A Cross-Sectional Study." *Anthrozoös* 29, no. 1 (2016): 123–136.

for the homeless who frequently suffer from isolating stigmatization.[58] Although some pedestrians respond negatively to homeless dog owners, more respond positively, including making donations that are directed to providing food for dogs.[59] Dogs in particular may provide some protection against risks encountered by those living on the street, especially for female youth.[60] Not surprisingly, like a majority of housed people, the homeless typically also see their dogs as family members to whom they feel a responsibility as well as attachment.[61] Research suggests that pets contribute to less negative behavior by the homeless. A fear of being separated from their pets through their institutionalization has been identified as contributing to sobriety and to avoidance of involvement in crime.[62]

We can conclude that the aggregate empirical research suggests that the homeless, as do most people, gain in a number of ways from pet ownership. However, some caution is warranted because these studies do not really deal with the direction of causality. That is, they are not designed in a way to show that the pets cause the observed improvements in the homeless quality of life. Therefore, although they do support helping the homeless keep their pets, they do not provide strong evidence that policy interventions to give the homeless pets would result in the positive benefits observed in the existing studies.

3.16 COVID AS A DEMAND SHOCK TO OWNERSHIP

The COVID pandemic spurred demand for pets. A survey by the American Society for the Prevention of Cruelty to Animals (ASPCA) estimated that almost a fifth of U.S. households added a dog or cat between March 2020 and May 2021.[63] An economic interpretation of the surge in the demand

---

[58] Interestingly, an experimental study conducted in Northern Ireland found that the type of dog makes a difference. A Rottweiler was less effective than a puppy or an adult Labrador in prompting positive responses to a homeless person by passing pedestrians. Deborah L. Wells. "The Facilitation of Social Interactions by Domestic Dogs." *Anthrozoös* 17, no. 4 (2004): 340–352.

[59] Leslie Irvine, Kristina N. Kahl, and Jesse M. Smith. "Confrontations and Donations: Encounters between Homeless Pet Owners and the Public." *Sociological Quarterly* 53, no. 1 (2012): 25–43.

[60] Rhoades et al., pp. 6–7.

[61] Louise Scanlon, Pru Hobson-West, Kate Cobb, Anne McBride, and Jenny Stavisky. "Homeless People and Their Dogs: Exploring the Nature and Impact of the Human–Companion Animal Bond." *Anthrozoös* 34, no. 1 (2021): 77–92.

[62] Kerman et al., p. 108.

[63] ASPCA Pandemic Pet Ownership Survey Memo, May 26, 2021. www.aspca.org/about-us/press-releases/new-aspca-survey-shows-overwhelming-majority-dogs-and-cats-acquired-during. Accessed August 23, 2023.

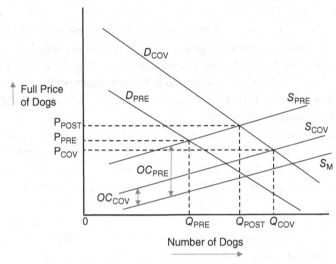

FIGURE 3.1 COVID shock to the supply and demand for dogs

for dogs would attribute it to either an increase in the perceived benefits or a reduction in the perceived costs of dog ownership. Social distancing, lockdowns, and working from home each could very well have increased the benefits of having a dog: canine companionship would substitute for forgone companionship with other people.[64] Spending more time at home and anticipating less travel reduces the *opportunity costs* of adopting a dog, especially puppies, who seem to need almost constant attention. However, the rapid and large response to these changes in the benefits and costs of dog ownership may have been faddish.

Figure 3.1 illustrates the change in the level of dog ownership resulting from the COVID pandemic. The horizontal axis shows the number of dogs owned by households. The vertical axis shows the full price to households of owning dogs, which includes opportunity costs such as time required for dog care and the reduction in schedule flexibility. The line labeled D_{PRE}, the *demand schedule*, shows the quantity of dogs demanded at each full price pre-pandemic. The line labeled S_{PRE}, the *supply schedule* as seen by potential dog owners, shows the quantity of dogs supplied at each full price pre-pandemic. The full price has two components. One component is the price consumers pay to breeders or shelters

---

[64] Cori Bussolari, Jennifer Currin-McCulloch, Wendy Packman, Lori Kogan, and Phyllis Erdman. "'I Couldn't Have Asked for a Better Quarantine Partner!': Experiences with Companion Dogs During COVID-19." *Animals (Basel)* 11, no. 2 (2021): 330–344.

to obtain a dog. These costs are determined by the market supply schedule, S_M. The second component is the opportunity cost of owning a dog beyond the purchase price. Prior to COVID, the supply schedule as seen by consumers is the market supply schedule, S_M, plus these opportunity costs, OC_{PRE}. The market equilibrium in normal times occurs at full price P_{PRE} and quantity of dogs Q_{PRE}, the point at which the quantity supplied equals the quantity demanded.

The pandemic shifts the demand schedule from D_{PRE} to D_{COV} because the companionship value of dogs increases as access to human companionship declines during the pandemic. It also shifts the supply schedule from S_{PRE} to S_{COV} by reducing the opportunity costs of owning dogs from OC_{PRE} to OC_{COV}. The new equilibrium occurs at Q_{COV} and P_{COV} where D_{COV} and S_{COV} intersect. As drawn, the combination of the increased benefits and reduced costs of dog ownership substantially increases ownership. The full price is lower than pre-pandemic, though the market price of dogs increased: the upward slope of S_M means that the increase in the quantity of dogs bought and sold increases the market price of dogs. Because of the change in opportunity costs, COVID results in the full price declining even though the market price increases.

The assessment of the impact of COVID on the market for dogs illustrates how economists carry out what they call *comparative statics*. The analysis begins with an equilibrium, which in this case was the pre-COVID supply and demand schedules. Something exogenously changes, which in this case are both the supply and demand schedules, so that a new equilibrium results. The original and final quantities can then be compared, which in this case was a decline in the full price and an increase in the quantity of dogs purchased.

The increase in the quantity of dogs purchased from Q_{PRE} to Q_{COV} in this simple model of the market is consistent with the observed increase in dog ownership during the pandemic. Although most of social science involves applying models that predict the past in the sense of explaining what has been observed, we often want to use these models to predict what will happen in the future. In the context of this market model, it is reasonable to expect the supply schedule to move toward S_{PRE} as the opportunity costs return to pre-pandemic levels now that the worst of the pandemic has passed. However, it remains a question as to what will happen to post-pandemic demand and, therefore, post-pandemic ownership of dogs?

The ASPCA fielded a survey for a period of over 1 year during which the pandemic was still affecting behavior: 90 percent of those who acquired dogs during that period still had them and 85 percent of dog and cat owners stated that they intended to keep their new family members.[65] Since then, however, the isolationist effects of the pandemic have been dramatically reduced within the United States, with many people returning to in-person employment and schooling. The resulting loss of schedule flexibility generally increases the costs of keeping a dog at home. People may have to secure market services, such as paid dog walkers, and perhaps efforts to deal with dogs' separation anxiety.[66] It may also have adverse effects on dogs who became familiar with around the clock human companionship.[67]

Although only infants can be surrendered under state safe harbor laws, dogs of any age can be surrendered to shelters.[68] Because the wave of additional dog adoptions began during the pandemic, people have expressed concern about large increases in shelter populations once it subsides. Data from the nonprofit organization, Shelter Animals Count, shows that the number of dogs entering shelters from within the shelters' communities decreased by 18 percent from 2019 to 2022.[69] Compared to 2021, however, 2022 has seen a 5-percent rise in the number of dogs entering shelters.[70] But both the fraction of dogs relinquished by owners and the adoption rate remain fairly constant. Thus, although there have been news

---

[65] Ibid.

[66] In big cities like New York, the receding of the pandemic has increased demand, and therefore the earnings, of dog walkers. See Alyson Krueger. "How These Dog Walkers Make Over $100,000 a Year: It's All Those Pandemic Puppies." *New York Times Section ST*, January 29 (2023): 8.

[67] Jessica Pierce, Marc Bekoff. "Home Alone: The Fate of Postpandemic Dogs." *Scientific American Opinion*, October 26 (2021). www.scientificamerican.com/article/home-alone-the-fate-of-postpandemic-dogs/. Accessed November 6, 2022.

[68] Most state safe harbor laws allow people to give infants under 6 months old to state foster care systems without any questions. However, Nebraska initially did not put an age limit in its safe harbor law but had to do so as people began moving to Nebraska to give their teenage children to the foster care because they could not afford necessary medical treatments. Nebraska History. Safe Haven Law, 2008 (n.d.). www.history .nebraska.gov/blog/safe-haven-law-2008#:~:text=Feeling%20that%20the%20law%20 was,up%20to%20thirty%20days%20old. Accessed November 6, 2022.

[69] Shelter Animals Count. "The National Database." www.shelteranimalscount.org/ industry-trends-dashboard/. Accessed February 2, 2023. The data are from 1,233 shelters, which is about a fifth of all U.S. animal shelters. The pandemic also appears to have increased fostering, which, unlike adoption, provides temporary shelter to dogs in people's homes. See Laura A. Reese, Jacquelyn Jacobs, Jordan Gembarski, Caden Opsommer, and Bailey Walker. "The COVID-19 Animal Fostering Boom: Ephemera or Chimera?" *Animals (Basel)* 12, no. 10 (2022): 1325–1336.

[70] Shelter Animals Count. "The National Database." www.shelteranimalscount.org/ industry-trends-dashboard/. Accessed February 2, 2023.

reports of some centers seeing dramatic increases in their populations of dogs, the available aggregate data suggest only a modest increase so far.

Note that economic conditions can also play a role. The most common reason for a household to move from pet ownership to nonownership is the death of the pet. However, for those whose pets did not die, 29 percent who give up pets reported doing so because they could no longer afford the pet.[71] The high inflation in 2022 may have contributed to the surrender of dogs to shelters by lower-income households. One can expect any future increases in the unemployment rate, which disproportionately affects lower-income households, to also contribute to the surrender of dogs. Just as human medical expenses often strain household budgets and are a major cause of personal bankruptcy in the United States,[72] unexpected veterinary expenses can also strain household budgets and contribute to the surrender of dogs.

The post-pandemic fate of newly acquired dogs potentially provides a number of tests of competing economic views about owner motivation and behavior. In the neoclassical economics perspective, the reversal of the reductions in cost and increase in benefits should generate a return of the quantity of dogs purchased and sold to pre-pandemic levels. That is, the post-pandemic equilibrium should be close to the pre-pandemic equilibrium in Figure 3.1 at Q_{PRE} and P_{PRE}. If ownership rates remain closer to those observed at the height of the pandemic, however, neoclassicists would seek an explanation in other changed factors: say, prior investments in knowledge and dog paraphernalia that lower continued ownership costs or perhaps a change in preferences like that in the rational addiction model.[73] Behavioral economists might seek to explain it in terms of the sort of endowment effect that we previously noted. In terms of Figure 3.1, they may predict that the post-pandemic demand remains at D_{COV}, so that dog ownership will be Q_{POST}, which is closer to pandemic demand than pre-pandemic demand. Someone with a non-economic perspective might also expect Q_{POST} because, "Well, they are members of the family so they must stay!"

[71] Based on data from the American Pet Products Association as cited by Jacob Bogage and Yiwen Lu. "People Are Giving Up Pets. Blame Inflation." *Washington Post*, December 27 (2022).

[72] David U. Himmelstein, Robert M. Lawless, Deborah Thorne, Pamela Foohey, and Steffie Woolhandler. "Medical Bankruptcy: Still Common Despite the Affordable Care Act." *American Journal of Public Health* 109, no. 3 (2019): 431–433.

[73] Gary S. Becker and Kevin M. Murphy. "A Theory of Rational Addiction." *Journal of Political Economy* 96, no. 4 (1999): 675–700.

3.17 CONCLUSION: BEYOND COMMODITY

A naive economic framing of dog ownership would treat dogs as consumer durables that provide streams of benefits over their lives, but also demand substantial upkeep and potentially involve costly disposal. However, this framing falls far short by not recognizing that for most dog owners, dogs are not just property but rather beings who have some sort of membership in the family. Most families do not even contemplate replacing their dog with a better model! It is natural then to consider dogs from the perspective of the economic theory of the family, where they appear to be substitutes for children in some situations and complements to them in others.

Understanding why people invite particular dogs into their families can benefit from both behavioral and neoclassical theories, especially with respect to the choice of breeds. People often seem to choose dogs without fully considering the future costs of their choices, especially with respect to their selection of a breed. Further, substantial evidence suggests that breed choice is faddish, which can be seen as resulting from either a rational informational shortcut or a shortsighted embracing of fashion.

The basic microeconomic approach to modeling market exchange helps explain why the COVID pandemic increased dog ownership. The pandemic increased the value of companionship with dogs as a replacement for lost companionship with other people. It also reduced the opportunity cost of owning a dog, so that the full price of dog ownership fell. The market analysis also facilitates predictions of the impact of the pandemic on future dog ownership rates as the opportunity cost increases with a return to work away from home and pre-pandemic opportunities for social interaction return. Whereas the neoclassical perspective suggests a shift in the demand schedule back to near pre-pandemic levels, the behavioral perspective suggests the possibility that the demand schedule will remain closer to pandemic levels.

4

How Much Is That Doggy in the Window?

Supply, Information Asymmetry, and Negative Externality in the Dog Market

Rather than being born within families, most pet dogs join their families as puppies purchased from for-profit suppliers. Older dogs entering families are usually rescued from municipal or nonprofit shelters. The quality of care provided to puppies affects both their physical and mental health as well as their socialization with people and other dogs. The quality of care provided to, and the genetic makeup of, puppies that for-profit suppliers sell varies greatly. Consequently, the fitness of the puppies they sell can also vary greatly. Potential purchasers usually cannot fully assess the quality of the care provided to puppies because it is difficult to observe at first inspection. Similarly, the genetic makeup of puppies, particularly any history of inbreeding, is not directly observable, and may even be unavailable or deliberately withheld. Because of any or all of these informational problems, purchasers can overestimate the fitness of their new puppies. Compensating for a lack of fitness can be costly for owners and can result in costs for others if the puppies are eventually given to shelters or cruelly abandoned.

In this chapter, we analyze the supply side of the market for dogs. To explain some of the economic consequences, we begin by setting out two kinds of market failure, *information asymmetry* and *negative externalities*, that lead to inefficiencies in the market for dog acquisition. As we explain, we are interested in efficiency – and inefficiency, the misallocation of resources or goods – from a societal perspective. Then we describe the organization of the industry that supplies dogs and assess the extent to which information asymmetry and negative externalities result in inefficiencies in the market for dogs. These inefficiencies are realized only as costs and benefits directly borne by people; we follow standard economic practice by assuming that only human preferences count. Nonetheless, it is important to keep in mind that these inefficiencies often manifest as dire consequences for dogs.

4.1 EFFICIENCY AND MARKET FAILURES

The normative branch of neoclassical economics, welfare economics,[1] focuses on conditions under which the decisions of self-interested economic actors result in *allocative efficiency*. Allocative efficiency is an equilibrium in which it would be impossible to reallocate the resources used in production or the goods they produce in such a way that someone could be made better off without making anyone else worse off. This definition of allocative efficiency, commonly referred to as *Pareto efficiency*, is attributed to the Italian economist Vilfredo Pareto. A policy increases efficiency if it produces a Pareto improvement, a reallocation that makes someone better off without making anyone worse off. Applied welfare economic analysis considers potential Pareto improvements – they provide sufficient gains so that it would be conceptually possible to compensate those who lose from the policy. Thus, a policy that produces positive net benefits provides a potential Pareto improvement.

Under certain (we think usually reasonable) assumptions about the preferences of purchasers and the technology of production, competitive markets achieve allocative efficiency. Government intervention in these markets could not improve allocative efficiency and therefore would have to be justified by the desire to promote some other value, such as achieving a fairer allocation of goods.

A market failure results when assumptions about the competitive economy do not hold so that markets do not achieve allocative efficiency.[2] We explain the two market failures that are most relevant to the supply of dogs, information asymmetry and negative externalities, with familiar supply and demand diagrams. To set the stage, however, we begin by illustrating allocative efficiency in an undistorted market.

---

[1] The term "welfare economics" often confuses noneconomists. Welfare is not used in the commonly assumed sense of wellbeing, but rather in the specific context of *allocative efficiency*. In most public policy contexts, efficiency is one of several values relevant to the choice of policy. Few economists would argue that it is the only important value, but almost all economists (and most policy analysts) would argue that it is usually one of the important values.

[2] David L. Weimer and Aidan R. Vining. *Policy Analysis: Concepts and Practice*, 6th ed. (New York, NY: Routledge).

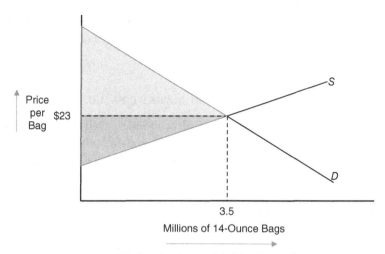

FIGURE 4.1 Market for freeze-dried beef liver dog treats

Figure 4.1 shows the market for freeze-dried beef liver dog treats. The downward sloping line, labeled *D*, is a demand schedule, like the demand schedules introduced in Chapter 3, which indicates how many 14-ounce bags of the treats dog owners will purchase annually at various prices. There is another way to think about (and interpret) this demand schedule: its height indicates the marginal value to consumers of purchasing one additional bag of treats.

The demand schedule, *D*, is downward slopping because as the price continues to fall, more consumers find that they value the treat at least as much as the price. If the supply offered is small and therefore the price is high, some consumers will decide to switch to other markets in order to buy less expensive treats or perhaps buy fewer treats of any kind (sorry Fido!). Thus, the downward slopping demand schedule indicates the declining value of the supply of additional bags of treats. As price declines, consumers who place less value on the treat will enter the market. That is, price indicates the marginal value of an additional, or marginal, bag of treats supplied to the market. Hence, the demand schedule can be interpreted as a *marginal valuation schedule*. Adding up these marginal values over a range from no bags to the actual number of bags purchased provides an estimate of the total value to consumers (again from our human perspective as the pleasure of observing dogs enjoy the treats) from the purchases.

The upward sloping line, labeled *S*, is a supply schedule. It indicates how many 2-ounce bags of the treat will be offered to purchasers at various prices. This supply schedule also has an alternative interpretation: its height indicates the marginal cost to suppliers of delivering that number of bags to the market. The upward slop of *S* indicates that in this market, it is more costly to produce successively larger numbers of bags of the treat. Over time, the supply schedule may flatten out as firms adjust to the higher level of demand. For example, adding another assembly line or just hiring more employees may enable the firm to avoid paying overtime. Absent any unique advantages, such as being adjacent to a slaughterhouse, the supply schedule would eventually become horizontal, indicating that additional bags could be provided at the same marginal cost.

At the level of the individual firm, the upward slope may result because workers have to be paid overtime. At the industry level, the upward slope may result because the beef livers have to be bid away from dog food manufacturers. At each number of bags, the supply schedule indicates the cost of producing an additional, or marginal, bag of the treat. Hence, the supply schedule is also a *marginal cost schedule*. Adding up the marginal costs of no bags to the number of bags purchased gives the total cost to suppliers of delivering the purchased bags.

In Figure 4.1, the equilibrium (between supply and demand) occurs at a price of $23 per 14-ounce bag, the price at which the quantity supplied equals the quantity demanded. It is at an annual quantity of 3.5 million bags.[3] At the equilibrium $23 price, the marginal value of another bag (given by the height of the demand schedule) exactly equals the marginal costs of another bag (given by the height of the supply schedule). It would not be possible to increase economic value in the market by either producing one more bag (marginal cost would exceed marginal value so a loss would occur) or producing one less (marginal value would exceed marginal cost so a gain would be forgone). In other words, the market equilibrium is allocatively efficient.[4]

The shaded area in Figure 4.1 represents the net gain to consumers and producers at the market equilibrium. The difference between marginal value and marginal cost for each unit of supply from zero to the

---

[3] We could not locate data on the actual sales of freeze-dried beef liver treats. The quantity reported is a guestimate based on the $8 billion annual spending on dog treats and the assumption that 1 percent of all dog treats are freeze-dried beef liver: ($8 billion) (0.01)/$23 ≡ 3.5 million.

[4] Chapter 5 considers a case in which the market for dog food was distorted by the addition of adulterated ingredients so that the market equilibrium was not allocatively efficient – sadly many dogs suffered and died.

equilibrium represents a gain to society called *social surplus*. The lighter-shaded area represents *consumer surplus*, the excess of the value of each consumed unit over the price paid. The darker-shaded area represents *producer surplus*, the excess of the price received for each produced unit over its production cost. A supply to the market of less than 3.5 million bags would forgo gain to consumers and producers; a supply to the market of more than 3.5 million bags would reduce gain because the additional units would involve production costs in excess of consumer value. In these sorts of market analyses, the price and quantity that maximize social surplus are allocatively efficient.

Goods vary in terms of the information that purchasers have about their quality attributes.[5] The quality of some goods can be assessed at the time of purchase fairly accurately. Purchasers may have to search to find the quality and price they seek, but they can verify both before purchase. For example, dog owners may have to engage in a search to find the most desirable combination of price and quality of dog treats before they purchase them. In contrast to these *search goods*, purchasers cannot fully assess quality of some goods until they, through their dog's behavior, have experience with the goods after purchase. These *experience goods* involve information asymmetry when sellers have information that buyers do not. If this information were provided to dog owners, then it would alter their assessment of the quality of the good. Likewise, puppies are most accurately categorized as experience goods because their fitness cannot be fully assessed at the time of purchase. The quality of some goods, called *post-experience goods*, may not be apparent to buyers until long after purchase. For example, the seller may know, but not reveal, that the lineage of the puppy puts it at risk of genetic disease as it matures.

There are two features of the puppy market that contribute to information asymmetry. First, as we explore in depth in the next section, very heterogeneous organizations supply the market. Different organizations produce puppies of very different quality. Because inputs, such as the quantity and quality of labor, determine the level of care that these organizations provide, and these can change over time, the quality of puppies produced by the same organization may vary over time as well. This temporal variability hinders the identification of high-quality producers through experience. Consumers who

---

[5] Aidan R. Vining and David L. Weimer. "Information Asymmetry Favoring Sellers: A Policy Framework." *Policy Sciences* 21, no. 4 (1988): 281–303.

purchase puppies directly from these firms often have difficulty determining if they are suppliers of high- or low-quality puppies. Further, consumers who purchase from retailers like pet stores usually do not know whether a particular puppy they are considering was bred by a low- or high-quality wholesale supplier.

Second, people usually buy puppies infrequently. About 60 percent of dog-owning families have one dog at a time.[6] With dogs having a life span of about a decade, these families have little opportunity to learn about the puppy market through direct experience. For some types of durable goods potentially subject to information asymmetry, consumers can hire experts who are able to assess quality by virtue of both their training and the tacit knowledge they gain through involvement in many purchases. For example, although most people buy houses infrequently, they can hire various sorts of inspectors to assess the quality of the house in terms of such attributes as mechanics (plumbing, electrics, and heating), termite damage, and earthquake risk. An inspector can make an assessment based on observing the house in its current state. Puppy inspectors, such as veterinarians, can assess the current physical health of a puppy but usually not the quality of care that was provided prior to its purchase, care that can have long-term consequences for both the health and temperament of the puppy as it ages. Further, because the market price of puppies is much lower than the market price of almost all houses, potential purchasers of puppies are generally not willing to pay large fees and, unlike the case of houses, a lender who would require inspections is not involved. Consequently, dedicated inspection services that assess the overall quality of puppies are not readily available.

The presence of an information asymmetry favoring puppy sellers results in an allocatively inefficient equilibrium in the puppy market. In sum, the sellers have more information about the care given to puppies before they are marketed than potential purchasers. Figure 4.2 illustrates the consequences of this information asymmetry by showing two distinct demand schedules. The uninformed demand schedule, D_U, is the demand for puppies before a purchase. The informed demand schedule, D_I, is the demand schedule for puppies after they are purchased, when

---

[6] About 60 percent of respondents reported having one dog in the PVL Survey (May 18–23, 2018). This is consistent with the estimate of 1.6 dogs per dog-owning household reported by the American Veterinary Medical Association for the same period. www.avma.org/resources-tools/reports-statistics/us-pet-ownership-statistics. Accessed February 8, 2023. The ratio has likely fallen because of the increase in first-time dog owners during COVID.

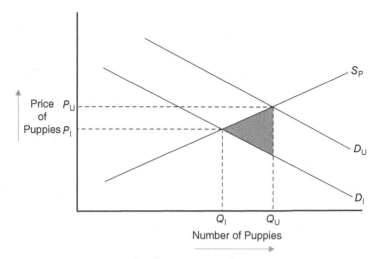

FIGURE 4.2 Market for puppies: Information asymmetry

their behavior and health can be directly observed. The market equilibrium is a price of P_U and a quantity of Q_U, which is determined by the intersection of D_U and the supply schedule S_P. However, the marginal value of the puppies is determined by D_I, that is, it represents the value that dog owners place on them after they are purchased. If they were fully informed about the fitness of the puppies, buyers would make purchases based on D_I, so that the equilibrium would occur at a lower price P_I and a lower quantity Q_I. This would represent an efficient allocation, as was the case for the equilibrium in Figure 4.1. What exactly is the efficiency problem? The allocative inefficiency is the sum of the area between the two demand schedules over the puppies purchased between Q_I and Q_U. This shaded triangular area captures the inefficiency of the marginal cost of the puppies purchased above Q_I have marginal values (the vertical height of D_I) less than marginal costs (the vertical height of S_P).

Ethical suppliers that provide high-quality care to the puppies that they raise will have difficulty distinguishing themselves from unethical suppliers that do not. Of course, all is not lost. Ethical suppliers that have been in business long enough to establish a track record may be able to brand their high quality of care, perhaps marketing their puppies by relying primarily on word of mouth from satisfied purchasers communicating with potential customers. They may also try to reassure potential buyers by giving them some degree of access to their facilities.

They can do so in a number of ways, including the use of webcams or by allowing customers to return puppies within a specified time period for partial refunds, voluntarily exceeding the reimbursement that is mandated under the "lemon laws" that apply in some states.[7] They may also seek certification from some third party that their practices and facilities are consistent with high-quality care.[8] Despite such efforts, ethical breeders must still compete with unethical breeders, including so-called puppy mills, that provide low-quality care to minimize costs.

Unethical breeders do not bear the full costs of their production of puppies. Puppies deemed unfit that are purchased and kept by their new owners incur unexpected costs, such as expenditures for exceptional veterinary care and coping with behavioral issues. These costs are captured by the lower demand schedule in Figure 4.2. However, some purchasers will decide not to keep unfit puppies and instead abandon them to shelters. The cost of caring for these dogs in shelters is a cost of puppy production that is not borne by the unethical breeders. These costs are a *negative externality* of the for-profit dog supply industry.

Negative externalities are the class of costs borne by all parties not involved in the market transactions that produce them (or the rest of society). The canonical example of a negative externality is pollution resulting from the production of electricity from fossil fuels: neither the producer nor the consumer bears the full social cost of the pollution, which adversely affects the health of nonconsumers. Perhaps more tangibly for most readers, a neighbor's persistently loud music or barking dog represents very common manifestations of a negative externality. Because the external effects like these are not directly traded in markets, negative externalities are often referred to as missing market problems. Sometimes, however, they show up in house prices. Public policies often attempt to internalize externalities through such approaches as taxing pollutants or creating markets through tradeable permits. However, as

---

[7] It is often difficult for consumers to obtain the refunds to which they are legally entitled. See Stephanie K. Savino. "Puppy Lemon Laws: Think Twice before Buying that Doggy in the Window." *Penn State Law Review* 114, no. 2 (2009): 643–666 and Jonathan T. Tortorici. "Puppies, Puppies, Puppies: Why Georgia Should 'Adopt' a Progressive Puppy Lemon Law and Engage in Much-Needed Statutory Reform." *Georgia Law Review* 55, no. 1 (2020): 431–466.

[8] Most states provide some certification, though often with little enforcement. There are several of private certification services that mainly certify that breeders have completed some course of study. The only national certification service that sets comprehensive standards is Canine Care, a program administered by the Purdue University, College of Veterinary Medicine. www.vet.purdue.edu/ccc/about.php. Accessed November 7, 2022.

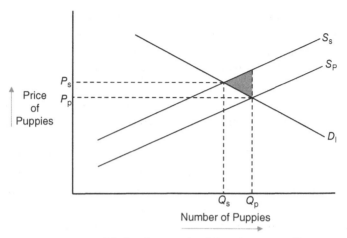

FIGURE 4.3 Market for puppies: Negative externality

we will see, these approaches have limited application in reducing the
negative externalities imposed on society by the least responsible puppy
producers.

Figure 4.3 shows the inefficiency resulting from this negative externality. The supply schedule labeled S_p indicates the marginal costs of puppy
production that are borne by the suppliers. The higher schedule labeled
S_s indicates the social marginal costs of puppy production, which include
the external costs of providing shelters that are not borne by the suppliers. The equilibrium, Q_p and P_p, is determined by the intersection of
the demand schedule with S_p; however, the efficient allocation is at Q_s
and P_s. The inefficiency of the equilibrium is represented by the shaded
triangle, which occurs because the marginal values of the consumption
above Q_s are smaller than the social marginal costs.

Unfortunately, both information asymmetry and negative externalities distort the aggregate puppy market. These market failures, however,
manifest in distinct ways for different segments of the market. Ethical
breeders who provide full information to potential purchases and internalize all the costs of the puppies they sell would facilitate an efficient
market if they were the only suppliers or if they could clearly distinguish
themselves from unethical breeders. If they could, there would be greater
efficiency, but a segmented market. Their segment of supply would be
efficient, while the segment of supply from unethical breeders would not.
To assess the overall efficiency of the puppy market, it is necessary to
take a closer look at how it is organized in view of the different types of
breeders who sell puppies.

4.2 TYPES OF PUPPY SUPPLIERS

To put it mildly, a heterogeneous collection of breeders supplies dogs to Americans. They range in motivation and scale from hobbyists who breed the occasional litter from their own pets to the operators of puppy mills that mass produce puppies in abhorrent conditions. In many, indeed most, industries, federal, or state regulatory requirements generate data that allow interested parties to identify and classify firms in ways that enable more efficient rulemaking and enforcement. Limited existing federal regulation and a patchwork of different regulations across states, however, does not currently provide a detailed enough census of the breeder industry for quality assessment.

Currently, the primary federal rules for puppy suppliers are issued under the Animal Welfare Act (Public Law 89–544). These rules apply to breeders with more than four female dogs who do not directly participate in sales where the buyer, seller, and dog are all physically present – basically only to firms that sell wholesale or on the internet. The existence and level of state regulation of dog breeders vary greatly; eighteen states have no regulations on breeders, and only five states have rules that cover most breeders.[9] The Humane Society of the United States provides a rough estimate of the scale of the industry. The Society estimates that there are 10 thousand active puppy mills in the United States, only about a quarter of which are registered under the Animal Welfare Act, and that these mills supply about 2.6 million puppies per year.[10]

We believe that any realistic assessment of the efficiency of the puppy market requires recognition of the heterogeneity of suppliers. To help understand how heterogeneity affects efficiency, Table 4.1 identifies six types of suppliers based on their organizational form and the ethical standards of their practices. Simplifying somewhat, organizational form distinguishes between commercial and so-called backyard breeders. Commercial breeders are for-profit firms that produce large numbers of puppies. Backyard breeders, in contrast, are typically individuals who breed only small numbers of puppies. Similarly, the ethics of their practice distinguishes among breeders in terms of the quality of care they

---

[9] Based on data from Table 6.1, pp. 212–213, of Susan Hunter and Richard A. Brisbin, Jr. *Pet Politics: The Political and Legal Lives of Cats, Dogs, and Horses in Canada and the United States* (West Lafayette, IN: Purdue University Press, 2016).
[10] Humane Society of the United States. "Puppy Mills: Facts and Figures." www.humanesociety .org/sites/default/files/docs/puppy-mills-facts-and-figures.pdf. Accessed November 7, 2022.

TABLE 4.1 *Types of puppy supplier and market failures*

		Organizational form	
		Commercial: large and professional	Backyard: small and amateur
Practice	Ethical	Compliant breeders	Hobbyists
	Ethically questionable	Purebred and pedigree breeders *Negative externalities*	Inadvertent breeders *Negative externalities*
	Unethical and often illegal	Puppy mills *Information asymmetry, negative externalities*	Gray and black-market breeders *Negative externalities*

provide to puppies and their parents. Ethical breeders provide high-quality care; unethical breeders do not. But to inject more realism, in an intermediate category, we place breeders whose practices are, let us say, ethically questionable.

4.2.1 Compliant Breeders

The desirable physical, mental, and social development of puppies and the humane care of their parents require a variety of economic resources. To operate effectively, breeders must construct and maintain appropriate facilities. Labor is required to provide appropriate sustenance, sanitation, exercise, and supervised interaction with other dogs. Breeders must arrange and document veterinary care. Compliant breeders are ethical in the sense that they are willing to expend these resources to increase the chances that their puppies will be healthy and become well socialized.

Regulations issued under the Animal Welfare Act set minimum standards for wholesale breeders. As indicated by those states with more exacting rules, the federal standards are minimal. For example, the minimum amount of floor space provided to a puppy 12 inches in length from the tip of the nose to the base of the tail is only 2.25 square feet, and there must be at least 6 inches of clearance above the head of the dog.[11] Many states have set more stringent standards. For instance, Wisconsin

[11] Code of Federal Regulations, Title 9, Chapter 1, Part 3, Subchapter A, Section 36(c) (1)(i): (i) Each dog housed in a primary enclosure (including weaned puppies) must be provided a minimum amount of floor space, calculated as follows: Find the mathematical square of the sum of the length of the dog in inches (measured from the tip of its

requires 8 square feet for a single dog of that size, as well as an additional 6 square feet for each additional dog of that size included in the enclosure, and there must be 12 inches of clearance above the head of the tallest dog in the enclosure.[12] Oregon has a functional requirement that would generally require more space than the federal standard: "Provide each dog with sufficient space to turn about freely, stand and sit, and lie down without the head, face, tail, legs, or feet of the dog touching the sides of the enclosure or touching any other dog."[13]

A current limitation of regulation is that most state standards apply only to larger-scale operations: Wisconsin standards apply to breeders who sells twenty-five or more dogs per year unless they come from no more than three litters; Oregon standards apply to breeders with ten or more sexually intact dogs; and Virginia standards apply to anyone who maintains thirty or more adult female dogs at any time in a 12-month period.[14] Some states do require inspections as part of the licensure process, and a few states specify periodic inspections, usually biannually. However, because of understaffed inspectorates, most states rely on complaints to trigger inspections.

Several factors effectively allow breeders to determine what care to provide and how to provide it: the minimal standards set out in the federal rules, the absence of any rules in many states, the high thresholds of the number of breeding dogs, litters, or puppies subject to rules in those states that have them, and the low levels of routine enforcement because of understaffed inspection units. As ethical breeders, compliant breeders make decisions that increase the fitness of their puppies, not just in terms of observable factors, such as the quality of enclosures, but also with respect to less observable factors, such as the amount of exercise puppies receive and their socialization to people and other dogs. Despite their potential difficulty in conveying full information about the quality of care that they provide, information asymmetry is generally not a problem for puppies supplied by compliant breeders. This is especially

---

nose to the base of its tail) plus 6 inches; then divide the product by 144. The calculation is: (length of dog in inches + 6) x (length of dog in inches + 6) = required floor space in square inches. Required floor space in inches/144 = required floor space in square feet.

[12] Wisconsin Administrative Code. "Agriculture, Trade & Consumer Protection." Chapter 16. 22(2).

[13] Oregon Revised Statutes, 167.376 (2)(a).

[14] Table of State Commercial Pet Breeders Laws, Animal Legal & Historical Center, College of Law, Michigan State University. www.animallaw.info/topic/table-state-commercial-pet-breeders-laws. Accessed November 7, 2022.

the case if they provide substantial refunds without dispute to dissatisfied purchasers who return puppies. If they ethically take care of returned puppies and adult dogs past their usefulness as breeders, then negative externalities are also likely to be small. However, providing high-quality and responsible care is costly, so that compliant breeders typically must charge more for puppies than other less ethical commercial breeders to be profitable and stay in business.

4.2.2 Purebred and Pedigree Breeders

Both purebred and pedigree breeders mate parents of the same breed to produce puppies. Pedigree breeders additionally document the genetic history of puppies through their family trees. (The family of one of your authors purchased, Ming, a wonderful parti standard poodle, from a purebred breeder, and in the process learning that poodle is a verb as well as noun!)

Selective breeding for various traits has transformed the wolf into varied breeds of dogs. Selective breeding accelerated over the last two centuries as dog shows became popular and breeders sought to accentuate specific characteristics that distinguish breeds. Selective breeding tends to reduce genetic diversity within a breed and can result in the prevalence of nonselected characteristics that are detrimental to dogs' health.[15] For example, Cavalier King Charles Spaniels have high risks of mitral valve disease, which can lead to premature death, and canine syringomyelia, which can cause severe pain and damage the spinal cord. Historically, English bulldogs selection induced large heads, flattened muzzles, and bandy legs. This makes it difficult for current cohorts English bulldogs to breathe and naturally breed.[16] An analysis of the 215 pedigree breeds recognized by the UK Kennel Club in 2015 found that, although the loss of genetic diversity has slowed in recent years, it continues because of preferences for favored sires.[17]

[15] Åke A. Hedhammar, Sofia Malm, and Brenda Bonnett. "International and Collaborative Strategies to Enhance Genetic Health in Purebred Dogs." *The Veterinary Journal* 189, no. 2 (2011): 189–196.

[16] Claire Maldarelli. "Although Purebred Dogs Can Be Best in Show, Are They Worst in Health?" *Scientific American (Scienceline)*, February 21 (2014). www.scientificamerican.com/article/although-purebred-dogs-can-be-best-in-show-are-they-worst-in-health/. Accessed November 7, 2022.

[17] T. W. Lewis, B. M. Abhayaratne, and S. C. Blott. "Trends in Genetic Diversity for All Kennel Club Registered Pedigree Dog Breeds." *Canine Genetics and Epidemiology* 2, no. 1 (2015): 1–10.

The high prices commanded by purebred puppies give pedigree breeders a financial incentive to provide high-quality care like that provided by compliant breeders. However, the incentive they face to accentuate the physical characteristics of the breeds encourages inbreeding. Pedigree breeders who contribute to inbreeding impose a negative externality: a reduction in genetic diversity that increases disease risk within breeds. There is also the potential for information asymmetry, even though the pedigree process provides a breeding record and high prices encourage purchasers to view the pedigree as well as learn about the breed in general, including health risks. Nonetheless, the genetic and epigenetic make-up of puppies, particularly a history of inbreeding, may not be observable by purchasers, and may even be deliberately withheld by sellers.[18] Even sellers may not have intergenerational genetic or epigenetic information, and so it is not an information asymmetry failure, but simply a problem of the lack of relevant information. Finally, some aspects of puppy fitness may remain unknown even after purchase and, indeed, throughout a dog's life, so these puppies are post-experience goods. Breeders, especially large-scale commercial breeders of purebred dogs, often have information about the level of inbreeding that is not observable to purchasers even after purchase or during the dog's life.

In summary, purebred and pedigree breeders who take appropriate steps to avoid inbreeding are ethical; those who do not are unethical. Consequently, Table 4.1 assesses their ethics as questionable.

4.2.3 Puppy Mills

The efforts of animal welfare advocates to expose the inhumane treatment of dogs by many commercial puppy breeders had limited success in gaining public attention until an episode of the Oprah Winfrey Show in 2008.[19] That episode painted a picture of abuse that is very difficult to watch. It popularized the term "puppy mill" to describe unethical

---

[18] As with humans, dogs pass along characteristics to their offspring through genes, segments of DNA that determine biological functions. Experiences during life can affect how genes are expressed. "Epigenetics refers to heritable modifications of gene expression, without any change to the DNA sequence," Katriina Tiira. "Resilience in Dogs? Lessons from Other Species." *Veterinary Medicine: Research and Reports* 10, November (2019): 159–168 at p. 164.

[19] The Oprah Winfrey Show: Lisa Ling Investigates the Hidden World of Puppy Mills, April 4, 2008. www.youtube.com/playlist?list=PLsg4a7bf-t61eUkxx2D9UsXAJn8YA2hLu. Accessed November 7, 2022.

commercial breeders who maximize profit by minimizing costs so that breeding dogs and their puppies receive cruel and harmful treatment.[20]

Puppy mills that avoid federal and state enclosure standards often have horrific caging practices. Poor sanitation and restricted movement result when small cages without solid floors are vertically stacked. Financial incentives to maximize the ratio of puppies to staff make it unlikely that puppies become appropriately socialized, either with other dogs or with people. This treatment increases the chances that puppies will have behavioral problems. These incentives also can result in health problems for puppies from a lack of exercise, and one can only speculate on the low quality of care provided by veterinarians who would participate in these operations.

People who purchase directly from commercial breeders may be able to identify the worst puppy mills by visiting their facilities. However, observing the quality of ongoing care is more difficult, so that many purchasers may unwittingly purchase from a puppy mill. People who purchase puppies in pet stores usually have no basis for knowing the quality of care the puppies received before they arrived in the store. Concern about pet stores enabling puppy mills by not providing full information about the puppies they sell has led several municipalities and eventually the State of California to prohibit pet stores from selling companion animals that are not obtained from shelters or rescue groups.[21] Consequently, the existence of puppy mills, and the difficulty people have in determining if puppies come from compliant breeders or puppy mills, creates a substantial information asymmetry in the puppy market.

This information asymmetry results in unexpected health and behavioral costs for purchasers who keep puppies. These costs induce a negative externality for those who ultimately end up surrendering puppies to shelters. The disposal of the adult dogs used in breeding by puppy mills can also involve negative externalities. When their fertility declines, female dogs are either killed or abandoned. Those that are abandoned often end up in shelters.

---

[20] Kailey A. Burger. "Solving the Problem of Puppy Mills: Why the Animal Welfare Movement's Bark Is Stronger than Its Bite." *Washington University Journal of Law & Policy* 43 (2013): 259–284.

[21] An initial ban set out in Assembly Bill 485 took effect on January 1, 2019. However, some pet stores replaced prices with "adoption fees" to circumvent the law. Bella's Act (Assembly Bill 2152), which closed this loophole, took effect on January 1, 2021. www.leginfo.legislature.ca.gov/faces/billNavClient.xhtml?bill_id=201920200AB2152. Accessed November 7, 2022.

Although our focus in this chapter is on the market for puppies as pets, it is worth noting that some suppliers of puppies for medical research also engage in the objectionable and inhumane practices of puppy mills, as illustrated by a recent case that captured national attention.[22] In 2022, agents from the Department of Agriculture inspected a Cumberland, Virginia facility with about 4 thousand beagles, a preferred breed for medical research because of its docility and relatively small size. The inspectors found about 300 dead puppies, insect infested food, dogs euthanized without anesthesia, many dogs with fight wounds, eye infections, dental problems, and inflamed paws, kennels polluted with urine and feces, and dogs stressed from confinement in buildings with high temperatures. In July 2022, a federal judge approved the transfer of dogs from the company to the Humane Society of the United States, which has worked to find them homes. (In Chapter 6, we return to the question of the appropriate use of dogs in medical research.)

The information asymmetry and negative externalities in the puppy market directly result in allocative inefficiency, as illustrated in Figures 4.2 and 4.3. Yet another market failure, the *public good* nature of the protection of dogs from cruelty, also brings into question the efficiency of the market. Pure public goods are both nonrivalrous in consumption (everyone consumes the same level of the good) and nonexcludable (no one can be excluded from consuming the good). Canonical examples of pure public goods are national defense and knowledge. We know from the historical evolution of anti-cruelty laws, which began as a prohibition against sadistic cruelty, but evolved to include passive cruelty,[23] and the voluntary contributions that people make to organizations like the Humane Society and Society for the Protection of Cruelty to Animals, that many people value protecting animals from cruel treatment. That is, most people, including those who do not make voluntary contributions to prevent cruelty, would be willing to pay something to prevent it. (In Chapter 6, we return to this issue as it arises in the use of dogs in medical research.) Anti-cruelty laws have been widely adopted, and they would apply to the worst practices of puppy mills. However, as we analyze it,

---

[22] Lizze Johnson. "Profit, Pain and Puppies: Inside the Rescue of Nearly 4,000 Beagles." *Washington Post*, October 17 (2022).

[23] On the evolution of views on cruelty to animals, see Susan Hunter and Richard A. Brisbin, Jr. *Pet Politics: The Political and Legal Lives of Cats, Dogs, and Horses in Canada and the United States* (West Lafayette, IN: Purdue University Press, 2016), Chapter 2. On the role of cruelty in shaping group identity, see Arnold Arluke. *Just a Dog: Understanding Animal Cruelty and Ourselves* (Philadelphia, PA: Temple University Press, 2006).

these practices persist because of the public good nature of public or private actions to prevent cruelty: public enforcement of existing laws against puppy mills is undersupplied; private contributions to organizations that work to identify and stop puppy mills are underprovided.

4.2.4 Hobbyists

The second column of Table 4.1 lists the types of "backyard breeders," typically involving small numbers of puppies whose sale is not the primary source of income for the breeder. Although the term tends to be used pejoratively, especially by commercial breeders who see them as amateurs (and competitors), we recognize that some of these breeders are ethical care givers to the dogs they mate, and the puppies that result. These backyard breeders are commonly called hobbyists. (The family of one of your author's obtained Matilda the dachshund from a hobbyist.)

Hobbyists typically breed one or two litters per year. Some hobbyists breed service dogs of various kinds, such as police or guide dogs. Other hobbyists simply breed their favorite pet. Although they usually sell puppies, hobbyists rely primarily on other sources for their income. As ethical breeders, they provide sustenance, sanitation, exercise, and socialization, as well as pay for and document appropriate veterinary care so that the puppies they sell are generally healthy.[24] Potential buyers are usually able to interact with hobbyists to assess the quality of care provided to puppies, and hobbyists will usually take back puppies that families find unfit for their circumstances. Consequently, neither information asymmetry nor negative externality is likely to create inefficiency in this segment of the market.

4.2.5 Inadvertent Breeders

Many puppies are born as the result of unintended pregnancies of pet dogs. The puppies in these litters often end up in shelters, whether surrendered to shelters either directly by their mothers' owners or by those who buy or receive them as gifts, or indirectly through abandonment.

---

[24] One comparison of owner assessment of the behavior of puppies purchased from pet stores versus those purchased from noncommercial breeders (hobbyists) favored the latter. Franklin D. McMillan, James A. Serpell, Deborah L. Duffy, Elmabrok Masaoud, and Ian R. Dohoo. "Differences in Behavioral Characteristics between Dogs Obtained as Puppies from Pet Stores and Those Obtained from Noncommercial Breeders." *Journal of the American Veterinary Medical Association* 242, no. 10 (2013): 1359–1363.

These consequences could be prevented by either sterilization or closer supervision of sexually intact dogs. Although even ethical dog owners can become inadvertent breeders, allowing these pregnancies to occur suggests the possibility of unethical behavior.

Sterilization effectively prevents inadvertent breeding. Although it is generally viewed as having positive health consequences for dogs, sterilization can also have negative health consequences, especially for male dogs.[25] Further, some would argue that routine sterilization is ethically questionable from several perspectives on the relationship between people and companion animals, especially when companions are not free roaming.[26] Despite these concerns, North American veterinarians and animal welfare advocates generally support routine sterilization of dogs that are not intended for breeding. They do so to avoid the burden of sheltering unwanted puppies. To encourage sterilization, many municipalities charge lower registration fees for sterilized dogs to incentivize sterilization by internalizing some of the external cost of unintended puppies. The exclusion of unneutered dogs by many doggy daycare centers also encourages sterilization. Nonprofit clinics promote sterilization for low-income dog owners;[27] these clinics appear to increase the total number of sterilizations, rather than simply substituting for private veterinary sterilizations.[28]

Nonetheless, many pet dogs remain sexually intact. Veterinary cost is likely a factor in decisions not to sterilize. Convenience costs aside, neutering and spaying fees typically fall in the ranges of $50–$250 and $100–$500, respectively. These fees discourage some low-income owners from sterilizing their dogs. Table 4.2 presents sterilization rates by income level based on data from the 2018 PVL survey of U.S. dog owners. The columns show income as a ratio of reported family income to the federal poverty level, which is based on family size. Very low-income families have incomes below the poverty line; low-income families have

---

[25] M. V. Root Kustritz. "Effects of Surgical Sterilization on Canine and Feline Health and on Society." *Reproduction in Domestic Animals* 47, no. 4 (2012): 214–222.

[26] Clare Palmer, Sandra Corr, and Peter Sandøe. "Inconvenient Desires: Should We Routinely Neuter Companion Animals?" *Anthrozoös* 25, no. sup1 (2012): S153–S172.

[27] Sara C. White, Janet M. Scarlett, and Julie K. Levy. "Characteristics of Clients and Animals Served by High-volume, Stationary, Nonprofit Spay-Neuter Clinics." *Journal of the American Veterinary Medical Association* 253, no. 6 (2018): 737–745.

[28] Joshua M. Frank and Pamela L. Carlisle-Frank. "Analysis of Programs to Reduce Overpopulation of Companion Animals: Do Adoption and Low-Cost Spay/Neuter Programs Merely Cause Substitution of Sources?" *Ecological Economics* 62, no. 3–4 (2007): 740–746.

TABLE 4.2 *Spaying/neutering as a function of income*

	Male dogs	Female dogs
	Neutered (percent) *n* = 2,571	Spayed (percent) *n* = 2,312
Very low income (≤1 FPL)*	42	51
Low income (>1 FPL&≤2 FPL)	65	75
Higher income (>2 FPL)	73	84

*FPL is the federal poverty level based on the number of people in the household. In 2018, the FPL was $25,750 in annual income for a family of four.
Source: PVL Survey, May 18 to 23, 2018.

incomes above the poverty line but below twice the poverty line. As indicated, both the rate of spaying for female dogs and neutering for male dogs increase with income, ranging from 42 percent for male dogs in very low-income families to 84 percent for female dogs in higher-income families.

Table 4.2 shows higher sterilization rates for female than male dogs within each income group, despite the higher cost and intrusiveness of spaying relative to neutering. The explanation almost certainly lies in the relative consequences of an unwanted pregnancy for the owners of male versus female dogs. Basically, these are none for the owner of the male dog and substantial costs for the owner of the female dog! In addition, spaying avoids the high costs of managing a sexually intact female, including dealing with the many potential sires who seek her out when she is in heat, typically for one to two weeks twice per year. Thus, even though the dollar and recovery costs are higher for spaying than neutering, the owner benefits are much larger for spaying than neutering.

In summary, inadvertent breeding often results in negative externalities. Owners of sexually intact male dogs inflict costs on the owners of sexually intact female dogs. Because unwanted puppies often end up in shelters, owners of sexually intact female dogs inflict negative externalities on the rest of society. So, although there may be ethical grounds for not sterilizing one's dog, unexpected pregnancies suggest refraining from doing so is generally unethical behavior.

4.2.6 Gray and Black-Market Breeders

Intentional backyard breeders can potentially be unethical in several different ways. Unlike hobbyists, they may not provide adequate nurturing and veterinary care for their puppies, instead seeking to maximize profits from selling puppies by minimizing their costs. They often produce numbers of puppies that legally require municipal, state, or federal registration, but they usually remain unregistered. These breeders may also engage in illegal practices, such as raising fighting dogs, or contribute to illegal activity by providing guard dogs to criminal enterprises.[29] In view of these latter activities, we label them "gray and black-market breeders." They participate in the gray market when they fail to provide ethically appropriate levels of care or fail to register or otherwise follow applicable laws; they are participating in the black market when they sell dogs for fighting or guarding illegal activities.

The substantial presence of larger dogs in shelters indicates that their breeding involves negative externalities. Lisa Milot has laid out the logic of this claim:[30] The evidence suggests that black-market breeders tend to raise larger, more muscular dogs with large heads, typically "bully" mixtures of various kinds. Puppy mills tend to avoid these larger breeds, instead favoring trendier and easily managed breeds. Therefore, it is likely that most of the larger dogs in shelters come from black-market breeders. As larger dogs make up a substantial fraction of dogs in shelters, the negative externalities created by black-market breeders are large.

4.3 SUPPLY FROM SHELTERS

In the United States, there are approximately 7 thousand animal shelters.[31] Both municipalities and nonprofit organizations operate shelters that provide refuge for companion animals. These shelters are funded from a number of sources: taxes, donations, and adoption and surrender fees.[32] Although the data are incomplete, it is likely that total annual shelter costs in the United States are about $2.5 billion.[33] The American Society for the Prevention of Cruelty to Animals (ASPCA) estimates the

---

[29] Lisa Milot. "Backyard Breeding: Regulatory Nuisance, Crime Precursor." *Tennessee Law Review* 85 (2017): 707–752.

[30] Ibid., pp. 710–712.

[31] Kimberly Woodruff and David R. Smith. "An Estimate of the Number of Dogs in US Shelters in 2015 and the Factors Affecting Their Fate." *Journal of Applied Animal Welfare Science* 23, no. 3 (2020): 302–314.

[32] Andrew Rowan and Tamara Kartal. "Dog Population & Dog Sheltering Trends in the United States of America." *Animals (Basel)* 8, no. 5 (2018): 68–88.

[33] Andrew N. Rowan. "Companion Animal Statistics in the USA." *Wellbeing International Studies Repository* (2018): 15. www.wellbeingintlstudiesrepository.org/cgi/viewcontent .cgi?article=1002&context=demscapop. Accessed November 7, 2022.

numbers of dogs entering and exiting U.S. shelters annually.[34] It is estimated that 3.1 million dogs enter shelters each year. About 2 million of
these dogs are adopted, and 710 thousand are returned to their owners.
However, about 390 thousand dogs are euthanized each year.[35] On the
one hand, shelters are a substantial source of supply of pet dogs, accounting for about 40 percent of the total supply. On the other hand, they are
the end of the line for many dogs.

The role of shelters has changed dramatically since the 1970s, when over
90 percent of sheltered animals were euthanized.[36] One factor in the decline
has been changes in owner behavior, which is now more protective of dogs
as they have become increasingly viewed as family members. Another factor
driving the decline has been increasing sterilization rates, both in the general
community and at shelters. A final factor in the decline, particularly relevant
to our assessment of the supply of dogs, has been the gradual increase in
adoptions from shelters. Indeed, these adoptions have accelerated in recent
years: since 2006, the fraction of pet dog acquisitions from shelters has risen
from 15 percent to the current level of about 40 percent.[37]

How do dogs get into shelters? About a quarter of dogs enter shelters
as strays and another 10 percent are seized by law enforcement. (Luis, a
shelter dog following his seizure by police, joined the family of one of your
authors.) Another quarter of shelter dogs are surrendered by their owners,
and about 5 percent are returns of adopted dogs. The remaining dogs are
transfers from other organizations.[38] Many of the strays and dogs seized
by law enforcement are manifestations of negative externalities resulting
from the irresponsible practices of suppliers to the puppy market. Some
surrendered dogs are almost certainly the consequence of information
asymmetry in the puppy market, though it is difficult to assess its importance because there are many reasons people surrender dogs to shelters.

Studies have identified several risk factors that raise the probability of the
surrender of dogs: move to a new residence, change in health status of the

---

[34] ASPCA Pet Statistics. www.aspca.org/helping-people-pets/shelter-intake-and-surrender/
pet-statistics. Accessed November 7, 2022.

[35] Centers in San Francisco, California, and Thompkins County, New York, pioneered
the idea of "no kill," in which outreach is used to save all healthy dogs from euthanasia
through adoption. See Nathan J. Winograd. *Redemption: The Myth of Pet Overpopulation and the No Kill Revolution in America* (Santa Clara, CA: Almaden, 2007). Today,
no-kill shelters can use the designation as long as they do not euthanize more than 10
percent of dogs in their care.

[36] Rowan and Kartal, p. 71.

[37] Ibid., Figure 12, p. 76.

[38] Rowan, pp. 9–10.

owner, cost, unmet human expectations about the relationship with the dog, and behavioral problems of the dogs.[39] Although it is commonly thought that the presence of behavioral problems exhibited by dogs is the most important risk factor, some recent research raises questions about its importance.[40] Evidence does suggest that aggressiveness toward family members, especially in the context of chronic diseases that create stress in grooming and medication, contributes to the likelihood of rehousing, including surrender to shelters, or euthanasia.[41] Nonetheless, overemphasis on behavioral problems can be problematic in two ways. First, it may discourage adoptions if potential owners overestimate the probability of encountering behavioral problems when adopting shelter dogs. Second, it may encourage staff to overinvest in changing the behaviors of sheltered dogs.

With apologies to fellow dog lovers, we characterize the supply of dogs from shelters in economic terms as the "used dog market." Although puppies can be found in shelters, most of the dogs are previously owned juveniles or adults. George Akerlof provided the seminal insight into the economics of the quality of goods in used markets in his assessment of information asymmetry.[42] He observes that an explanation for the large price differential between new and used cars at the time he wrote is the rational expectation that people will be more likely to trade-in relatively lower-quality vehicles whose defects will not be apparent on the car lot. Based just on this insight, one might reasonably expect the fitness of dogs in shelters to be low. However, he also points to the importance of trust in facilitating efficient exchange in such markets. In the case of the used market for dogs, the nonprofit status of most shelters can be reassuring that its employees are not pushing "lemons."[43] The relatively benign return policies of most shelters also provide reassurance to prospective owners.

---

[39] Kim Lambert, Jason Coe, Lee Niel, Cate Dewey, and Jan M. Sargeant. "A Systematic Review and Meta-Analysis of the Proportion of Dogs Surrendered for Dog-Related and Owner-Related Reasons." *Preventive Veterinary Medicine* 118, no. 1 (2015): 148–160.

[40] Gary J. Patronek, Janis Bradley, and Elizabeth Arps. "Saving Normal: A New Look at Behavioral Incompatibilities and Dog Relinquishment to Shelters." *Journal of Veterinary Behavior* 49, March (2022): 36–45.

[41] Carlo Siracusa, Lena Provoost, and Ilana R. Reisner. "Dog- and Owner-Related Risk Factors for Consideration of Euthanasia or Rehoming before a Referral Behavioral Consultation and for Euthanizing or Rehoming the Dog after the Consultation." *Journal of Veterinary Behavior* 22, November–December (2017): 46–56.

[42] George A. Akerlof. "The Market for "Lemons": Quality Uncertainty and the Market Mechanism." *Quarterly Journal of Economics* 84, No. 3 (1970): 488–500.

[43] Burton A. Weisbrod. *The Nonprofit Economy* (Cambridge, MA: Harvard University Press, 1988).

Yet some evidence suggests that the adoption decisions may not be fully rational, at least according to standard neoclassical precepts. For example, an experiment conducted at a shelter found that prospective adopters appeared to be more influenced by the physical characteristics of dogs than by their behaviors.[44] It also seems that there is a bias against black dogs![45] More generally, one can imagine that the decision to adopt a dog may be the result of some unexplainable chemistry of the sort that sparks romance between people. Would the same dog be chosen if the adopter had engaged in a more systematic search within the shelter? If not, an interesting question for an economist is whether the actual choice is efficient. A behavioral economist would likely argue that people almost never carry out systematic searches. In this case, the initial engagement already creates an endowment effect that makes it hard for the person to move on to the next dog. Alternatively, the initial engagement may be an ancillary factor that is relevant to the choice of dog but not the ultimate assessment of quality.[46]

4.4 CONCLUSION

The market for dogs has attracted suppliers of different sizes and motivations. Although varying in importance across types of suppliers, information asymmetries and negative externalities bring the allocative efficiency of the aggregate market into question. Such market failures provide justification for government interventions to increase efficiency. Some states have adopted laws more stringent than federal regulations, but the patchwork of regulations and lack of resources invested in enforcement still allow puppy mills and black-market breeders to distort the market, impose costs on others, and inflict much harm on dogs. In contrast to markets for most durable goods, however, the used market for dogs (shelters) is less prone to information asymmetry than the market for new dogs (puppy suppliers).

---

[44] Alexandra Protopopova and Clive D. L. Wynne. "Judging a Dog by Its Cover: Morphology but Not Training Influences Visitor Behavior Toward Kenneled Dogs at Animal Shelters." *Anthrozoös* 29, no. 3 (2016): 469–487.

[45] For example, see Laura A. Reese, Mark Skidmore, William Dyar, and Erika Rosebrook. "No Dog Left Behind: A Hedonic Pricing Model for Animal Shelters." *Journal of Applied Animal Welfare Science* 20, no. 1 (2017): 52–64.

[46] For an overview of such behavioral anomalies, see David L. Weimer, *Behavioral Economics for Cost-Benefit Analysis: Benefit Validity When Sovereign Consumers Seem to Make Mistakes* (New York, NY: Cambridge University Press, 2017).

5

You Bet Your (Dog's) Life

The Value of a Statistical Dog Life (VSDL)

We regularly face a great variety of risks to life and limb over the course of our lives. The magnitudes of many of these risks depend on the decisions we make and the actions we take. All decisions and actions in our lives involve trade-offs of various sorts. For example, driving faster than the speed limit saves you a little time, but increases the risk of a serious or, possibly, fatal accident. Observing how people make specific trade-offs between money and mortality risk enables economists to infer the implicit value people place on their own lives. The average of this implicit value for some specific population, such as that of the United States, has the label, the value of statistical life (VSL).[1] This label is somewhat unfortunate because it reinforces the image that economics is truly the "dismal science" that prices people's lives. But the VSL has very practical value because it allows economists and government agencies to monetize reductions in mortality risk that are predicted to result from potential policies, including rules developed by regulatory agencies, such as the Environmental Protection Agency (EPA) or the Food and Drug Administration (FDA). With this value in hand, analysts are able to compare the benefits of these reductions

---

[1] Trudy A. Cameron notes the unfortunate connotations of the VSL. Most importantly, it measures not what people would be willing to pay to avoid imminent death, but rather how they value small changes in mortality risk. She also notes that value does not adequately capture the notion that people themselves are making trade-offs, or willingly swapping things of value, usually money or time, for reductions in the risk of death. She recommends replacing VSL with the term "Willingness-to-Swap for a Microrisk Reduction." Unfortunately, VSL has become so engrained in the economics literature and regulatory practice that its replacement is unlikely. See Trudy A. Cameron. "Euthanizing the Value of a Statistical Life." *Review of Environmental Economics and Policy* 4, no. 2 (2010): 161–178.

to the costs required to implement them in their cost–benefit analyses. However, government policies sometimes also affect the mortality risks faced by our pets; a comprehensive accounting of costs and benefits should also monetize the value people place on the lives of their pets. Specifically, policy analysts seeking to value the benefits of policies that reduce mortality risk for dogs require a value of statistical dog life (VSDL) based on how people value these risks in their own decisions.

Mostly without thinking about it much, we all regularly make trade-offs that affect the mortality risks faced by our dogs. For example, buying more expensive pet food may reduce the risk that our dogs will develop a particular cancer. In the same way that the trade-offs we make between money and our own mortality risk provide leverage for estimating the economic value of policies that reduce human mortality, and the trade-offs we make between money and the mortality risks faced by our dogs provide leverage for estimating the economic value of policies that reduce dog mortality. In other words, they help us to estimate the VSDL – the average monetary value U.S. households implicitly place on their dogs based on the trade-offs they make between money and the mortality risks faced by their dogs.

In this chapter, we present and discuss how to get to a plausible estimate of the VSDL. We begin by first reviewing the ways economists have developed estimates of the VSL for you and me over the last few decades. The analytical need for a theoretically grounded canine VSL was highlighted by the challenges that FDA economists faced in valuing proposed rules intended to reduce mortality risks to pets from adulterated food. The estimate of the VSDL that we later present involves the application of the contingent valuation method. Economists now regularly use the contingent valuation method to value goods, like reductions in human mortality risk, that are not traded in markets. Similarly, risk reduction for canines is not directly traded. Estimating the VSDL involves applying it to how people value their dogs. Beyond its application in the assessment of proposed regulations by government agencies, the VSDL can be employed in the valuation of companionship in cost–benefit analyses of policies to promote zooeyia, as well as potentially in legal cases involving the wrongful death of dogs or determining which spouse gets to keep Fido in a divorce case.

5.1 OUR VSL

Adam Smith presciently observed that workers may demand higher wages for riskier jobs; however, until the mid-1970s, his insight was not acted upon to estimate the implicit value people place on their own lives.[2] Since then, however, numerous studies have found ways to estimate the VSL for the U.S. population, as well as for the populations of an increasing number of other countries. They mostly do so based on data from labor markets, but increasingly from a variety of other sources.[3] Bolstered by reviews of this rich empirical literature, various U.S. regulatory agencies have adopted broadly similar values of the VSL, which they use as a *shadow price* for avoided deaths in their cost–benefit analyses of proposed rules.[4] The fundamental idea behind this shadow price is an assumption that individuals value small changes in their own mortality risk as if they were valuing their own lives at the VSL. Aggregating changes in mortality risk across the given population yields a prediction of the number of lives that would be saved or lost under the proposed rule. For example, a rule that would reduce the probability of mortality risk by 1/1,000,000 for each of the 10 million people in the population would be predicted to save 10 lives. In comparing the costs and benefits of the proposed rule, the 10 saved lives would be monetized using the estimated VSL, say $10 million per person, to yield a benefit of $100 million. The economic principle behind this approach is that individuals are usually the best judges of the risk trade-offs that they make in life. Although we see this as an appropriate conceptual approach, its actual application requires consideration of whether individuals have sufficient information and cognition to make rational choices in complex situations; an issue we address in the design of the contingent valuation for estimating either the VSL or the VSDL.

Figure 5.1 shows the conceptual framework for estimating the VSL or the VSDL. The estimation is shown as a decision tree, where the square box indicates the choice to be made, the circles indicate random events, and the triangles indicate dollar valuations of the outcomes, either life or death. The lower branch shows the choice as a gamble with a $1-p$

[2] Richard Thaler and Sherwin Rosen. "The Value of Saving a Life: Evidence from the Labor Market." In Nestor E. Terleckyj, ed., *Household Production and Consumption* (New York, NY: Columbia University Press, 1976), 265–302.

[3] For an excellent overview by one of the eminent contributors to the study of the VSL, see W. Kip Viscusi. *Pricing Lives: Guideposts for a Safer Society* (Princeton, NJ: Princeton University Press, 2018).

[4] Resources and goods not traded in markets do not have readily observable prices. Rather, their prices are in the shadows in that they must be inferred in some way. For a list of commonly used shadow prices, see Anthony E. Boardman, David H. Greenberg, Aidan R. Vining, and David L. Weimer. *Cost–Benefit Analysis: Concepts and Practice*, 5th ed. (New York, NY: Cambridge University Press, 2017), Chapter 17.

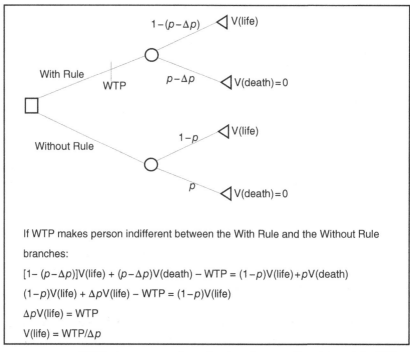

If WTP makes person indifferent between the With Rule and the Without Rule branches:

$[1- (p-\Delta p)]V(\text{life}) + (p-\Delta p)V(\text{death}) - WTP = (1-p)V(\text{life}) + pV(\text{death})$

$(1-p)V(\text{life}) + \Delta pV(\text{life}) - WTP = (1-p)V(\text{life})$

$\Delta pV(\text{life}) = WTP$

$V(\text{life}) = WTP/\Delta p$

FIGURE 5.1 Willingness to pay for reductions in mortality risk and the VSL

probability of living and a p probability of dying. The upper branch offers a reduction in the probability of death by a small amount, Δp, for some payment, WPT, that an individual is willing to make. Consequently, on the upper branch, the probability of living increases to $1 - (p - \Delta p)$ and the probability of dying falls to $p - \Delta p$. We are interested in the willingness to pay (WTP) for this improvement in life expectancy. Assuming that the WTP is just large enough to make the individual facing the risk indifferent between the two branches, we can equate the expected values of the two branches and solve for V(life), the VSL, to be WTP/Δp. For example, if the WTP were $100 and $\Delta p = 1/1,000,000$ (1 in a million reduction in mortality risk), then the VSL would be $10 million, which is the approximate value that most U.S. regulatory agencies currently use.

Economists employ two general approaches in estimating WTP and Δp. One approach infers people's preferences by observing their actual choices (the *revealed preference method*). For example, they observe the expenditures that car purchasers make on optional safety devices that reduce mortality risk. The other approach infers people's preferences from their responses to questions in survey experiments that randomize some variable relevant to estimating an economic value of interest (the *stated preference method*). For example, survey respondents may be offered different (randomly assigned) prices for a product that reduces their mortality risk, such as a new safety device that has not yet been marketed. When well done, these approaches yield quite similar results, though the stated preference method tends to yield somewhat smaller estimates of WTP than the revealed preference method.[5]

The revealed preference method has been the most common approach of empirical economics and remains so currently. Its great strength is its basis in data on actual decisions made by individuals, whether in their roles as consumers, workers, or executives. The great challenge in doing this kind of analysis convincingly is collecting data that allow researchers to isolate the impact of interest. Many VSL studies rely on employment data of various kinds to determine the relationship between WTP and Δp. They primarily do so by observing the additional pay, the wage premium, that must be paid to workers in riskier jobs. In other words, the wage premium for risk is the amount of higher pay, holding all other job characteristics the same, that workers demand to take the riskier jobs. However, other characteristics besides mortality risk, such as morbidity risk, local labor market conditions, and pleasantness, almost always also vary across jobs, so isolating the relationship between WTP and Δp often requires sophisticated statistical (econometric) methods. Even using the best statistical methods, it is sometimes reasonable to raise doubts about the extent to which those workers who are observed correctly perceive the relevant probabilities, though market wages can often be assumed to reflect the choices of marginal workers who are well informed.[6]

The stated preference method was originally developed by environmental economists who faced the problem of valuing environmental amenities that are not traded in markets and often leave no behavioral traces of choices that would generate the data needed for revealed preference methods. The most widely used stated preference method, contingent valuation, a type of survey experiment, elicits willingness to pay by offering survey respondents a hypothetical choice in some structured, but lifelike scenario (economists call this setup the elicitation). The major advantage for researchers is

---

[5] W. Kip Viscusi and Elissa Philip Gentry. "The Value of a Statistical Life for Transportation Regulations: A Test of the Benefits Transfer Methodology." *Journal of Risk and Uncertainty* 51, no. 1 (2015): 53–77, p. 56.

[6] Colin F. Camerer. "Do Biases in Probability Judgment Matter in Markets? Experimental Evidence." *American Economic Review* 77, no. 3 (1987): 981–997.

that the scenario can be carried out as an experiment in which respondents either accept or reject a randomly assigned dollar amount for the good that they are valuing. However, in addition to all the challenges of conducting a valid survey, the contingent valuation survey designer faces the additional task of trying to structure the scenario so that respondents treat it as if they are confronting it as a real economic choice involving a trade-off of some sort. The survey format also allows researchers to set up a variety of different scenarios that can be used to help assess the extent to which respondents are indeed making economic trade-offs. However, designing valid scenarios is challenging. Indeed, an early application of what was to become the field of behavioral economics was a critique of stated preference studies. These studies were criticized for not sufficiently accounting for problems resulting from the various cognitive biases of survey respondents.[7] In response to these criticisms, researchers have gradually improved the contingent valuation method so that it is now widely used beyond environmental policy, including in studies to estimate the VSL.

Mainstream economics only gives standing to *Homo sapiens* in assessing values! Some notable pioneers of economics, however, such as Jeremy Bentham, questioned this limiting of standing to our own species.[8] (Some people find the mainstream assumption disturbing, although it does not stop many of them from eating animals.) Therefore, the VSDL we present here is based on the willingness of human owners to pay for reductions in the mortality risk faced by their dogs. As people expend both money and time to improve the health and safety of their dogs, clever researchers will probably find a way to apply revealed preference methods to estimate the VSDL. However, we know of no such study. Later in this chapter, we report extensively on a contingent valuation used to estimate the VSDL. But, first, we explain the crisis and federal response that prompted its estimation.

5.2 THE MELAMINE PET FOOD DISASTER

The pet food industry exhibits the supply-chain globalization that permeates most economies today: a Canadian firm produces pet food under

---

[7] David L. Weimer. *Behavioral Economics for Cost-Benefit Analysis: Benefit Validity When Sovereign Consumers Seem to Make Mistakes* (New York, NY: Cambridge University Press, 2017).

[8] Bentham includes the pleasure and pain of animals in his utilitarianism. However, he did not argue for equal treatment of the pleasure and pain of humans and animals. See Johannes Kniess. "Bentham on Animal Welfare." *British Journal for the History of Philosophy* 27, no. 3 (2019): 556–572.

a variety of labels with ingredients from China at U.S. plants for sale in domestic and international markets. Just such an arrangement led to a pet disaster in 2007: many dogs and cats died from the consumption of adulterated pet food. The political response was federal legislation that substantially increased the responsibilities and authorities of the Food and Drug Administration (FDA) to regulate the safety of pet food.

This story has economic, legal, and regulatory dimensions. It began in 2006. The Canadian firm Menu Foods ordered wheat gluten for use in its Emporia, Kansas, pet food plant from the U.S. firm ChemNutra. In turn, ChemNutra imported the gluten from the Chinese firm, Xuzhou Anying.[9] In early 2007, Menu began receiving complaints from customers that their cats and dogs suffered kidney failure after eating its brands. Menu also received an early report from an owner of five dogs who reported that one had died and four were ill after eating its products. The company that did palatability testing for Menu reported high rates of death among cats and illness among dogs who were fed food from the Kansas plant. In response, Menu issued a recall for "60 million units of 42 cat food brands and 53 dog foods made in its Emporia plant between December 2006, and March 2007."[10] The firm soon expanded its recall to include products produced at its Ontario plant. Recalls from other pet food companies followed, as these firms also discovered contamination in imported rice and corn products.

The nature of the contamination was not immediately obvious, but eventually it became clear that the culprit was melamine and one of its byproducts, cyanuric acid, both of which are found in wastewater from plastic production. These chemicals are rich in nitrogen, so they can appear to be proteins when examined using common chemical tests. Both U.S. and Chinese investigators found that Xuzhou Anying added inexpensive melamine and cyanuric acid to wheat flour so that it could pass as gluten, a more valuable and expensive protein-rich substance. They also eventually discovered that other Chinese firms had even adulterated milk and infant formula with melamine to make it appear they had higher protein contents. Many Chinese children suffered kidney damage as a result.

The harm to pets from the adulteration was substantial. Between 30 thousand and 50 thousand U.S. pets became ill. The U.S. Attorney for the Western District of Missouri, who successfully prosecuted ChemNutra

[9] This account is based on the very detailed chronology provided by Marion Nestle. *Pet Food Politics: The Chihuahua in the Coal Mine* (Berkeley, CA: University of California Press, 2008).
[10] Nestle, Table 2, p. 34.

for supplying the adulterated gluten, claimed that 1,950 cats and 2,200 dogs died.[11] The recall also created a great deal of anxiety among pet owners – the FDA received over 18 thousand calls about the 2007 pet food recalls, more than for any pet or human food recall up to that time.[12] Although the Chinese government initially denied the claims that its exports of gluten were adulterated, it eventually participated in the investigation of the incident. Subsequently, it revoked Xuzhou Anying's license, strengthened its own food safety systems, committed to greater monitoring of food exports, and executed the former head of its food and drug agency.

5.3 U.S. PUBLIC POLICY RESPONSE

Prompted largely by the melamine pet disaster, Congress made substantial changes to FDA authorities and responsibilities through the Food and Drug Administration Amendments Act of 2007 (Public Law 110–85) and the FDA Food Safety Modernization Act (P.L. 111–353) in 2011.[13] Alongside provisions that strengthened the regulation of human food, these acts required the FDA to develop pet food processing and ingredient standards, to improve pet food labeling, to initiate new preventive measures, and to improve inspection, compliance, and response procedures. In sum, these provisions made the regulation of pet food more like the existing regulations of human food. Further, rather than being limited to requesting that firms conduct recalls, the FDA gained the additional authority to mandate them.

As with almost all major changes in U.S. domestic public policy, the substantive content of these laws had to be filled out through rulemaking,

[11] Mark A. Fox and Robert Kenagy. "Commercial Pet Food Recalls: Incentives to Improve Pet Food Safety." *Contemporary Readings in Law & Social Justice* 7, no. 2 (2015): 17–39.
[12] Sophie L. Rovner. "Anatomy of a Pet Food Catastrophe." *Chemical & Engineering News* 84, no. 19 (2008): 41–43.
[13] The history of legislative changes to food and drug regulation in the United States shows a pattern of long periods of unsuccessful efforts to strengthen regulation punctuated by public events that opened "policy windows" for major change: Upton Sinclair's *The Jungle* helped precipitate the 1906 Pure Food and Drug Act, the Elixir Sulfanilamide deaths set the stage for Food, Drug, and Cosmetic Act of 1938, and the thalidomide birth defects prompted the 1962 Kefauver-Harris Amendments. David L. Weimer. "Organizational Incentives: Safe – and Available – Drugs." In LeRoy Gramer and Frederick Thompson, eds., *Reforming Social Regulation: Alternative Public Policy Strategies* (Beverly Hills, CA: Sage Publications, 1982), 19–69. The melamine disaster adds to this list of precipitating events, perhaps giving some solace to those who lost pets.

which involves agencies publishing proposed rules for public comment and then responding to the comments with revisions or responses in the final rules they publish. The pet food safety rules proposed by the FDA were finalized in 2015.[14]

These rules were subject to Regulatory Impact Analysis (RIA). Beginning with Executive Order 12291 issued by President Reagan and strengthened by President Clinton's Executive Order 12866 and President Obama's Executive Order 13563, federal executive agencies, including the FDA, must conduct Regulatory Impact Analyses of major proposed rules, primarily rules that would involve annual costs, benefits, or transfers of more than $100 million. Two components of the RIA are the requirement for a statement of the rationale for the rulemaking and a cost–benefit analysis that, at least in principle, monetizes all the impacts of the proposed rule.

The 2015 pet food rules were predicted to have annual costs that were sufficiently large to qualify them as a major rulemaking. The FDA analysts argued there were two market failure rationales that justified the proposed rule changes.[15] The first rationale was that, because pet food firms were not legally liable for all the morbidity and mortality costs that they impose on pet owners, they did not have a sufficiently strong incentive to minimize risk. (We return to the liability issue later in this chapter.) The second rationale was that consumers have difficulty distinguishing among firms in terms of the safety of their products. In other words, the information asymmetry market failure discussed in Chapter 4 that leads to inefficiency in the puppy market also leads to inefficiency in the pet food market.

The FDA analysts faced something of a challenge in plausibly predicting the benefits of the rules because they lacked a way of valuing the avoided pet deaths. They went about the task by predicting that the proposed rules would reduce the risk of feces contaminating pet food so that humans would be less likely to get salmonellosis from handling it. They used the average cost of medical treatment for salmonellosis to monetize this benefit. They then predicted how many avoided illnesses and deaths to pets the agency believed would result from the rules. Quite

---

[14] Food and Drug Administration. "Current Good Manufacturing Practice, Hazard Analysis, and Risk-Based Preventive Controls for Food for Animals. Final Rule." *Federal Register* 80, no. 180 (2015), 56170–56356.

[15] Department of Health and Human Services, Food and Drug Administration. FSMA Final Rulemaking for Current Good Manufacturing Practice, Hazard Analysis, and Risk-Based Preventive Controls for Food for Animals. Docket No. FDA-2011-N-0922, September 17 (2015).

reasonably, the analysts monetized the avoided injuries using estimates of owners' veterinary expenses, but they did not have an available VSDL for monetizing avoided dog deaths. Thus, in the end, the impact that owners likely valued most highly, reduced risk of their pets dying, was not actually included in the FDA's estimate of monetized benefits.

5.4 GENESIS OF THE VSDL ESTIMATE

At the 2015 annual meeting of the Society for Benefit-Cost Analysis, one of your authors had breakfast with Clark Nardinelli, who was the FDA economist overseeing the RIA for the pet food rules. He commented that, unlike the case of human mortality risks, he had no shadow price for monetizing changes in mortality risks for dogs and other pets. Your author sagely (other author's comment) suggested that he could carry out a contingent valuation study to develop an estimate of the VSDL. He asked if the FDA would provide the approximately $50 thousand needed to do the survey. Unfortunately, Nardinelli had nothing but praise for the proposed study! After several years of searching for funding, your author decided to use his professorship account. He recruited former students who were dog owners, as well as experts in survey research and the contingent valuation method, to work with him on the project. Their study was published in 2019 in the *Journal of Benefit-Cost Analysis* where it can be accessed without charge.[16]

5.5 ESTIMATING THE VSDL

Implementing any contingent valuation survey poses quite a few design challenges. Applying it in a unique context is especially challenging. The following sections describe how these challenges were addressed to estimate the VSDL.

5.5.1 Selecting the Survey Sample

Using a contingent valuation survey to develop a shadow price like the VSDL involves estimating the mean WTP of a random sample of the relevant population for a hypothetical reduction in their dog's mortality risk.

---

[16] Deven Carlson, Simon Haeder, Hank Jenkins-Smith, Joseph Ripberger, Carol Silva, and David Weimer. "Monetizing Bowser: A Contingent Valuation of the Statistical Value of Dog Life." *Journal of Benefit-Cost Analysis* 11, no. 1 (2019): 131–149. www.cambridge.org/core/journals/journal-of-benefit-cost-analysis/issue/FEF31134CBB73FAF3AF93346D9BC9624. Accessed November 8, 2022.

The relevant population in cost–benefit analysis (CBA) consists of those people who have standing in the sense that their costs and benefits count.[17] The team decided that in this particular context, the relevant population with standing was U.S. residents who kept dogs as pets, as this shadow price was their primary interest. Consequently, the team excluded dog owners who keep their dogs primarily to provide service in agriculture, as guides, breeders, or guards; the services of these working dogs have their own market values. (We consider the economics of working dogs in considerable detail in Chapter 7.)

The research team drew the initial sample of all dog owners from the Qualtrics panel of willing respondents in an internet survey fielded in May 2018. Of the initial 4,975 respondents, 4,682 responded that they considered their dogs to be primarily pets, and so the latter number constituted the sample for estimating the VSDL. Previous chapters presented data from this survey, which we labeled the PVL Survey. Some of the respondents had more than one dog. They were asked questions only about the dog with whom they spend the most time. If they reported spending equal time with more than one dog, then they were asked to answer questions about the dog with whom they most recently interacted. The respondents were asked to provide the name of this dog. Asking for a dog's names had three purposes. First, it allowed the team to phrase questions using the dog's name to personalize the survey so that respondents would be more likely to be fully engaged. Second, it increased the likelihood that respondents with multiple dogs would focus only on the one they initially identified. Third, the distribution of respondents' dog names could be compared to the most common names reported in commercial sources as a check on the representativeness of the dog owners in the survey. Indeed, the team did find the same commonest names in 2018: Max for male dogs and Bella for female dogs.[18]

---

[17] On the issues involved in determining standing, see Anthony E. Boardman, David H. Greenberg, Aidan R. Vining, and David L. Weimer. "Standing in Cost-Benefit Analysis: Where, Who, What (Counts)?" *Journal of Policy Analysis and Management* 41, no. 4 (2022): 1157–1176.

[18] The comparison for the full sample was made to Rover, a dog-walking and dog-sitting network (www.rover.com/blog/dog-names/) and the comparison for respondents who had pet insurance was Embrace Pet Insurance (www.embracepetinsurance.com/waterbowl/article/most-popular-dog-names-of-2018). The overlap in the top ten female names for both comparisons was six. The overlap for male dogs in general was seven and the overlap for respondents with pet insurance was five. The research team viewed these overlaps as reassuring that it had obtained a random sample of dog owners. Accessed March 31, 2019.

5.5.2 Using the Dichotomous Choice Method

Not surprisingly, the hardest questions to develop were those about willingness to pay for changes in the mortality risk faced by respondents' dogs. These questions had to have premises that were sufficiently plausible so that respondents would answer as if they were making real choices – the more realistic and familiar, the better. Further, questions also had to clearly specify the change in mortality risk (the Δp) that respondents were being asked to value. To frame a concrete risk, the team constructed questions about the value of a vaccine against canine influenza. This flu was first found in the United States in 2015, and by the time of the study, had infected dogs in thirty states. It could certainly cause canine mortality, although the mortality rate was estimated to be less than 10 percent. Vaccines were available to protect against the two most common strains of the flu: $H3N2$ and $H3N8$.[19]

What is the best way to get realistic answers to these sorts of unusual questions? The team followed common practice and picked the dichotomous choice format. In this method, respondents, to some degree, mimic consumers in that they are offered the vaccination (the good) at some randomly stated price. Respondents either accept the hypothetical offer or refuse it. If a respondent accepts the offer, then he or she has a WTP for the vaccination of at least that amount. This, admittedly hypothetical, choice tries to mimic the economic decisions consumers engage in routinely when they make purchases at prices specified by sellers. With the dichotomous choice methods, rather than having to decide the most they would be willing to pay for the good or the amount to offer, dog owners only have to ask themselves a simpler question: is the vaccination worth more to me than the price? If they think the answer is yes, then they express the willingness to (hypothetically!) purchase; if they think the answer is no, then they do not express a willingness to purchase.

Dichotomous choice has largely replaced the "open-ended" question format, which was the more commonly used method when contingent valuation was first introduced. That format would simply ask the respondent to state some notional WTP. However, most individuals are not used to making purchases thinking about possible prices in this way, especially for novel goods. Researchers often tried to help them arrive at a WTP through one of two iterative-bidding processes. First, like an English

[19] American Veterinary Medical Association. "Canine Influenza FAQ". www.avma.org/canine-influenza-faq. Accessed November 8, 2022.

auction, a very low bid was initially stated, then successively increased in a series of bids until the respondent rejected a bid. Second, like a Dutch auction, a very high bid was initially stated, then successively reduced in a series of bids until the respondent accepted a bid. Unfortunately, respondents tended to anchor their final WTP toward the initial starting value: increasing bids from a low level tended to result in lower final bids than decreasing bids from a high level. Beyond these behavioral issues, an open-ended format tends to encourage so-called strategic responses. Originally, the suspicion was that those who favored public provision of the good being valued would strategically overstate their WTP to increase the average WTP reported by the study. In practice, however, this turned out not to be a big problem and could be controlled by limiting the WTP to an estimate of respondents' disposable income. The strategic responses that did occur, however, tended to be respondents stating a zero WTP when they anticipated that their true WTP was less than the amount they would have to pay if the goods were provided.

The two advantages that the dichotomous choice format offers – familiar type of choice and little susceptibility to strategic responses – come, however, at a price. Unlike in an open-ended format where each response provides quite a bit of information in the stated WTP value, the dichotomous choice format provides much less information per respondent, a yes or no answer. Consequently, large samples are needed to obtain a reliable mean WTP for the population. Large sample sizes are also required to compare alternative scenarios because each respondent should see only one scenario to avoid an anchoring effect in which the bid offered to the respondent in the initial scenario affects the respondent's response to bids in subsequent scenarios.

5.5.3 Specifying the Elicitation Scenario

Effectively conveying the attributes of the good being valued in a contingent valuation is usually challenging. Respondents, not surprisingly, find it difficult to sensibly value a new and unfamiliar good. Understanding and valuing changes in risks, which involve probabilities, is especially challenging for most of us. Working out exactly how individuals perceive, and, just as importantly, misperceive, probabilities and risks was an early impetus in the field of behavioral economics.[20]

---

[20] Amos Tversky and Daniel Kahneman. "Judgment under Uncertainty: Heuristics and Biases." *Science* 185, no. 4157 (1974): 1124–1131.

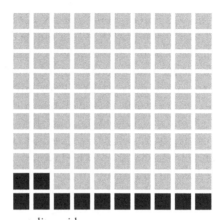

FIGURE 5.2 Basic mortality grid
Source: Deven Carlson, Simon Haeder, Hank Jenkins-Smith, Joseph Ripberger,
Carol Silva, and David Weimer. "Monetizing Bowser: A Contingent Valuation
of the Statistical Value of Dog Life." *Journal of Benefit-Cost Analysis* 11, no. 1
(2019): 131–149, p. 135. Reprinted with permission.

Some of this research, for example, has focused on how to more effectively communicate risk so that people misperceive it less.[21] One guide-
line for the effective presentation of risks is to use the probability metric
consistently, the team chose to present all probabilities as percentages.
Research also suggests that graphics help people better understand probabilities. Therefore, the team supplemented statements about probabilities with grids that conveyed differences and changes in mortality risk.
Figure 5.2 illustrates the grid presentation. Light gray squares (shown
as green to respondents) represent life and dark gray squares (shown
as red to respondents) represent death. With 100 squares, the number
of dark gray squares corresponds to the percentage points of mortality risk. The team also wanted to avoid the kinds of inconsistencies
that often arise when people are asked to compare certain to uncertain
outcomes – the evidence shows that people tend to place more weight
on risk reductions resulting in certain outcomes than on risk reductions
of comparable magnitude that do not result in certainty. This regularity
is inconsistent with the expected utility hypothesis, which posits that
people weight the values of outcomes by their respective probabilities

[21] For an overview of the risk communication research, see Vivianne H. M. Visschers, Ree
M. Meertens, Wim W. F. Passchier, and Nanne N. K. de Vries. "Probability Information
in Risk Communication: A Review of the Research Literature." *Risk Analysis* 29, no. 2
(2009): 267–287.

and use them to arrive at an overall assessment.[22] Taking account of this, the team decided to frame the choice so that the good being valued would be a vaccine that substantially reduced the mortality risk from canine influenza but did not completely eliminate it. Specifically, the primary scenario asked respondents if they would purchase a vaccine that reduced the mortality risk from 12 percent to 2 percent if it cost X (the "bid"). The value of X for each respondent was randomly drawn from a uniform distribution ranging from \$5 to \$3,000; that is, dollar amounts within this range were equally likely to be assigned to X.

In the primary elicitation scenario that follows [X] indicates where the random dollar amount appears and [name] indicates where the name of the respondent's dog appears.

Imagine that scientists have identified a new strain of canine influenza that will threaten dogs in your area during the coming year. Most dogs that contract the influenza over the next year will only show mild symptoms, but some dogs will die suddenly from the virus. Veterinarians estimate that a dog in your area will have a 12-percent chance of contracting the new influenza strain and dying from it over the next year. Fortunately, it is not expected that this strain of influenza will remain a threat beyond the next year.

The squares in this diagram represent the risk a dog in your area has of dying from the influenza virus over the next year. Each square represents one dog. Light gray squares represent dogs that do not die from the influenza; dark gray squares represent dogs that do die from the influenza. Assume that the mortality risk for your dog is represented by the chance of randomly drawing a dark gray square.

Now imagine that a vaccine is available to provide some protection against the influenza. The vaccine would reduce the risk that [name] would contract the new influenza strain. Specifically, the vaccine would reduce the chance of [name] dying from the influenza during the next year from 12 percent to 2 percent.

The diagrams were next displayed side-by-side as shown in Figure 5.3.

The diagram on the left represents the risk a dog in your area has of dying from the influenza virus over the next year if the dog receives the vaccine. For comparison, the diagram on the right represents the risk of dying from the influenza virus over the next year if the dog does not receive the vaccine.

---

[22] Daniel Kahneman and Amos Tversky. "Prospect Theory: An Analysis of Decision under Risk." *Econometrica* 47, no. 2 (1979): 263–291.

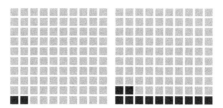

FIGURE 5.3 Comparative mortality grids
Source: Carlson et al., p. 136. Reprinted with permission.

Imagine that your out-of-pocket costs to have [name] vaccinated against the new strain of influenza would be [X]. *This is the amount you would have to pay whether or not you have either pet insurance or a prepaid plan with a veterinarian. Remember that this amount of money would not be available to you to use for other expenses such as grocery bills, utilities, recreation, or savings. Would you pay* [X] *to purchase the vaccine for [name]?*

Note that respondents are reminded that money spent on the vaccine would not be available to spend on other goods. This "budget reminder" is routine in elicitations; it encourages respondents to think of the scenario in economic terms; that is, it reminds them that their choices involve trade-offs!

Yet will respondents who say that they agree to pay the stated amount actually do so if confronted with a real choice? Studies that were able to compare results from stated and revealed preference methods have, indeed, found that hypotheticality bias, the tendency to overstate a willingness to purchase at the bid price, is quite common.[23] These studies also suggest, however, that researchers can correct for the bias in the estimation of WTP by converting acceptances to rejections for respondents who do not express high levels of certainty in their acceptances. To enable this adjustment, contingent valuations following best practice include a follow-up question for respondents who accept the offer that asks them how certain they are that they would indeed accept it. The team asked accepting respondents about how certain they were of their

---

[23] See Patricia A. Champ, Richard C. Bishop, Thomas C. Brown, and Daniel W. McCollum. "Using Donation Mechanisms to Value Nonuse Benefits from Public Goods." *Journal of Environmental Economics and Management* 33, no. 2 (1997): 151–162 and Karen Blumenschein, Glenn C. Blomquist, Magnus Johannesson, Nancy Horn, and Patricia Freeman. "Eliciting Willingness to Pay without Bias: Evidence from a Field Experiment." *Economic Journal* 118, no. 525 (2008): 114–137.

acceptance using an 11-point scale ranging from 0 (not at all confident) to 10 (extremely confident). The team converted acceptances with certainty responses of less than 8 as rejections in the subsequent statistical analysis.

5.5.4 Alternative Scenarios: Scope, Discretionary Spending, and Externality Tests

Good practice requires contingent valuations to use more than one scenario to help assess the validity of the results. Respondents were randomly assigned to either the primary scenario or one of four others. Two of the scenarios were what are called "scope tests" that vary the good being valued. If respondents are making economic choices, then we expect that they would be more willing to pay for either larger quantities or higher qualities of the good being valued. Standard practice is to include at least a quantitative scope test that offers a different amount of the good. The quantitative scope test offered a less effective vaccine that only reduced the mortality risk from 12 percent to 6 percent, rather than to 2 percent. If respondents do treat the questions about their purchase of the good as involving an economic choice, then the estimated WTP should be lower for the less effective vaccine. The qualitative scope test replaced the sentence in the primary scenario "*some dogs will die suddenly from the virus*" with "*are expected to suffer severe and painful respiratory symptoms including coughing and choking prior to death.*" Again, if respondents treat the scenario as posing economic choices, then the estimated WTP should be higher for the scenario involving suffering than for the less painful death.

Another scenario introduced the issue of flu contagion (in economic terminology, external effects, in this case positive externalities): "*The vaccine would also greatly reduce the risk that [name] would spread the influenza to other dogs. On average, for each dog that gets the vaccination, one additional dog will be saved from dying from the influenza.*" If dog owners have concerns about dogs in general, and if respondents treat the scenario as posing a real economic choice, then that estimated WTP should be higher than in the primary scenario.

The final scenario added a question to the primary scenario that asked respondents about their discretionary income. The team expected this question to make respondents more sensitive to the price of the vaccine, so that their estimated WTPs would be lower. However, it had no effect, so these respondents were pooled with those who were given the primary scenario in the subsequent analysis. The increased sample size from this pooling facilitated a more precise estimate of WTP.

5.5.6 Behavioral Considerations in Reducing Hypotheticality

As already noted, the early use of contingent valuation drew criticisms from scholars who contributed to what would become the field of behavioral economics. These criticisms contributed to the development of better contingent valuation craft. Use of the dichotomous choice method, careful presentation of probabilities, one elicitation per respondent, and the inclusion of scope tests are examples of better craft that grew out of behavioral criticisms. However, concerns related to the level of engagement respondents have in responding to hypothetical questions remain. Some of these concerns can be addressed with data from questions that assess respondents' perceptions of the plausibility of the presented scenarios.

The team anticipated that respondents who viewed their scenario as particularly plausible would be more fully engaged and therefore more likely to treat the hypothetical choice as if they were actually making it. To explore this conjecture, respondents were asked about the plausibility of their dog facing a threat like canine influenza and the plausibility of the existence of a vaccination against it. As some people are skeptical about vaccines (as recently made so apparent during the COVID pandemic), the team also asked a question about whether local governments should make canine vaccination mandatory.

5.5.7 Sociodemographic Factors Potentially Affecting WTP

One could suppose that the probability of accepting the vaccine might depend on the ages of respondents' dogs and how many additional years they expected their dogs to live. As the team was worried that people would have difficulty understanding and answering a question about expected longevity, it first asked respondents for the current ages and weights of their dogs. (Smaller dogs tend to live longer.) The team referred to a life table for dogs to find the number of additional years of life expected for a dog of that weight and age [expected_life].[24]

---

[24] Absent a table specifically for the United States, the look-up table was based on Mai Inoue, A. Hasegawa, Y. Hosoi, and K. Sugiura. "A Current Life Table and Causes of Death for Insured Dogs in Japan." *Preventive Veterinary Medicine* 120, no. 2 (2015): 210–218.

That expected life was reported to respondents. With this information in hand, the respondents were then asked about expected longevity: *On average, a dog with [name's] weight and age would be expected to live [expected_life] more years. Note that this is only an average, so that [name] could live more or fewer years. Barring an accident, and given your knowledge of [name's] health, what is your best guess about how many more years [name] will live?*[25]

The team also included questions that allowed it to create other variables that could potentially affect the probability of accepting the offered price. Respondents were asked to report their approximate income through several questions. To take account of different family sizes, respondents' incomes were divided by the federal poverty line, which depends on family size. Respondents were asked if they viewed their dogs as companions. To get at respondents' degree of risk aversion (but also indirectly their income), respondents were asked if they had pet health insurance or a prepaid plan for their dog. Respondents were asked if they lived alone. The team also created a variable to indicate if people owned more than one dog because the responses of those with more than one dog might reflect their anticipation of having to pay to vaccinate all their dogs.[26]

5.5.8 Statistical Analysis Strategy

What was the team's overall strategy for analyzing the resulting survey data? It involved estimating a curve representing the probability of acceptance of the bid as a function of the size of the bid [X], while statistically controlling for the other variables that the team hypothesized would affect WTP. The area under this curve gives the mean WTP for the sample. The team used it to develop a "random utility model," which allowed it to make inferences about the unmeasured factors that might influence acceptance. The team employed a common functional form for the curve: a logistic regression, where acceptance is the dependent variable and the natural log of the bid and the controls are explanatory

---

[25] The correlation between the life table and the respondents' estimates was 0.63; 54 percent of respondents expected their dogs to outlive the life table.

[26] Data on several demographic characteristics of the respondents were collected, including gender, whether other pets were kept, respondent age, working status, living in a rural or urban area, number of children, and presence of young children. As robustness checks, variables for these characteristics were created and included in versions of the model. However, so to speak, none of these dogs barked!

variables. The results of estimating this functional form can be translated into a curve for estimating mean WTP.[27]

The team was relieved to find a strong statistical relationship between the probability of acceptance and the bid size across all scenarios. This is the expected price effect: all other things equal, consumers are expected to demand less of a good the higher the price. If this relationship had not been found, the whole premise that respondents' acceptances fundamentally represent economic decisions would be undermined. If only a much weaker relationship had been found, then it could be seen as consistent with economic theory, but not sufficiently so as to support a confident estimation of the mean WTP. As bids are randomly assigned to respondents (and therefore uncorrelated with the other explanatory variables), their relationship to acceptance largely drives the mean WTP estimation for the sample. Nonetheless, the estimated effects of the other explanatory variables can contribute to confidence in the model if they are consistent with prior expectations. Including these other explanatory variables also facilitates the investigation of the mean WTP for subsets of the sample population.

The team found that several of the other explanatory variables were statistically significantly positive rather than zero in increasing the probability of acceptance of the bid in all scenarios. The expected years of remaining life of the dog, views that the described influenza and the vaccine were plausible, and the belief that local government should require canine vaccinations all contributed to a higher probability of acceptance. Viewing one's dog as a companion had consistently positive effects but was only statistically significant in two scenarios. The purchase of health insurance or a prepaid veterinary plan also had a positive effect across scenarios but was not statistically significant in the externality scenario. The dog's age was also statistically significantly positive in two scenarios. Although living alone had a consistently positive effect, it was only statistically significant in one scenario.

---

[27] On this functional form, see Michael Hanemann and Barbara Kanninen. "Statistical Analysis of Discrete Response CV Data." In Ian J. Bateman and Kenneth G. Wells, eds., *Valuing Environmental Preferences* (New York, NY: Oxford University Press, 1999), 300–441. Buckland et al. provide formulas for converting the results from the logistic regression to the density curve for acceptances, the area corresponding to mean WTP, and the standard deviation of WTP. See Stephen T. Buckland, Douglas C. MacMillan, Elizabeth I. Duff, and Nick Hanley. "Estimating Mean Willingness to Pay from Dichotomous Choice Contingent Valuation Studies." *Journal of the Royal Statistical Society: Series D (The Statistician)* 48, no 1 (1999): 109–124.

One finding that concerned the team was the absence of a statistically significant positive effect of income on the probability of bid acceptance. Economists expect that, all other things equal, higher-income consumers should demand more of any normal good at any given price (the income effect). One possible explanation for the absence of an income effect is that having health insurance or a prepaid veterinary plan is a proxy for income, capturing at least some of the direct effect of income. Also, the survey measures income with a degree of error, which tends to bias it toward no effect.[28] Theoretically, if respondents viewed the protection of their dogs as an altruistic act rather than as consumption for themselves, then WTP would not necessarily be positively related to income.[29] For these reasons, as well as evidence that the absence of an income effect is not unusual in contingent valuation surveys,[30] the team concluded that the absence of an income effect was not a serious problem.

5.5.9 Interpreting WTP Results to Estimate the VSDL

Turning to statistical results, Table 5.1 summarizes the pattern of mean WTP amounts across the scenarios; this pattern is important in assessing the validity of the results. The scenario that offered a relatively less effective vaccine (compared to the primary scenario), resulted in a smaller mean WTP estimate. In contrast, the scenario involving suffering rather than sudden death resulted in a larger estimate of mean WTP. These results are comforting to economists because they are consistent with respondents making economic decisions rather than simply expressing a "warm glow" for the idea of providing protection for their dogs. The externality scenario also provided a larger estimated mean WTP as expected.

Table 5.1 shows the implied VSDL from both the primary and the two scenarios providing scope tests. As the externality scenario provides an estimated mean WTP for each respondent's own dog as well as one other, it is not possible to infer the VSDL directly without knowing the relative weight placed on each of the dogs. Although the WTP pattern across

---

[28] As is common practice, respondents were asked first to place themselves in a broad income category and then asked questions to further narrow the range. Mid-points of the final categories, which were $10,000 wide, were used as estimates of income.

[29] Nicholas E. Flores and Richard T. Carson. "The Relationship between the Income Elasticities of Demand and Willingness to Pay." *Journal of Environmental Economics and Management* 33, no. 3 (1997): 287–295.

[30] Felix Schläpfer. "Survey Protocol and Income Effects in the Contingent Valuation of Public Goods: A Meta-analysis." *Ecological Economics* 57, no. 3 (2006): 415–429.

TABLE 5.1 *Initial estimates of mean WTP and the VSDL*

		Elicitation		
	Primary	Quantitative scope test	Qualitative scope test	Externality
Mean WTP	$676	$603	715	784
Δp	0.10	0.06	0.10	0.10
Implied VSDL	$6,760	$10,050	$7,150	$6,270*
Sample size	1836	918	905	923

*Arbitrarily assuming valuation of other dog at 25 percent of value of own dog.
Source: Calculated from Carlson et al., Table 2, p. 141.

scenarios was reassuring, the team had concerns that the VSDL values summarized in Table 5.1 were too low for various reasons.

The team had concerns about internal validity; first, about the extent to which the estimated VSDL is the true value for the sample. As discussed earlier, calculating a mean WTP requires measuring the area under the curve relating the probability of acceptance to the magnitude of the bid. This, in turn, requires setting an upper cutoff point for calculating the area. In the mean WTP amounts shown in Table 5.1, the team assumed that nobody would have been willing to pay more than $15,000 for the vaccine. This cutoff amount is five times the highest bid offered and so it is plausible. However, the acceptance rate for bids in the highest offered range, $2,500–$3,000, was 14 percent. This quite high percentage suggests that there may very well have been owners who would have accepted much higher bid prices.

The other reason for concern was that treating uncertain acceptances as equivalent to rejections might be too stringent. Further, the VSL literature shows that stated preference methods tend to give lower estimates than revealed preference methods. To address these issues, Table 5.2 shows the VSDL estimates for a higher upper bound and not converting uncertain acceptances to rejections.

A final concern was about external validity: that is, is it reasonable to treat the VSDL estimated for the sample as the VSDL for the general population of U.S. dog owners? Within the sample, those who viewed both the threat of influenza and a vaccine to counter it as plausible had a much higher estimated mean WTP than those who did not. The team thought that it was likely that these owners were more fully engaged in their scenarios. They were more likely to view the (hypothetical) situation as real and relevant to the mortality of their own dogs. If this is the case,

TABLE 5.2 *VSDL estimates under alternative technical assumptions*

		Recoding	
		None	High certainty
Assumed WTP upper limit	$15,000	$12,910	$6,760
	$20,000	$16,230	$8,320

Source: Adapted from Table 3, Carlson et al., p. 143.

then these respondents probably provide estimates that are more representative of the general population in terms of WTP than the full sample. The VSDLs for receptive respondents in the primary scenario who did, and did not, view their dogs as companions were $13,010 and $12,350, respectively. Thus, the team believed that the most plausible value for the VSDL fell somewhere between about $7 thousand and $13 thousand.

The team wanted to propose a specific dollar VSDL to complement the VSL as a shadow price for use in economic and regulatory analyses. After considering all the various estimates and some plausible adjustments to them, the team decided on $10,000 as the VSDL. They hoped that this deliberately very round number would avoid conveying more precision than was warranted but nonetheless would provide a convenient benchmark number for comparison with additional studies that may follow.

5.6 WHAT DOES THIS ALL MEAN? APPLICATIONS

The absence of a shadow price for valuing reductions in dog mortality from FDA pet food manufacturing regulations prompted the team to estimate the VSDL. It is now available for use in RIAs for future regulations of dog food and other products that affect canine mortality risk. The shadow price may also prove useful to other regulatory agencies. For example, the EPA regulates chemicals that pose morbidity and mortality risks to people. It is likely that many of these chemicals also pose risks to dogs. Indeed, in view of dogs' closer proximity to the ground and their constant sniffing and tasting to satisfy their curiosity, some chemicals may pose even greater risks to dogs than to humans. No federal agency currently regulates pet toys or grooming products. However, one can easily imagine some precipitating disaster prompting Congress to expand the mandate of the Consumer Product Safety Commission to include regulating risks to pets as well as humans.

5.6.1 Companionship Value in Zooeyia Programs

Zooeyia refers to the implications of people's interaction with animals on human health. A growing body of evidence suggests that pets contribute to better human health.[31] Dogs, especially, offer potential health benefits to their owners and to assignees by encouraging more outdoor exercise, serving as a focal point for social interaction, and providing companionship. Public (both government and nonprofit) programs that facilitate dog keeping by people with physical or mental health challenges appear to provide health benefits. These benefits could be monetized in cost–benefit analyses as the avoided cost of medical care, and through other proxies for better health. However, participants in these programs often also value the time they spend with their dogs beyond the value they place on any direct health benefits. Ideally, this value should also be included in cost–benefit analyses of such programs.

An estimate of the implicit value that people place on each year of additional life, the value of a statistical life year (VSLY), can be obtained by converting the VSL to an annuity over the person's remaining life that has the same present value[32] as the VSL.[33] A similar approach can be used to convert the VSDL to a value of a dog life year (VDLY). The team estimated this value for its sample by using its statistical model to predict the VSDL for each respondent, converting it to a VDLY by taking account of the expected number of remaining years of dog life and the discount rate, and then averaging across respondents. At a 3.5 percent discount

---

[31] For overviews, see Kate Hodgson, Luisa Barton, Marcia Darling, Viola Antao, Florence A. Kim, and Alan Monavvari. "Pets' Impact on Your Patients' Health: Leveraging Benefits and Mitigating Risk." *Journal of the American Board of Family Medicine* 28, no. 4 (2015): 526–534 and Deborah L. Wells. "The State of Research on Human–Animal Relations: Implications for Human Health." *Anthrozoös* 32, no. 2 (2019): 169–181.

[32] Present value in cost–benefit analysis takes account of the preferences of people generally to consume sooner rather than later. The commonly assumed exponential discounting reduces the value of consumption that will occur k years in the future by dividing it by $(1 + d)^k$ where d is the discount rate. For a fuller explanation, as well as an overview of the controversy over the appropriate value of the discount rate, see Anthony E. Boardman, David H. Greenberg, Aidan R. Vining, and David L. Weimer. *Cost–Benefit Analysis: Concepts and Practice,* 5th ed. (New York, NY: Cambridge University Press, 2017), Chapters 9 and 10.

[33] The VYL can be thought of as what constant annual annuity payment the person could receive in return for an amount equal to the VSL. It is obtained by dividing the VSL by an annuity factor that depends on the number of years (n) the annuity will be paid and the discount rate (d): $a_d^n = \dfrac{\left[1 - (1+d)^{-n}\right]}{d}$.

rate, the team concluded that the VDLY for receptive respondents would be approximately $2,400. An alternative estimate based on the VSDL and the average of respondents' expectations of additional years of life of their dogs (9 years) is $1,310.[34] A value between these amounts, say $1,500, would be a plausible shadow price for years spent with the dog.

5.6.2 Valuing Veterinary Care

A VDYL estimate could also be used to assess the efficiency of veterinary treatment strategies. For example, an investment in veterinary technology, such as capacities for advanced imaging and chemotherapy, would be efficient and therefore should be made from an efficiency perspective if it can provide an additional year of dog life for less than the VDLY. The relative efficiency of alternative treatment strategies that provide different contributions to canine longevity can also be assessed using the VDLY. Note that these applications of the VDLY apply to treatment strategies rather than to decisions about the treatment of specific dogs. As we discuss in the next chapter, many people are willing to spend much more on veterinary care than on preventive measures like those used to estimate the VSDL.

5.6.3 Potential Legal Applications

Two other potential applications of the VSDL are more contentious. They would move beyond the valuation of changes in risks to the valuation of the life of a specific dog. A classic manifestation of the distinction appears in the way society treats the safety of coal miners: society does not insist on high levels of investment in mine safety, yet once specific identifiable miners are trapped below ground, society expends whatever resources are available to save them. At a personal level, once grandma is hospitalized after a fall, most of us spend whatever it takes to save and extend her life. However, fallible as we are, we may not have invested very much in remodeling her home to reduce the chances that she would fall. Nonetheless, we raise these potential applications, compensation for the wrongful death of dogs and valuation of dogs in the division of property in divorces, because on balance use of the VSDL can contribute to socially desirable improvements over current practice.

---

[34] The conversion of VSDL to VDLY is very nonlinear in the number of years. Consequently, the average of VDLY values across individuals differs substantially from one calculated using the average VSL and average number of years of expected life.

In almost all legal systems, the survivors of people who suffer wrongful death can seek compensation in the courts for both economic and (so-called) noneconomic damages. It is relatively straightforward to estimate direct economic damages, typically based on loss of future income. Noneconomic damages are more difficult to estimate, as they often include "pain and suffering" and loss of companionship.[35] Some economists have advocated for the use of the VSL to value companionship, or what is referred to as hedonic damages, in wrongful death cases.[36] Although the sum of traditional economic and hedonic damages may provide an appropriate total damage amount for efficiently deterring risky behavior, it may provide on average too much compensation because it captures the willingness to pay of the deceased rather than the survivor.[37] Nonetheless, it would provide some standardization of loss of companionship awards if it were to be adopted by the courts.

Courts currently do not provide compensation for the loss of companionship of dogs. American tort law (and English common law, its progenitor) considers dogs and other domesticated animals to be property. As a consequence, the wrongful death of one's dog can generally only result in the award of economic damages.[38] The usual legal practice of assessing the economic loss as the "fair market value" of the dog typically results, therefore, in very small damage awards, especially when calculated as the replacement cost of mixed-breed dogs (poor mutts!). An important legal rationale for limiting compensation to fair market value is the subjective nature of owners' valuations of the economic value of companionship with their pet dogs and therefore the difficulty courts would face in assessing it.

Remember that the VSDL is an estimate of the mean implicit dollar value U.S. owners place on their pet dogs. It could provide an alternative,

---

[35] For a critique of the way courts value lives, see Howard S. Friedman. *Ultimate Price: The Value We Place on Life* (Berkeley, CA: University of California Press, 2020).

[36] Eric A. Posner and Cass R. Sunstein, "Dollars and Death." *University of Chicago Law Review* 72, no. 2 (2005): 537–598.

[37] W. Kip Viscusi. "Extending the Domain of the Value of a Statistical Life." *Journal of Benefit-Cost Analysis* 12, no. 1 (2021): 1–23 and W. Kip Viscusi. "The Flawed Hedonic Damages Measure of Compensation for Wrongful Death and Personal Injury." *Journal of Forensic Economics* 20, no. 2 (2008): 113–135.

[38] See, for example, Sonia S. Waisman and Barbara R. Newell. "Recovery of Non-Economic Damages for Wrongful Killing or Injury of Companion Animals: A Judicial and Legislative Trend." *Animal Law* 6 (2001): 45–74 and Lynn A. Epstein. "Resolving Confusion in Pet Owner Tort Cases: Recognizing Pets' Anthropomorphic Qualities under a Property Classification." *Southern Illinois University Law Journal* 26, no. 1 (2001): 31–51.

and credible, measure of economic damage to supplement "fair market value." Indeed, it does not suffer from the problem of the VSL as a hedonic damage measure because it is the loss to the survivor. Of course, as an average it would be an overestimate of economic loss for some dog owners and an underestimate for others. In comparison, however, fair market value is likely an underestimate for almost all pet dogs. We think it is most appropriate that the VSDL be the standard compensation for the wrongful death of pet dogs.

Several objections have been raised against any movement away from assessing damages as fair market value in cases involving the tortious death of dogs.[39] One objection is that any dollar caps on categories of damages that can be awarded in tort cases tend to increase over time. However, using the VSDL as a default (and therefore as a cap) means that changing the cap would emerge through the accumulation of research, a process that has led to widespread consensus about the appropriate use of the VSL in the regulation of human mortality risks.

Another objection is that both increased awards and the increased litigation it would induce would hurt pets and owners by raising veterinary costs. This objection seems to undervalue one of the important legal and economic functions of tort law: providing incentives for economically efficient risk reduction. A closer correspondence between actual economic damages and compensation would be consistent with better tort incentives; in turn, this would result in more efficient levels of risk taking in veterinary care. We thus see assessing economic damages in terms of the VSDL as a desirable, if imperfect, alternative to assessment through fair market value.

In divorce settlements, custody of dogs can be as contentious as custody of children! Some courts have begun deviating from the treatment of dogs as simply property in divorce cases, sometimes assessing which party has the closer attachment to dogs, specifying visiting rights, and even "petimony" payments to share the costs of care.[40] Most courts, however, continue to treat dogs as property that must be allocated in settlements. Reaching agreement on the division of property may be especially contentious when dogs are involved because the party getting custody has an incentive to understate the dollar value of custody and the

---

[39] Victor E. Schwartz and Emily J. Laird. "Non-Economic Damages in Pet Litigation: The Serious Need to Preserve a Rational Rule." *Pepperdine Law Review* 33, no. 2 (2005): 227–271.

[40] Christopher D. Seps. "Animal Law Evolution: Treating Pets as Persons in Tort and Custody Disputes." *University of Illinois Law Review* no. 4 (2010): 1339–1373.

party not getting custody has an incentive to overstate it. We recommend using the VSDL as at least a starting point for negotiation, if not a default value, in jurisdictions that continue to treat dogs as property.

5.7 SOME CONCLUDING THOUGHTS ON VALUATION

Many of the rules issued by federal regulatory agencies seek to reduce human mortality risks. Unfortunately, all risk cannot be eliminated – we don't get out of this world alive – and reductions in risk usually come at the cost of other things we value. Economic analysis identifies the trade-offs involved in achieving reductions in human mortality risk and monetizes these trade-offs using the VSL. Rules can also affect the mortality risk faced by our dogs. The VSDL enables regulators to take account of the implicit values we place on changes in the mortality risk to our dogs. It is possible to estimate the VSDL through a stated preference method: we explained how the method was done and presented a value, $10,000, that we see as the starting point for additional studies. We hope that other researchers will make estimates so that regulators will be able to use the VSDL as confidently as they now use the VSL. We also hope that some analysts who are cat keepers will be sufficiently motivated by our presentation to develop a VSCL!

6

A Doggone Shame

Hard Decisions about Euthanasia and Dogs' Lives

Most people can expect to live longer than their dogs. This biological reality means that most owners and caregivers will eventually confront difficult choices about how their dogs will spend their last days. They will have to decide whether or not to euthanize their dogs to reduce their suffering when they become seriously ill or severely injured. Unlike the case of caring for a person with a terminal illness, dog owners have to make decisions about the nature of treatment and the circumstances of their dogs' end of life without being able to ask them about their preferences – alas, Cervantes' Ensign did not really overhear the two old dogs philosophizing about death in the Resurrection Hospital.[1] When a dying person can no longer communicate, sometimes the caregiver can receive instructions from a living will or at least seek guidance from prior conversations. In the absence of specific guidance, however, caregivers of persons who can no longer communicate tend to err on the side of demanding any or all available treatments. Indeed, social norms in most societies generally encourage them to do so.[2] The default option for dogs is less clear; many owners often must consider both suffering and expense in making decisions about treatment and euthanasia. We also recognize that many dogs are owned by corporations, such as pharmaceutical companies, or by not-for-profits,

---

[1] Miguel de Cervantes. *The Dialogue of the Dogs* (Brooklyn, NY: Melville House Publishers, 2008). First published in 1613, this novella is generally credited as being the first instance in Western literature of conversing dogs. For a more contemporary canine soliloquy, see Peter Mayle. *A Dog's Life* (New York, NY: Knopf Publishing Group, 2013).
[2] Rachael Spalding, JoNell Strough, and Barry Edelstein. "What Would People Think? Perceived Social Norms, Willingness to Serve as a Surrogate, and End-of-Life Treatment Decisions." *Palliative & Supportive Care* 19, no. 1 (2021): 46–54.

such as universities and shelters, that may have interests that do not necessarily coincide with the interests of the dogs under their care. Nonetheless,
these organizations also often make end-of-life decisions for dogs.

End-of-life decisions made for dogs are hard and often raise challenging ethical issues. We do not claim that other animals and pets do not
raise the same or similar issues, but we focus here on dogs. The legal status
of dogs as property in most countries, including the United States, only
restricts owners to terminating their lives in ways considered humane,
but their common social status as family members makes them more akin
to a person, or at least a being worthy of respect and protection. Other
legal jurisdictions may place other restrictions on owners; in the context
of property rights, the reality is that it is the legal regime, rather than
implicit norms, that is usually determinative. A decision about providing medical care for a dog confronts the owner with questions about the
appropriate trade-off between suffering and longevity. Owners can also
face considerable uncertainty: is an illness really terminal? Almost all of
these decisions also have nontrivial economic consequences; the out-of-
pocket financial costs of veterinary care and providing in-home care to an
ill or injured dog can be substantial and even impractical for households
with either tight finances or inflexible work schedules.[3]

In this chapter, we explore some of these hard end-of-life issues. We
begin by framing the explicit decision to end life, euthanasia, in terms of
the differing fiduciary responsibilities it involves across alternative property rights regimes. We next explore the appropriateness of euthanasia
as an end-of-life option and how perspectives on it have changed over
time. We then turn to the growth in pet health insurance and prepaid
veterinary plans and how they affect the choice between medical care and
euthanasia by making advanced treatment more financially feasible for
subscribers. We conclude by considering how individual and societal attitudes toward the use of dogs in medical research, which often involves
their suffering and sometimes their death, have changed.

6.1 PRINCIPALS AND AGENTS

Economists believe that considerable insight into the production and
consumption of things people value can be gained by observing the

---

[3] Caring for ill dogs can involve stresses from "practicalities like extra care, changes in use of
the home, and restrictions relating to work, social life, and finances." Stine B. Christiansen,
Annemarie T. Kristensen, Peter Sandøe, and Jesper Lassen. "Looking After Chronically Ill
Dogs: Impacts on the Caregiver's Life." *Anthrozoös* 26, no. 4 (2013): 519–533 at 519.

choices of individuals in impersonal markets. Yet much economic activity involves complex and often sequenced interactions that require relationships among individuals that go beyond anonymous one-time transactions – buying a kitchen appliance can be done without a great amount of interaction with a salesperson, but remodeling a kitchen typically requires an extensive amount of interaction with contractors before, during, and even after the work is done. The complexity and sequencing of such cooperative endeavors often make it impossible to specify fully the responsibilities of any particular participant, so that it is virtually impossible to spell out a contract that specifies the rights and duties of the parties under all the possible contingencies. For example, what are the responsibilities of a contractor delayed because of supply chain problems caused by COVID? We inevitably have *incomplete contracts*.

We can often usefully frame relationships and behaviors based on incomplete contracting situations as involving an agent acting on behalf of a principal. This framing is somewhat different from many, or indeed most, contractual relations where the contracting parties are fully aware of their own interests and can effectively pursue civil, and even criminal, legal remedies for breaches of contract. In principal–agent contracts, in contrast, there is some fundamental asymmetry, usually of information but also sometimes, as we will see, of capacity. In an asymmetric information situation, one contracting party is an agent with private information not available to the principal (so-called *hidden information*) or the opportunity to act without being observed by the principal (so-called *hidden action*). Because of their informational advantage, agents may be able to increase their gains at the expense of the principal. These deviations from the interests of the principals are referred to as *agency loss*.[4]

Economic transactions, whether they consist of atomistic market exchanges or contracts that embody principal–agent relationships, take place within a specific property-rights regime that determines who has rights and who bears duties to honor them. The resources that need to be employed to establish and maintain property rights are known as *transaction costs*, as are any costs resulting from agency loss.[5] The collection of property rights that determine transaction costs in an economy makes up

---

[4] On agency loss as a central concept for understanding organizational design, see Michael C. Jensen and William H. Meckling. "Theory of the Firm: Managerial Behavior, Agency Costs, and Ownership Structure." *Journal of Financial Economics* 3, no. 4 (1976): 305–360.

[5] Douglas W. Allen. "What Are Transaction Costs?" *Research in Law and Economics* 14 (1991): 1–18.

the property rights regime, a central concept of the field of *institutional economics*. Any regime has both formal and informal components. The formal components are mostly defined by political authorities through law; indeed, property rights are the fundamental nexus between the political and the economic aspects of society.[6] The informal components arise from social norms. However, there are important caveats to this simple dichotomy. Property rights can be formal but still be ineffective because they are not enforced because they are not enforceable in practice or not enforced for political or social reasons. For example, there may be a right to clean public spaces expressed in an ordinance that imposes a duty on dog owners to scoop their dogs' poop, but enforcement without a social norm of compliance is unlikely to be very effective. Property rights may also be informal but effective: a strong social norm at a dog park may effectively impose a duty on the owners of aggressive dogs to prevent them from harassing other dogs.

One way or another, any property rights regime specifies the duties of the parties in principal–agent relationships.[7] In some cases, an agent must meet the higher standard of a fiduciary. Fiduciary relationships apply some combination of standards, default rules, and mandatory rules to structure principal–agent relationships. Unfortunately, in general, no bright line distinguishes normal agents from agents with fiduciary responsibilities. But professional standards do typically indicate the level of care and loyalty that agents with expertise must show. Perhaps of most relevance to dog and dog-owner welfare, veterinarians are expected to provide care according to professional standards. Known default rules do apply unless the contracting parties agree to waive them. For example, veterinarians normally receive specified payments for particular services – there may even be a fee guide – but they can waive payment in special circumstances, such as in ministering to strays. Mandatory rules cannot be waived. For example, in many states, lemon laws allow purchasers to return puppies for rebates within specified periods of time and do not allow the seller to require the buyer to agree to forgo the use of the law.

[6] See William H. Riker and David L. Weimer. "The Economic and Political Liberalization of Socialism: The Fundamental Problem of Property Rights." *Social Philosophy and Policy* 10, no. 2(1993): 79–102 and Aidan R. Vining and David L. Weimer. "Informing Institutional Design: Strategies for Comparative Cumulation." *Journal of Comparative Policy Analysis* 1, no. 1 (1998): 39–60.

[7] Tamar Frankel. "Fiduciary Law." *California Law Review* 71, no. 3 (1983): 795–836 and Robert H. Sitkoff. "An Economic Theory of Fiduciary Law." In Andrew Gold and Paul Miller, eds., *Philosophical Foundations of Fiduciary Law* (New York, NY: Oxford University Press, 2014), 197–208.

6.2 FIDUCIARY RESPONSIBILITIES IN EUTHANASIA

Simplifying somewhat the variegated world in which we live, the rows of Table 6.1 show three different property rights regimes. The rows show what we perceive to be the typical fiduciary responsibilities for "owners," for veterinarians, and for society with respect to the determination of the appropriateness of euthanasia and how it is carried out. We put owner in quotes because we believe the meaning of ownership is an open question when dogs have the status of quasi-personhood.

Prior to the adoption of anti-cruelty laws in the United Kingdom and the United States in the nineteenth century, all animals were viewed in law simply as property.[8] In this regime, dogs are unregulated commodities; the owner is the principal for both deciding the process and the appropriateness of euthanasia. In a commodity regime, veterinarians are agents with respect to owners in making decisions about euthanasia and carrying them out. Veterinarians are also agents of their professional societies, which expect them to follow established professional standards. Society does influence individual decisions about euthanasia, but only through widely held norms about how dogs should be treated.

TABLE 6.1 *Fiduciary responsibilities in property rights regimes for dog euthanasia*

		"Owner"	Veterinarian	Society
	Unregulated commodity	Principal for both process and appropriateness	Agent for owner; agent for profession	Express norms
Property status of dogs	Commodity as currently regulated	Agent for process; principal for appropriateness	Coagent for process; owner's agent for appropriateness; agent for profession	Express norms; modify and enforce process rules
	Quasi-person	Agent for both process and appropriateness	Coagent for both process and appropriateness; agent for profession	Express norms; create and enforce both process and appropriateness rules

[8] David Favre and Vivien Tsang. "The Development of Anti-cruelty Laws during the 1800's." *Detroit College of Law Review* no. 1 (1993): 1–35.

The second row, dogs as regulated commodities, best describes the current property rights regime in the United States and in many, if not most, other countries. Of course, that is inevitably a fairly wide category with a variety of standards of practice. Anti-cruelty laws most directly regulate the process of euthanasia, as do professional veterinary standards. In this regime, owners are effectively coagents with veterinarians with respect to the process of euthanasia. However, the owner remains the principal with respect to the appropriateness of euthanasia. This separation can be a source of ethical tension for veterinarians because they are agents for both their client and their profession when making decisions about whether a dog should be euthanized.[9] These decisions are also almost certainly affected by societal norms, which, when widely held, may lead to their formalization through changes in law. Note that in this kind of regime, there may be differences between what the law mandates and practice that results in dogs effectively being unregulated commodities, despite laws on the books: as we discuss in Chapter 4, lax enforcement of laws in some states allows some puppy mills to euthanize dogs through neglect and other cruel means.

Before elaborating in the next section on the consequences of dogs having the status of regulated property, consider the situation in which dogs gain the status of quasi-person, as shown in the third row of Table 6.1. In this case, the "owner" switches roles from principal to agent. The role of the veterinarian also shifts from agent for the "owner" for the determination of the appropriateness of euthanasia to coagent with the "owner" for both process and appropriateness. As coagents the "owner" and veterinarian now have a fiduciary duty to make decisions in the best interests of the dog. Euthanasia for nonmedical reasons becomes much less justifiable. For instance, do changes in family circumstances that will make it difficult to provide adequate care justify either direct euthanasia of the dog by the veterinarian or the high risk of euthanasia if it is surrendered to a shelter?

Although not shown in Table 6.1, some philosophers and animal advocates go as far as to argue for the full personhood of dogs.[10] Now a

---

[9] See, for example, J. W. Yeates and D. C. J. Main. "Veterinary Opinions on Refusing Euthanasia: Justifications and Philosophical Frameworks." *Veterinary Record* 168, no. 10 (2011): 263–263.

[10] Although cast in terms of animal suffering rather than rights, an argument for treating animals more like persons is provided by Peter Singer. *Animal Liberation: A New Ethics for Our Treatment of Animals* (New York, NY: Harper Collins, 1975). For a general overview on animal rights from the legal perspective, see Cass R. Sunstein. "The Rights of Animals." *University of Chicago Law Review* 70, no. 1 (2003): 387–401.

(so-called) "owner" would become a guardian with a fiduciary responsibility to its ward, the dog, in the same way a person becomes a guardian for another person with severe cognitive impairment. Just as guardians of persons cannot currently select euthanasia to stop suffering, dog personhood would likely severely limit or even eliminate euthanasia for dogs. Of course, the issue would arise about why that status is conferred on companion animals but not on other animals. An extension of this position to all vertebrates, say, would have severe implications for meat eaters (perhaps including dogs!), hunters (who play an important role in wildlife management), and some medical researchers (a topic we address later in the chapter).

6.3 EUTHANASIA PROCESS AND APPROPRIATENESS

Existing professional guidelines relating to the euthanasia of animals reflect a nearly universal consensus that their lives should be ended humanely by methods that are as distress-free, rapid, and painless as possible. In contrast to wide agreement about how euthanasia should be carried out, less societal consensus exists on the conditions that make euthanasia appropriate. This requires veterinarians to weigh competing values in advising pet owners and deciding when to agree to euthanize. Consider the guidance the American Veterinary Medical Association provides about when euthanizing is appropriate: "... current AVMA policy supports the use of animals for various human purposes, and also recognizes the need to euthanize animals that are unwanted or unfit for adoption. When evaluating our responsibilities toward animals, it is important to be sensitive to the context and the practical realities of the various types of human–animal relationships. Impacts on animals may not always be the center of the valuation process, and there is disagreement on how to account for conflicting interspecific interests ... raising concerns across a large number of domains, including scientific, ethical, economic, environmental, political, and social."[11] This statement does not provide much practical guidance. Some veterinary ethicists argue that, for the killing of an animal to be considered euthanasia, it should be done in the best interests of the animal rather than just done humanely.[12] In other words, following

---

[11] American Veterinary Medical Association. "AVMA Guidelines for the Euthanasia of Animals: 2020 Edition." www.avma.org/sites/default/files/2020-02/Guidelines-on-Euthanasia-2020.pdf. pp. 6–7. Accessed November 8, 2022.
[12] James Yeates. "Ethical Aspects of Euthanasia of Owned Animals." *In Practice* 32, February (2010): 70–73.

TABLE 6.2 *Dog owners who would consider euthanasia of a suffering pet*

	Pet Dog Owners (percent) (*n* = 4,602)	Females (percent) (*n* = 2,319)	Males (percent) (*n* = 2,282)
Strongly disagree	3	3	3
Disagree	1	2	1
Somewhat disagree	2	3	2
Neither agree nor disagree	14	17	11
Somewhat agree	17	18	16
Agree	30	27	33
Strongly agree	32	30	33

Source: PVL Survey, May 18 to 23, 2018.

this line of reasoning would shift the property rights regime from one of regulated commodities toward one of quasi-personhood.

Veterinarians and a majority of the public state that they share the view that ending the suffering of dogs does justify euthanasia. The PVL Survey asked dog owners about their agreement with the statement: "I would consider euthanizing a suffering pet." Table 6.2 reports the distributions of responses for all dog owners who considered their dogs to be pets, as well as broken out by owner's gender. The responses show substantial support for considering euthanasia for suffering pets, with little difference between genders. Only very small percentages of respondents would not consider euthanizing their suffering dogs. Although not shown in Table 6.2, the responses are similar across party affiliation and ideology.[13] Most of us accept euthanasia as an option for relieving the suffering of ill or injured dogs. However, the actual decision is a hard one because it requires one to assess whether the suffering is sufficiently severe to justify euthanizing.

Readers may be surprised or even shocked to hear that veterinarians often face direct requests from clients to euthanize dogs that are either

---

[13] Do attitudes of dog owners cross the partisan divide more generally? Political scientists have taken advantage of the absence of an Obama family dog in the 2008 election and its presence in the 2012 election to see if there is an independent effect of dog ownership on presidential preference. Although dog ownership may have had an independent negative effect on support for Barack Obama in 2008 because his family did not have a dog, see Diana C. Mutz. "The Dog that Didn't Bark: The Role of Canines in the 2008 Campaign." *PS: Political Science & Politics* 43, no. 4 (2010): 707–712, subsequent research suggests dog ownership did not have an independent effect in either election. See Matthew L. Jacobsmeier and Daniel C. Lewis. "Barking Up the Wrong Tree: Why Bo Didn't Fetch Many Votes for Barack Obama in 2012." *PS: Political Science & Politics* 46, no. 1 (2013): 49–59.

healthy or have illnesses or injuries that could be effectively treated. Veterinarians usually honor requests from shelters to euthanize healthy dogs that cannot be accommodated. Some veterinarians may view complying with such requests as consistent with protecting the welfare of the dogs, perhaps because the family circumstances have changed, or are expected to change, in ways that would substantially reduce the quality of the dogs' lives. Vikings often expected their dogs to accompany them to Valhalla in the longship.[14]

An extreme example of anticipatory euthanasia occurred in September 1939 in Britain at the outset of World War II. Families in the London area had over 400,000 dogs and cats, a quarter of the total population of these pets, euthanized over four days. Historian Hilda Kean provides an account of this mass euthanasia of healthy animals.[15] She writes: "On the first weekend of the war people in the London area did indeed "do things." These included sending away children to the apparent safety of the country, making blackout curtains, digging up flower beds to create vegetable patches – and killing the family pet."[16] Why did so many people euthanize their dogs and cats? Although the horrific bombing of London did not occur until the following year, fear that bombing would adversely affect dogs and cats seems reasonable, especially as they could not be fitted with gas masks. There might also have been a fear that pets would disproportionately suffer under the expected rationing. However, Kean notes contemporary writing in newspapers at the time arguing that this euthanasia was neither necessary nor consistent with government propaganda about the country being able to cope with the war but rather occurred because some owners found it inconvenient to keep their pets alive.[17]

Kean documents that neither animal charities nor the government encouraged this mass euthanasia. She points out that there was an increase in requests for euthanasia first during the Munich crisis the prior September. Anticipating a need for increased euthanasia if bombing were actually to occur, the Royal Society for the Prevention of Cruelty to Animals and other animal charities increased their capacities for providing euthanasia. Nonetheless, they discouraged owners

[14] Kaitlyn A. Gutierrez. "Animals in the Viking World: Dogs in Society and Burial." Dissertation, Archaeology Department, University of Glasgow (2017).
[15] Hilda Kean. *The Great Cat & Dog Massacre* (Chicago, IL: University of Chicago Press, 2017).
[16] Ibid., p. 47.
[17] Ibid., p. 50.

from euthanizing their pets, both generally and in response to specific requests. Similarly, the government-sponsored National Air Raid Precautions Animals' Committee had published the recommendation, "Those who are staying at home should not have their animals destroyed. Animals are in no greater danger than human beings."[18] Why so many dogs were euthanized remains a puzzle, but Kean suggests that it may have been a displacement of the anticipated general panic that did not occur.[19]

In contemporary America, although they may not fully realize it, dog owners indirectly choose euthanasia, or at least the risk of euthanasia, for healthy dogs when they surrender them to shelters. As Chapter 4 notes, the American Society for the Prevention of Cruelty to Animals (ASPCA) estimates that 390 thousand dogs in U.S. shelters are euthanized each year. Some of these dogs do suffer from physical ailments, but the majority die because of limited shelter capacity. Even so-called no-kill shelters can use that designation as long as they euthanize no more than 10 percent of the dogs in their care. Older, brachycephalic (e.g., pugs and bulldogs), and larger dogs are more likely to be euthanized.[20] The distress among dog lovers from awareness of the euthanasia risk for shelter dogs has undoubtedly contributed to the increased rate of adoption from shelters. There is good evidence to suggest that the need to euthanize shelter dogs also stresses shelter workers and volunteers.[21]

Veterinarians cannot avoid ethical conflicts in their role as agents for owners and their profession. On the one hand, they face some requests from owners for euthanasia when the veterinarian believes that it is not in the best interests of the dog. In some of these cases, a dog may have only a mild illness or correctable behavioral problem. In other cases, owners may not authorize treatment that the veterinarian considers

---

[18] As cited in Kean, p. 68.

[19] Kean, p. 52.

[20] Cassie J. Cain, Kimberly A. Woodruff, and David R. Smith. "Factors Associated with Shelter Dog Euthanasia versus Live Release by Adoption or Transfer in the United States." *Animals (Basel)* 11, no. 4 (2021): 927–935.

[21] Charlie L. Reeve, Steven G. Rogelberg, Christiane Spitzmüller, and Natalie DiGiacomo. "The Caring-Killing Paradox: Euthanasia-Related Strain among Animal-Shelter Workers." *Journal of Applied Social Psychology* 35, no. 1 (2005): 119–143. Participation in euthanasia may also be a factor in the relatively high suicide rate for veterinarians. See Rebekah L. Scotney, Deirdre McLaughlin, and Helen L. Keates. "A Systematic Review of the Effects of Euthanasia and Occupational Stress in Personnel Working with Animals in Animal Shelters, Veterinary Clinics, and Biomedical Research Facilities." *Journal of the American Veterinary Medical Association* 247, no. 10 (2015): 1121–1130.

desirable for the dog. On the other hand, owners sometimes request treatments that the veterinarian believes would either have too low a chance of producing a meaningful improvement or would involve undue suffering for the dog.

For many owners, cost is inevitably an important consideration in choosing between treatment and euthanasia: 40 percent of respondents to a recent national survey indicated that cost was a barrier to obtaining veterinary care for their dogs.[22] Another recent survey found that almost a quarter of pet owners actually went into debt to pay for veterinary expenses.[23] Beyond contributing to higher veterinary costs overall, the increasing availability of "advanced veterinary care" complicates end-of-life decisions in several ways.[24] First, it expands the range of illnesses and injuries that can be treated. Second, these treatments are typically more expensive than the "existing standard of care" treatments, thus increasing the chances that owners will be unable or unwilling to purchase them. Third, the evidence for predicting the quality of life that these treatments will produce, whether successful or unsuccessful, is not yet strong. This makes it more difficult to assess whether a treatment is in the best interest of the dog.

In their role as agents, veterinarians may also be subject to cognitive dissonance. Treatment is financially rewarding, especially if they have invested in expensive equipment or training to carry out these advanced treatments. Like their colleagues who treat humans, many U.S. veterinarians graduate with large debts that put pressure on them to engage in high-revenue practices – a mean debt of over $150 thousand for graduating students in 2020.[25] They may also share an understandable desire to be on the cutting edge of treatment.[26] But set against these factors,

---

[22] Courtney Bir, Mario Ortez, Nicole J. Olynk Widmar, Christopher A. Wolf, Charlotte Hansen, and Frederic B. Ouedraogo. "Familiarity and Use of Veterinary Services by US Resident Dog and Cat Owners." *Animals (Basel)* 10, no. 3 (2020): 483–510.

[23] Katie Kuehner-Hebert. "Americans Willing to Spend as Much on Pets' Health Care as their Own." *Alm Benefits Pro*, August 16 (2019). www.benefitspro.com/2019/08/16/americans-willing-to-spend-as-much-on-pets-health-care-as-their-own/. Accessed August 23, 2023.

[24] Anne Quain, Michael P. Ward, and Siobhan Mullan. "Ethical Challenges Posed by Advanced Veterinary Care in Companion Animal Veterinary Practice." *Animals (Basel)* 11, no. 11 (2021): 3010–3026.

[25] Bridgette Bain and Sandra L. Lefebvre. "Associations between Career Choice and Educational Debt for Fourth-Year Students of US Veterinary Schools and Colleges, 2001–2021, *Journal of the American Veterinary Medical Association* 260, no. 9 (2022): 1063–1068.

[26] Advanced veterinary care technologies developed in universities are more likely to be familiar to recent graduates. Anne Quain, Michael P. Ward, and Siobhan Mullan, p. 3018.

veterinarians may suspect that many of these treatments are not in the best interests of dogs or their owners.[27]

6.4 PET HEALTH INSURANCE AND
END-OF-LIFE DECISIONS

Insurance can be individually and socially valuable because it takes advantage of the pooling of risk across individuals to reduce their individual risk. As one learns in an introductory statistics course, the variance of the average of independent random variables is inversely proportional to the number of random variables being summed. In the context of insurance, the pooling of clients with independent risks allows the insurer to reduce both the risk to individuals and the uncertainty in its average payout as the number of clients increases.[28] Premiums include the expected payout as well as a markup for administrative costs.[29] Nonetheless, risk averse individuals – people who are only willing to pay less than the expected value of a gamble – often find insurance attractive because it reduces their risk. Pet insurance covering veterinary expenses is now widely available to reduce the financial risk of providing veterinary care to dogs and cats.

Health insurance for horses and cattle began being offered in the nineteenth century.[30] Although pet insurance was subsequently offered in a number of countries, it was not until 1982 that Veterinary Pet Insurance promoted its introduction to the U.S. market by writing a policy for

[27] Economists often see large medical bills in the last month of people's lives as potentially indicating futile care. A study of dogs treated for lymphoma at a California animal hospital showed the same kind of skewed pattern of medical charges in the last month of life compared to preceding months – median charges in the last month were close to earlier months but, as is the case for people, mean charges were much higher, suggesting heroic care for some of the dogs. Liran Einav, Amy Finkelstein, and Atul Gupta. "Is American Pet Health Care (also) Uniquely Inefficient?" *American Economic Review* 107, no. 5 (2017): 491–495.

[28] Imagine that individual j faces a risk v_j with expected value (mean) loss of μ and variance σ^2. The expected value of the average loss for a pool of n individuals is μ but the variance of this average loss is σ^2/n and the standard deviation is $\sigma/\sqrt{n}$. Thus, the insurer can indemnify losses to the n individuals with its own uncertainty about the average indemnification declining as n increases.

[29] The administrative costs include marketing of policies and settlement of claims. Also, because the variance of the total payouts increases with the number of policies, insurers must set aside reserves to avoid bankruptcy in unusual situations of especially large numbers of claims. Because premiums are collected before claims are paid, their investment can earn returns that reduce administrative costs. Changes in the returns to investment may therefore affect premiums.

[30] Jill M. Bisco and Stephen G. Fier. "Licensing and Reporting in the US Pet Insurance Market." *Journal of Insurance Regulation* 39, no. 2 (2020): 1–19 at 4.

former TV star Lassie.[31] Since then, the supply side of the market for pet health insurance has grown to over 20 firms writing over $2.6 billion in premiums.[32] On the demand side, about 80 percent of policies cover dogs, though only about 2.6 million U.S. dog owners (with less than 4 percent of dogs) currently purchase pet insurance. However, this market continues to grow rapidly[33] and an estimated 15 percent of U.S. firms now subsidize pet insurance as an employee benefit.[34] Experimental evidence suggests that as owners become better informed about veterinary costs and the risks of diseases, such as canine cancer, they are more likely to purchase pet insurance.[35]

6.4.1 The Pet Insurance Market

Pet insurance involves one or more of three types of coverage: injury, illness, and wellness. Injury and illness coverage reimburses policyholders for veterinary expenses for treatment of adverse health events. Policyholders pay a certain premium to avoid potentially large veterinary costs that often result from injury or illness. Injury insurance is often purchased as standalone coverage, while illness coverage is usually bundled with injury insurance. Bundled injury and illness coverage is not unlike the coverage persons receive from their health insurance.

Wellness coverage plans, often referred to as prepaid plans, reimburse policyholders for regular veterinary care. This coverage is usually purchased as an add-on to injury or illness coverage. Although it is marketed as insurance, it does not provide risk reduction. Rather, it sometimes offers a discount on services because it guarantees the availability of visits to a veterinarian or reduces the risk insurers face in their illness coverage. Some policyholders may see it as one way of spreading payments evenly through the year rather than paying larger amounts when routine visits

---

[31] United Press International. "TV's Lassie First Dog to Have Health Insurance." *UPI Archives*, April 7 (1982). This was likely the last of the nine dogs who played the part over the show's run from 1954 to 1974. Interestingly, although Lassie was portrayed as female, all the actors were male.

[32] North American Pet Health Insurance Association. *State of the Industry Report 2021.* https://naphia.org/industry-data/. Accessed November 8, 2022.

[33] Kari Steere. "How Many Pet Owners Have Pet Insurance in 2021?" Pawlicy Advisor. www.pawlicy.com/blog/how-many-pet-owners-have-pet-insurance/. Accessed November 8, 2022.

[34] Bisco and Fier, p. 8.

[35] Leslie J. Verteramo Chiu, Jie Li, Guillaume Lhermie, and Casey Cazer. "Analysis of the Demand for Pet Insurance among Uninsured Pet Owners in the United States." *Veterinary Record* 189, no. 1 (2021): 243–250.

actually occur. Policyholders may also see wellness coverage as a commitment mechanism: a way of committing to routine visits, which are tempting to skip as they involve not only monetary expense but also time and scheduling costs.

Insurance underwriting involves classifying potential policyholders into different risk categories to set premiums proportional to expected claims. Underwriters generally consider multiple factors in assessing the risk of illness coverage. Older dogs have higher risks of illness, and so premiums generally increase for a dog as it ages. Larger dogs, where size is usually assessed in terms of weight, also face higher premiums because they tend to develop more costly illnesses, die earlier, and therefore risk end-of-life treatment earlier, than smaller dogs. Premium differences also usually reflect known differences in health risks across breeds, with above-average premiums for French bulldogs, bulldogs, and Rottweilers and (pay attention now) lower-than-average premiums for beagles, Yorkshire terriers, and even those quirky Australian shepherds. Finally, premiums tend to vary by the location of policyholders; these geographic differences reflect price and cost variations across local veterinary markets and differences in state regulations.

6.4.2 Consequences of Adverse Selection and Moral Hazard

We discuss market failures in a number of places in earlier chapters. Two potential responses to the availability of insurance interfere with its efficient provision from a societal perspective: *adverse selection* and *moral hazard*. The presence of hidden information facilitates adverse selection because owners generally have more information about the health of their dogs and their own propensity to use veterinary services than do insurers. Unlike the information asymmetry that favors sellers that we discuss in Chapter 4, adverse selection in insurance contexts can favor buyers. If insurance is priced in terms of average loss for the entire population of dog owners, those who expect to incur larger than average veterinary bills will be more likely to buy it and those who expect to incur less than average bills will be less likely to buy it. In the absence of mechanisms to sort potential buyers, adverse selection can result in an unraveling of the market as premiums rise in response to the more costly dog owners, which in turn makes the insurance less attractive for owners of relatively healthier dogs.

One should not be surprised to hear that potential insurers are aware of this problem. Pet insurers employ several mechanisms in order to counter adverse selection. First, they may require records of recent examinations conducted by licensed veterinarians to help them identify prior health conditions. The identification of prior conditions may lead to a denial of coverage or an exclusion from coverage of future veterinary expenses related to the prior condition. Second, insurers typically impose waiting periods between the time the policy is issued and the time coverage actually begins. These waiting periods are typically measured in weeks for illness insurance and days for accident insurance.

Some behavioral responses to risk may also help to attenuate the impact of adverse selection. As in other markets, myopia and overconfidence may lead to an underestimation of the risk of loss, while owner affection toward dogs may result in them valuing compensated veterinary treatment above its dollar value.[36] Adverse selection may also be offset by so-called propitious selection: especially risk averse owners who demand insurance are more careful and so also take special care to avoid health problems in their dogs. Consequently, they tend to have lower losses than the average for their risk category.[37] The ready availability of pet insurance certainly suggests that the combination of insurer mechanisms and some owner behavioral responses to insurance adequately address adverse selection.

Hidden action facilitates moral hazard: policyholders have reduced incentives to avoid insured loss, or service providers have increased incentives to provide too much billable care.[38] The term actually arose in a more sinister context: beneficiaries hastening the death of a life insurance policyholder. This form of moral hazard helps explain the absence of life insurance for pets! More generally, in the case of pet insurance, as with other types of casualty insurance, owners may not be as careful about their dogs' health as they would be if they were not insured. For example, if a policy covers veterinary dental services, holders may be less conscientious about cleaning their dogs' teeth themselves. (Would you floss less if your insurance covered routine dental cleanings?) Incentives for behavior displaying moral hazard may be stronger for veterinarians

---

[36] On behavioral influences on insurance demand, see Francisco Pitthan and Kristof De Witte. "Puzzles of Insurance Demand and Its Biases: A Survey on the Role of Behavioural Biases and Financial Literacy on Insurance Demand." *Journal of Behavioral and Experimental Finance* 30 June (2021): 1–8.

[37] David Hemenway. "Propitious Selection." *Quarterly Journal of Economics* 105, no. 4 (1990): 1063–1069.

[38] Isaac Ehrlich and Gary S. Becker. "Market Insurance, Self-Insurance, and Self-Protection." *Journal of Political Economy* 80, no. 4 (1972): 623–648.

than they are for owners. A veterinarian profits from performing any tests or procedures that are covered by the owners' policies, even if they are of questionable, or no, value to the pet.

Do not lose too much sleep over insurer profits, however. Insurers use several mechanisms to reduce moral hazard. Most directly, they nearly always require co-payments that require policyholders to continue to bear some of the financial cost of service utilization. Co-payments provide policyholders with an incentive to temper their demand for services as well as to monitor the services provided by their veterinarians. Pet insurance co-payment are typically set at 10 or 20 percent of the price of covered services. Insurers also place a cap on the total amount they will pay for veterinary care. Caps both prevent exceptionally expensive care and incentivize policyholders to monitor service bills as costs accumulate toward the cap. Although most pet insurance policies allow owners to obtain services from any licensed veterinarian, some require policyholders to secure services from specified veterinarians who constitute a network. Just as the insurers of human health care may be able to negotiate more favorable prices with medical providers in their networks, pet insurers may be able to negotiate more favorable prices with veterinarians in their networks. Networks may also enable insurers to more effectively monitor service patterns to detect questionable care.

Like human health insurance, pet insurance policies may also have deductibles, amounts that must be expended before expenses are indemnified. Rather than a response to either adverse selection or moral hazard, deductibles are generally used to reduce administrative costs by reducing the number of claims that have to be processed.

In a fictional world where everyone had the financial resources and flexibility to pay large veterinary bills, we could reasonably interpret an increase in veterinary expenditures from the introduction of insurance as an indication of moral hazard. In contrast, in a world where people do not have the financial resources and flexibility to pay for large veterinary bills, an increase in veterinary expenditures could be plausibly interpreted as increased access. The real world lies between these extremes. Some of the increased expenditure indicates moral hazard, but some also results from an expansion of access, especially to rare but high-cost care. Indeed, for very serious illnesses and injuries, increased access may make treatment a financially feasible alternative to euthanasia.

Does the purchase of pet insurance result in larger expenditures on veterinary care? A 2017 survey of dog owners found that the availability of insurance did increase annual veterinary expenditures.[39] We can also estimate the impact of pet insurance on veterinary expenditures using the 2018 PVL Survey data. Survey respondents spent on average $366 in the prior year on veterinary care for their dog. We can assess the marginal impact of pet insurance on veterinary expenditures by statistically controlling for other factors that may also affect veterinary expenses: in this instance, family income, wellness coverage, and age and size of the dog. The analysis indicates that the presence of insurance contributes to a (statistically significantly) larger expenditure of $94, which is a substantively large effect. Family income, dog age, and dog size all have statistically significant but smaller effects on veterinary expenditures; having a wellness plan did not affect expenditures.[40]

The presence of increased veterinary expenditures, however, provides only indirect support for the hypothesis that pet insurance results in fewer dogs being euthanized. A study of decisions regarding the treatment of dogs with gastric dilatation-volvulus provides more direct evidence that supports this hypothesis.[41] This disease threatens the life of the dog. Its surgical treatment has a success rate of between 80 and 90 percent. However, the surgery is expensive, usually costing several thousand dollars. The researchers convincingly argue that owners' decisions between surgery and euthanasia are primarily driven by economics. Owners without pet insurance decided to euthanize in 37 percent of cases, while those who did have insurance decided to euthanize in only 10 percent of cases. In a comprehensive model that included statistical controls for the dog's age and sex, the size of the deposit requirement

---

[39] Angelica Williams, Brian Williams, Charlotte R. Hansen, and Keith H. Coble. "The Impact of Pet Health Insurance on Dog Owners' Spending for Veterinary Services." *Animals (Basel)* 10, no. 7 (2020): 1162–1175.

[40] Income was measured as the ratio of family income to the Federal Poverty Line to take account of family size. Each unit increase in the ratio increased veterinary expenditures by $33. Each year of dog age contributed $6 to expenditures. Very large dogs (over 88 pounds) had expenditures $117 higher relative to small dogs (under 23 pounds); large dogs (between 45 and 88 pounds) had expenditures $102 higher relative to small dogs; medium-sized dogs (23 to 44 pounds) did not have statistically different expenditures than small dogs. Overall, these results indicate a positive income elasticity of demand for veterinary care and is consistent with underwriters charging higher premiums for older and larger dogs.

[41] Manuel Boller, Tereza S. Nemanic, Jarryd D. Anthonisz, Magdoline Awad, Joshua Selinger, Elise M. Boller, and Mark A. Stevenson. "The Effect of Pet Insurance on Presurgical Euthanasia of Dogs with Gastric Dilatation-volvulus: A Novel Approach to Quantifying Economic Euthanasia in Veterinary Emergency Medicine." *Frontiers in Veterinary Science* (2020): 1039–1049.

prior to surgery, and a measure of disease severity, the odds of electing euthanasia were 7.4 times higher for those without insurance than for those with insurance. The researchers (as do we) interpret their results as strong evidence of the presence of insurance coverage reducing the risk of euthanasia.

6.5 DOGS IN MEDICAL RESEARCH

Victorian England saw the emergence of both modern medicine and growing public concern about the morality of using animals in medical research. Although the government's first draft of the Cruelty to Animals Act of 1876 would have completely banned the use of dogs and cats in medical research, a goal sought by the anti-vivisectionists, the final draft only required professional review of experimentation on dogs, cats, horses, mules, and asses, similar to the requirements put in place to regulate painful experiments on animals without anesthesia.[42] Almost a century later, the Animal Welfare Act of 1966 set out a framework for U.S. federal rules governing the use of animals in research. The rules on the supply side require that the suppliers of animals for research to be licensed (Class A licenses for firms that breed and raise dogs within their own facilities and Class B licenses for so-called "random source" firms that purchase or resell dogs). The primary rules on the demand side require every research organization using animals in research to have at least one Institutional Animal Care and Use Committee (IACUC) that reviews proposed research involving warm-blooded animals and conducts at least semiannual inspections of animal facilities. IACUCs must include members who can assess the care, treatment, and experimental use of animals as well as members who *"represent society's concerns regarding the welfare of animal* subjects used at such facility."[43]

6.5.1 Changing Public Attitudes toward Animal Research

Society's concerns have evolved over the decades. In a 1948 national survey, 84 percent of respondents supported the use of live animals

---

[42] Richard D. French. *Antivivisection and Medical Science in Victorian Society* (Princeton, NJ: Princeton University Press, 1975), pp. 115 and 127.

[43] Lenore M. Montanaro. "The Heart of Animal Research and Testing Law: A Study of the Animal Welfare Act, the Health Research Extension Act, and Proposed Solutions Supporting the Three Rs." *UIC Law Review* 55, no. 1 (2022): 1–39 at 24–25, emphasis in the original.

in medical teaching[44] and research.[45] However, 22 percent of those who supported the use of animals in medical research responded that some species of animals should not be used in research, and 45 percent of these respondents indicated dogs as one of these species. That is, even among the majority that stated they favored the use of animals in research, about 10 percent opposed the use of dogs. More recent surveys show increasing concern about the use of animals in research. A 1985 national survey asked respondents if they approved or disapproved of dogs being used in medical experiments; 40 percent of respondents disapproved.[46] However, in response to the follow-up question, "What if dogs were the only kind of animals suitable for certain life-saving medical experiments," 60 percent expressed approval, suggesting that about 16 percent of respondents favored a complete ban on the use of dogs in research. Respondents to a 2008 national survey were asked about their approval of the statement: "Scientists should be allowed to do research that causes pain and injury to animals like dogs and chimpanzees if it produces new information about human health problems"; 36 percent disagreed and 22 percent strongly disagreed, suggesting a further increase in those favoring a ban on the use of dogs in research.[47] In general, younger people, women, vegetarians, and nonrural residents are less likely to support the use of animals in medical research than are others.[48]

---

[44] In 2008 the last U.S. medical school abandoned the use of dogs in medical school teaching. Nicholas Bakalar. "Killing Dogs in Training of Doctors Is to End." *New York Times*, January 1 (2008): F5. Concerns about pet dogs being kidnapped and sold for use by medical students was a factor in both the British and U.S. laws cited at the beginning of the section. As an aside, in 1983 one of your authors had a fellowship to audit medical school toxicology and pharmacology courses. In one of these courses, a laboratory exercise involved teams of medical students observing various biological markers of dogs as they received increasing doses of a drug. They were ultimately euthanized.

[45] National Opinion Research Center (NORC), NORC Survey: Animal Experimentation, Question 20, USNORC.480246.R13A, National Opinion Research Center (NORC) (Ithaca, NY: Roper Center for Public Opinion Research, Cornell University, 1948).

[46] Media General/Associated Press, Media General/Associated Press Poll: National Poll #8 – Telephone Service/Animal Testing/School Prayer, Question 14, USAPMGEN.8.R22, Media General/Associated Press (Ithaca, NY: Roper Center for Public Opinion Research, *Cornell University*, 1985).

[47] NORC GSS, with funding from NSF, National Opinion Research Center General Social Survey 2008, Question 9784, USNORC.GSS08F.Q1176, National Opinion Research Center [NORC] (Ithaca, NY: Roper Center for Public Opinion Research, Cornell University, 2008).

[48] Elisabeth H. Ormandy and Catherine A. Schuppli. "Public Attitudes toward Animal Research: A Review." *Animals (Basel)* 4, no. 3 (2014): 391–408.

6.5.2 Professional Norms Regarding Animal Research

The so-called "three Rs" are now widely accepted as directives for ethical experimentation using animals: "…replacing sentient animals with other models where possible, reducing the number of animal subjects to what is needed for statistical adequacy, and refining techniques to reduce animal pain and distress."[49] Acceptance by the research community of the three Rs, perhaps propelled by changing public attitudes, means fewer dogs are now used in medical research in the United States. The annual number of dogs used in medical research has fallen from about 200 thousand in the 1970s to about 60 thousand today.[50] Over half of these dogs are used in private-sector industries, primarily in pharmacological and toxicological studies.[51] These dogs may suffer from both experimental treatment and isolation and, often, stressful confinement in laboratories. Although some states now have laws requiring that dogs no longer being used in experiments at universities and research institutes be listed for adoption,[52] many dogs are euthanized either as subjects in experiments or when no longer useful to researchers.

Veterinary researchers also use dogs and other animals. Like the recruitment of patients into human research, veterinary researchers also recruit dogs, through their owners, to participate in clinical trials and other research. This involvement of companion dogs in research may offer them a direct benefit, as well as potentially risk, along with contributions to knowledge. Dogs may also participate in "One Health" research, which recognizes that there is often a close relationship between animal and human health.[53] For example, both humans and dogs are

---

[49] On the three Rs and their shortcomings as ethical guidance, see David DeGrazia and Tom L. Beauchamp. "Beyond the 3 Rs to a More Comprehensive Framework of Principles for Animal Research Ethics." *ILAR Journal* 60, no. 3 (2019): 308–317 at 310.

[50] National Academies of Sciences, Engineering, and Medicine. "US Department of Agriculture Statistics on the Use of Dogs and Other Animals in Research." In *Necessity, Use, and Care of Laboratory Dogs at the US Department of Veterans Affairs* (Washington, DC: National Academies Press, 2020), 143–148 at 144.

[51] Ibid., p. 146.

[52] In 2014, Minnesota became the first state to adopt a "Beagle Freedom Law." (Beagles are often bred for and used in research because of their docile nature.) The Minnesota law only applies to research at public universities: "… a publicly-funded higher education facility that confines dogs or cats for science, education, or research purposes and plans on euthanizing a dog or cat for other than science, education, or research purposes must first offer the dog or cat to an animal rescue organization." Animal Legal and Historical Center, College of Law, Michigan State University. www.animallaw.info/content/map-beagle-freedom-laws. Accessed November 8, 2022.

[53] Centers for Disease Control and Prevention. "One Health." www.cdc.gov/onehealth/in-action/index.html. Accessed November 8, 2022.

prone to antibiotic resistance. When dogs and humans suffer from the same or very similar diseases, dogs may serve as "sentinels" that provide early warning of the spread of these diseases.[54]

6.5.3 Economic Perspective on Dogs as Research Subjects

Economics cannot fully resolve the conflicts and dilemmas that arise in choosing between human and dog welfare in medical research. However, we think we can offer a few insights, even within the property rights regimes in which dogs are considered to be commodities. Specifically, this analysis shows how even considering only human welfare, economic efficiency would require some restrictions on animal use in medical research.[55] To do so, we adapt a framework first introduced by Glenn Boyle in which dogs have standing in the sense that their welfare would be directly included in assessing allocative efficiency.[56] We consider the case in which dogs do not have any independent standing from a property rights perspective, but people's welfare is affected by the treatment of dogs, so that the dogs gain standing indirectly through people.

Figure 6.1 illustrates the implications of people's valuation of dog welfare for economic efficiency. We label the horizontal axis as "harm to dogs." How might it be operationalized? If the harm were to humans rather than dogs, health economists would define the scale as the loss of quality-adjusted life-years (QALYs).[57] Human QALYs weight each year lived by a utility index of health status. For example, living 1 year in perfect health would equal 1 QALY. Living 1 year with a health condition assigned a utility of 0.5 would equal 0.5 QALYs. If analysts were similarly willing to estimate the utility of various statuses of dogs in research, then it would be possible to calculate QADLYs, or quality-adjusted dog

[54] Peggy L. Schmidt. "Companion Animals as Sentinels for Public Health." *Veterinary Clinics of North America: Small Animal Practice* 39, no. 2 (2009): 241–250.

[55] The seminal work in the modern economic literature is Charles Blackorby and David Donaldson. "Pigs and Guinea Pigs: A Note on the Ethics of Animal Exploitation." *Economic Journal* 102, no. 415 (1992): 1345–1369.

[56] Glenn Boyle. "The Dog that Doesn't Bark: Animal Interests in Economics." Working Paper Series No. 4017, The New Zealand Institute for the Study of Competition and Regulation, Victoria University of Wellington (2008).

[57] See Anthony E. Boardman, David H. Greenberg, Aidan R. Vining, and David L. Weimer. *Cost–Benefit Analysis: Concepts and Practice,* 5th ed. (New York, NY: Cambridge University Press, 2018), Chapter 18.

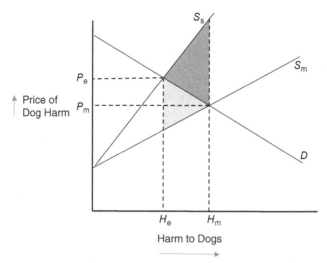

FIGURE 6.1 Economic efficiency when the use of dogs in research imposes nega-tive externalities
Source: Adapted from Figure 2 in Glenn Boyle. "The Dog that Doesn't Bark: Animal Interests in Economics." Working Paper Series No. 4017, The New Zealand Institute for the Study of Competition and Regulation, Victoria University of Wellington (2008) with permission.

life-years. The harm of a medical experiment that euthanized a dog without laboratory confinement or painful treatment could be approximated as a loss of QADLYs equal to the expected number of years of life forgone because of the euthanasia. The loss of QADLYs from an experiment that involved inflicting pain on an otherwise healthy dog would be approximated as the difference between 1 (the QADLY for 1 year of a dog living with normal health) minus the QADLY for the year of painful treatment. Following this approach, the horizontal axis could then be thought of as the lost QADLYs from the use of dogs in medical experiments.

We label the vertical axis in Figure 6.1 as the price of "dog harm." The line D represents the demand schedule for use of dogs in medical research and, therefore, the level of dog harm. The line S_m represents the supply schedule for dog harm as a function of the price actually paid by researchers. The market equilibrium occurs at the intersection of D and S_m: H_m units of dog harm are demanded and supplied at price P_m. The substantial decline in the number of dogs used in medical research since the 1970s can be explained by the shifts in D and S_m. D has shifted downward because of efforts by researchers to implement the three Rs. At the same time, more stringent oversight by IACUCs of research proposals to reduce the pain suffered by dogs in research shifts the supply schedule up.

Yet the equilibrium, H_m and P_m, is not allocatively efficient if the use of dogs in research negatively affects people who are aware that it is taking place. That is, harm to dogs is a negative externality in the sense that it affects those who are not party to decisions about the research that causes it.[58] In Figure 6.1, S_s, the social supply schedule, incorporates the externality by adding its dollar value to the market supply schedule, S_m. As explained in Chapter 4, supply schedules can be interpreted as marginal cost schedules: S_s indicates marginal cost from the social perspective. Similarly, demand schedules can also be interpreted as marginal value schedules. From the social perspective, the efficient allocation occurs at the intersection of the demand schedule and the supply schedule, inclusive of the externality: P_e and H_e. The loss resulting from ignoring the externalities is represented by the shaded area, which captures harm inflicted on dogs because the equilibrium is H_e rather than H_m. The net loss to society, taking account of the reductions in surplus to researchers and dog suppliers, is the darker shaded area above the demand schedule.

How could one operationalize and estimate these external costs? We could estimate the willingness of the population to pay for reductions in the use of dogs in research.[59] Although it would be very difficult to implement successfully, the contingent valuation method described in Chapter 6 could be used to estimate an average willingness to pay for the sample; we could then apply it to the overall population. Once such a QADLY is developed, the willingness to pay for a QADLY could be estimated and considered in deliberations by IACUCs. Of course, this approach can only be applied in a property rights regime in which dogs are viewed as a commodity. If instead dogs are quasi-persons, then the community would effectively be agents for the welfare of the dogs. As such, their fiduciary

---

[58] There may also be negative externalities in the supply of dogs for research. There continues to be concern that Class B "random source" suppliers sometimes secure pet dogs who were lost or stolen. More recently, as suggested by the case of the Virginia Beagles noted in Chapter 5, some Class A suppliers do not provide ethical care, causing harm to dogs and imposing costs on organizations that rescue them.

[59] Leslie and Sunstein suggest that if all consumers were fully informed about the treatment of animals in food production, one could imagine asking them about their willingness to pay for improvements in the quality of life of the animals. Jeff Leslie and Cass R. Sunstein. "Animal Rights without Controversy." *Law and Contemporary Problems* 70, no. 1 (2007): 117–138.

responsibility might be interpreted as not allowing them to make trade-offs between the welfare of humans and the welfare of dogs.[60]

6.6 CONCLUSION

In the current property rights regime, owners of dogs can decide when to euthanize them, either directly with the assistance of a veterinarian or indirectly by surrendering them to a shelter. Euthanasia to end suffering is widely viewed by the public and, unanimously, by veterinarians as appropriate. Less consensus exists about euthanasia as an alternative to expensive veterinary care. Pet insurance, which primarily covers dogs, increases the affordability of unexpected veterinary expenses, thereby potentially reducing resort to euthanasia. However, the economics of insurance warn of moral hazard, most likely occurring for pet insurance through veterinarians being too willing to engage in heroic care that may not necessarily be in the best interests of a suffering dog.

The current property rights regime also allows medical research that inflicts pain and often euthanasia on dogs. The economic perspective recognizes the value of the contributions of such research to human welfare. However, it also recognizes that harm to dogs in research imposes a negative externality on many people, suggesting that, even with institutional controls that have reduced the number of dogs involved annually in research, too many dogs are still being used.

---

[60] If we adopt fiduciary responsibility in the quasi-person property regime, we could interpret it as allowing trade-offs. Then the proper metric would be willingness to accept rather than willingness to pay. That is, not what they would be willing to pay to avoid harm but rather how much compensation would have to be given to make them indifferent about accepting the harm. The conceptual problem arises if some members of the community do not accept any trade-offs, effectively setting their willingness to accept at an infinite amount, which would prevent averaging over the sample. There would also be practical challenges because of the difficulty of eliciting willingness to accept because of the absence of a budget constraint that makes elicitation of willingness to pay feasible. See David L. Weimer. *Behavioral Economics for Cost-Benefit Analysis: Benefit Validity when Sovereign Consumers Seem to Make Mistakes* (New York, NY: Cambridge University Press, 2017), Chapter 5.

7

Working for the Man

Canine Occupations

As Chapter 2 discusses, the contribution of dogs to the production of goods and services for human consumption played a role in their early domestication and the subsequent development of breeds. However, the chapters that followed focus primarily on dogs as pets, their most common contemporary role. We return here to the consideration of dogs' labor as a productive input like other resources such as land, capital, and human labor. Applying economic concepts to canine labor and to the various types of canine occupations completes the basic foundation for dogonomics.

Dogs' labor is both multifaceted and complex, and so we would expect both the nature and magnitude of its costs and benefits to vary across occupations. Additionally, as we discuss later in the chapter, many canine occupations offer services to disadvantaged people suffering from physical or mental disabilities. Although our focus in this book is primarily on economic efficiency, we also recognize benefits to these disadvantaged groups that may be socially desirable even when they impose net economic costs on the rest of society.

We organize this chapter as follows. First, we explain in some detail the concepts of absolute and comparative advantage and the potential application of the theory of comparative advantage to interspecies mutualism. Second, we consider the costs of preparing dogs for entry into different types of occupations, recognizing that these costs consist of both selection (of dog) and direct training costs. Third, we present a categorization of canine occupations in terms of type of advantage and training and selection costs. Fourth, we move from concepts and costs to two applied social value questions. We examine the evidence on the costs and benefits of guide dog teams and the economics (and inevitably the politics) of the rise of the, now seemingly ubiquitous, emotional support dog.

7.1 COMPARATIVE AND ABSOLUTE ADVANTAGE

Many economic theories produce predictions that seem reasonably logical to normal people without any formal economics training. A few theories, however, produce predictions that seem surprising to many. Perhaps the most prominent of these is the theory of *comparative advantage*.[1] To understand it, it is also necessary to understand *absolute advantage*. In some canine occupations (e.g., guiding), the labor provided by dogs is fungible with human labor but with different costs that make it relatively attractive in some circumstances. In other canine occupations (e.g., drug sniffing), the labor of dogs is a distinct input because it cannot be economically replaced by human labor or capital. In a few canine occupations (e.g., detecting imminent human seizures), their labor is a unique input that currently cannot be replaced with another equivalent input. After illustrating the theory of comparative advantage in the context of international trade, we use it to better understand and categorize the exchange between *Homo sapiens* and *Canis lupus familiaris* in working contexts.

We recognize that most exchange in productive activity between humans and dogs is not free trade, limiting the usefulness of the theory of comparative advantage, though not its underlying mechanism of opportunity cost. We previously introduced the principal–agent model to frame potential duties and responsibilities with respect to human decisions about the euthanasia of dogs. We return to the principal–agent framework in this chapter to better understand decisions about when and how to employ canine labor. In this framework, the dog is the agent, and, like human agents, has an incentive to shirk or (shocking though that might be) even cheat. Breed choice and training can be seen as approaches to controlling canine shirking.

7.2 COMPARATIVE ADVANTAGE IN INTERNATIONAL TRADE

The theory of comparative advantage was first set out in the context of international trade. David Ricardo provided the most comprehensive

---

[1] For an introduction to comparative advantage, see Jonathan Eaton and Samuel Kortum. "Putting Ricardo to Work." *Journal of Economic Perspectives* 26, no. 2 (2012): 65–90.

statement of *comparative advantage*, but the basic idea can be found in the writings of Adam Smith and in the work of James Mill (the father of J. S. Mill) and in that of other enlightenment scholars.[2] Comparative advantage seeks to explain how two countries can realize mutual benefits through trade even if one of them is more efficient than the other in every type of economic activity. However, the concept of comparative advantage also helps us understand the nature of exchanges between organizations, between individuals, and between employers and employees when certain assumptions are satisfied. The required assumptions are very plausible in some exchange contexts but more of a stretch in others. Further, the theory of comparative advantage may provide insights into interactions, exchanges if you will, between different species. Obviously, we are most interested in exchanges between humans and dogs.

An application of comparative advantage in the canonical international trade context helps us set out the concept. Imagine a simple world of two countries, Sylvania and Freedonia. These countries can make either squeaky toys or dog beds, or both (but nothing else – they are obviously populated by dog lovers). There are two important assumptions underlying this simple illustration: first, there are constant returns to scale in both industries and so in both countries, and second, there is a commonly valued currency, or medium of exchange, between them. For purposes of this example, assume that each of the two countries, Sylvania and Freedonia, has 2,000 worker-hours available, but Sylvania is more productive, or efficient, than Freedonia. Reflecting this difference in efficiency, Sylvania needs 2 worker-hours while Fredonia needs 5 worker-hours to make a squeaky toy. To make a dog bed, Sylvania requires 4 worker-hours, while Freedonia needs 25. In the absence of trade and with each country employing half its worker-hours in each industry, Sylvania will produce 500 toys and 250 beds, and Freedonia will produce 200 toys and 40 beds, so that their combined output is 700 toys and 290 beds. As one can see, Sylvania makes both toys and beds more efficiently than Freedonia. Thus, Sylvania has an *absolute advantage* in producing each of these products. The crucial difference, however, is that Sylvania has a much bigger relative advantage over Fredonia in making beds: Sylvania must give up two toys to produce an additional bed (4/2) while Fredonia must give up five toys to produce an additional bed (25/5). Comparative advantage exists, however, because of differences in

---

[2] John Aldrich. "The Discovery of Comparative Advantage." *Journal of the History of Economic Thought* 26, no. 3 (2004): 379–399.

TABLE 7.1 *Absolute and comparative advantages in
international trade*

No trade (closed economy)		
	Sylvania	Freedonia
Squeaky toys	500	200
Dog beds	250	40
Specialization		
	Sylvania	Freedonia
Squeaky toys	400	400
Dog beds	300	0
Specialization and trade at 3 toys per bed		
	Sylvania	Freedonia
Squeaky toys	535	265
Dog beds	255	45
Gains in production from specialization and trade		
	Sylvania	Freedonia
Squeaky toys	35	65
Dog beds	5	5

the *opportunity costs* that the countries face in terms of how much of one good they must forgo to produce an additional unit of the other good.

If Sylvania recognizes its comparative advantage and the possibility of trading, it could focus production on beds and employ 1,200 worker-hours to produce them and 800 worker-hours to produce toys. This raises the bed output of Sylvania to 300 but reduces its production of toys to 400. If Fredonia now stops producing beds completely, it could produce 400 toys. These adjustments would increase the total output of toys from 700 to 800 and the total output of beds from 290 to 300. Thus, if Sylvania and Fredonia can trade, there is the potential for both countries to expand their consumption of both squeaky toys and dog beds.

At what price will they exchange toys for beds? Sylvania requires at least two toys for each bed; Freedonia will not give up more than five toys for a bed. If the exchange rate is set at, say, three toys per bed, which is favorable to both countries, and Sylvania trades 45 beds for 135 toys, Sylvania ends up with 535 toys and 255 beds, and Freedonia with 265 toys and 45 beds. As summarized in Table 7.1, both are better off from adjusting production and engaging in the exchange, even though Sylvania has an absolute advantage in making both squeaky toys and dog beds. It is straightforward to see how a market might establish an exchange rate and so a price, which in this case would fall between 2 and 5 toys per bed.

7.2.1 Application of Comparative Advantage
to Interspecies Mutualism

We now switch to interspecies exchanges. But what might species exchange with each other? There are numerous examples, ranging from plants providing homes in their roots for bacteria that have an advantage in fixing nitrogen to predators who protect smaller fish providing cleaning services.[3] In Chapter 2, we briefly introduce the cognitive trade-off hypothesis, which explains how the brains of different species have evolved to specialize in different capabilities. This kind of species specialization is at the core of Darwinian evolution. Darwin understood well that reproductive fitness was always relative, not absolute. Many evolutionary biologists have recognized the underlying parallels between the cognitive trade-offs that all species must make and comparative advantage theory. One important area where differential specialization is most striking is in the brain. For example, human cortical growth has evolved around language and categorization at the expense of other capacities retained by other species, such as olfactory capability in canines.[4] Their specialized capacities are critical for many species in their social interaction in the absence of language or for competitive activities such as hunting.

Two ecologists, Jason Hoeksema and Mark Schwartz, apply the comparative advantage model directly to interspecies resource trade.[5] They show how the innate differences between two species, both in terms of their abilities to acquire resources and in their need, or demand, for those resources, should largely determine the net benefit of participating in interspecies resource exchange. The benefits from resource trading also depend strongly on the trade-off between the cost of the acquisition of one resource versus the cost of acquisition of another resource.

---

[3] Peter Hammerstein and Ronald Noë. "Biological Trade and Markets." *Philosophical Transactions of the Royal Society B: Biological Sciences* 371, no. 1687 (2016):1–12.

[4] Agata Kokocińska-Kusiak, Martyna Woszczyło, Mikołaj Zybala, Julia Maciocha, Katarzyna Barłowska, and Michał Dzięcioł. "Canine Olfaction: Physiology, Behavior, and Possibilities for Practical Applications." *Animals (Basel)* 11, no. 8 (2021): 1–26. However, the domestication process resulted in enhanced communication between dogs and humans. See Hannah Salomons, Kyle C. M. Smith, Megan Callahan-Beckel, Margaret Callahan, Kerinne Levy, Brenda S. Kennedy, Emily E. Bray et al. "Cooperative Communication with Humans Evolved to Emerge Early in Domestic Dogs." *Current Biology* 31, no. 14 (2021): 3137–3144.

[5] Jason D. Hoeksema and Mark W. Schwartz. "Expanding Comparative-Advantage Biological Market Models: Contingency of Mutualism on Partner's Resource Requirements and Acquisition Trade-Offs." *Proceedings of the Royal Society of London. Series B: Biological Sciences* 270, no. 1518 (2003): 913–919.

The shape of the relevant cost curves can vary considerably across interspecies "markets" and could be linear, convex, or concave. Hoeksema and Schwartz conclude that for any species, the expected benefits from resource exchange primarily depend on three factors. First, the benefits depend on the relative difference between the species in their ability to acquire the resource in question. Second, the benefits depend on the relative differences between the species in their need, or demand, for the resource. Third, the benefits depend on variations in the shape of the relevant resource acquisition cost and the resulting trade-offs. As we stress whenever we enter the territory of evolutionary biology, these evolutionary strategies are, in most instances, driven by natural selection. The big exception is the selective breeding of other species by humans. For our purposes, in the case of dogs, the exception is as important as the rule.

7.3 MINIMIZING AGENCY COST: SELECTION AND TRAINING

Although perhaps a bit of a stretch, we can frame canine occupations as representing a principal–agent relationship in which the interests of the agent (the dog) and the principal (person) can, and sometimes will, differ. For example, it is the rare dog that does not desire to chase squirrels or frequently nap, activities that may interfere with occupational responsibilities. Effective training reduces the likelihood that dogs will follow their own (natural) interests while doing their work. The training cost and any subsequent behavior inconsistent with the canine occupational tasks constitute an *agency cost* along the lines we introduce in Chapter 6.

Canine occupations require dogs. Many of these occupations require substantial training that can be thought of as a costly investment in a dog to produce a worker. It is also an investment with uncertain payoffs because not all dogs complete the training required for the occupation – note the high dropout rate for dogs that begin guide training. The problem of efficiently recruiting and training canine labor has parallels in human labor markets. Michael Spence, who identified education as providing a signal about the trainability of job candidates that reduces hiring risk, provided one of the most influential insights about the economics of human labor markets.[6] Dogs do not have a choice about schooling, but they do have breeds that many believe signal trainability for specific tasks.

---

[6] Michael Spence. "Job Market Signaling." *Quarterly Journal of Economics* 87, no. 3 (1973): 355–374.

It is important to recognize that signals need not be perfect to be useful. College graduates have demonstrated at least the capacity to complete a set of requirements that generally convey some capacity to learn, yet it does not guarantee that they will thrive in on-the-job training – we have known graduates of even elite colleges who have not been occupationally successful. Analogously, a dog's breed does not have to perfectly predict traits necessary for a particular task to serve as a useful signal. However, if intra-breed variation swamps inter-breed variation, the signal may often be misleading.

Although breeding through much of human history was driven by a desire to produce more effective working dogs, breeding over the last few centuries has been driven more by the human desire to produce dogs with particular physical characteristics that may be unrelated to functional roles. Breeds historically bred to be herders, racers, hunters, or fighters likely provide useful signals about performance in occupations for which these sorts of tasks are central. However, the signaling value of breeds for success in less specialized occupations may be relatively small because of the great individual variation within breeds.

Kathleen Morrill and colleagues assessed the relationship between breed and behavioral traits using data from the Darwin's Ark project, a nonprofit collaborative of scientists and pet owners created to advance medicine through the study of animal behavior and genetics.[7] Based on an impressive study that drew on survey responses from over 18 thousand pet owners and sequenced the DNA of over 2 thousand dogs, the researchers were able to assess the inheritability and breed-specific distribution of traits.[8] On the one hand, one of these traits relevant to canine occupations, biddability (responsiveness to direction and command), showed some relevant differences across breeds. On the other hand, the distributions of this trait by breed largely overlapped, so that breed itself was only a weak predictor of the trait for individual dogs.[9]

In view of the weak predictive power of breed for many of the desirable traits for service dog training, a large literature concerns the early

---

[7] Darwin's Ark. www.darwinsark.org/. Accessed March 2, 2023.

[8] Kathleen Morrill, Jessica Hekman, Xue Li, Jesse McClure, Brittney Logan, Linda Goodman, Mingshi Gao et al. "Ancestry-Inclusive Dog Genomics Challenges Popular Breed Stereotypes." *Science* 376, no. 6592 (2022): 1–15.

[9] The researchers provide a dashboard that can be used to explore the distributions of traits across breeds. www.darwinsark.org/muttomics_viz_dashboard/. Accessed March 2, 2023.

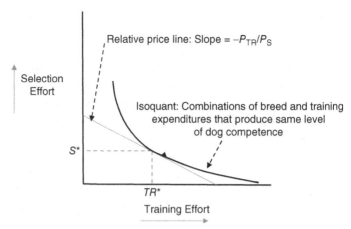

FIGURE 7.1   Trade-offs between selection and training costs

identification of these traits in individual dogs.[10] Early identification allows for the recruitment of promising dogs or the diversion of dogs already in training but unlikely to succeed before the full costs of training accrue. Although there are a number of tests available for assessing behavioral characteristics, their predictive values have not been adequately assessed for them to be considered reliable tools for selecting dogs for training.[11]

Figure 7.1 illustrates the trade-off between investments in selection and training to prepare dogs for an occupation. The horizontal axis indicates the level of investment in training. The vertical axis indicates the level of investment in selection, both in terms of choice of breed and screening of dogs within breed. The solid curved line, an isoquant, indicates the various combinations of training and selection needed to prepare the dogs for a particular occupation. The relative price line has a slope equal to minus the ratio of the prices of selection and training, $-P_{TR}/P_S$, where P_{TR} is the price of a unit of training and P_S is the price of a unit of selection. The greater the price of training or the smaller the price of selection, the steeper is the line.

[10] Emily E. Bray, Cynthia M. Otto, Monique A. R. Udell, Nathaniel J. Hall, Angie M. Johnston, and Evan L. MacLean. "Enhancing the Selection and Performance of Working Dogs." *Frontiers in Veterinary Science* 8 (2021): 1–21.

[11] Karen Brady, Nina Cracknell, Helen Zulch, and Daniel S. Mills. "A Systematic Review of the Reliability and Validity of Behavioural Tests Used to Assess Behavioural Characteristics Important in Working Dogs." *Frontiers in Veterinary Science* 5, no. 103 (2018): 1–10.

The point at which the relative price line is just tangent to the isoquant gives the combinations of selection and training that minimize the cost of preparing dogs for the occupation. In this illustration, costs would be minimized by the combination of TR^* units of training and S^* units of selection. Improvements in the identification of likely adult traits in puppies that lowered P_S would make the relative price line steeper, so that more selection and less training would minimize cost. If innovations make more effective training methods available, then the relative cost curve would be less steep, so that more training and less selection would minimize costs. In our classification of occupations, we assume that the procurers of canine labor choose combinations of selection and training to minimize costs.

7.4 CLASSIFYING CANINE OCCUPATIONS

When we look at dogs' working roles, we can observe a great deal of variety, as well as many changes over time. Therefore, there are also a number of different ways we can define the various roles, depending on our purpose. For example, we can define an economic role very broadly as olfactory detection or very narrowly as the olfactory ability to detect human cancer. Conceived very narrowly, the dog's ability relative to a human's is likely to be seen as an absolute advantage. Indeed, it may be a *unique advantage* that allows the dog to provide a service that currently cannot otherwise be provided. Conceived very broadly, the dog's ability relative to a human's is more likely to be seen as a comparative advantage. There are several ways to consider and define the nature and scope of the market for a dog's labor. This choice is an issue that economic analysis must confront in defining the scope of markets for use in a number of applied policy areas. For example, essentially the same issue arises when defining the scope of markets for assessing a firm's degree of monopoly power. If we define a market narrowly enough, it is easy to observe a monopolist and the exercise of monopoly power. In contrast, if we define a market broadly enough, most markets appear quite competitive.[12]

For our purposes, it is not crucial to specify the exact nature of the dog's advantage, as long as a market or society recognizes that advantage. While it is not crucial to decide between absolute and comparative advantages, we think it is nearly always interesting to consider it. Why?

---

[12] Jonathan B. Baker. "Market Definition: An Analytical Overview." *Antitrust Law Journal* 74, no. 1 (2007): 129–174.

Thinking about the scope of relevant markets facilitates thinking about future potential roles for working dogs in the presence of both technological changes and changes in (human) labor markets.

We classify important canine occupations in terms of two dimensions. First, we assess the nature of the advantage dogs bring to the production of goods and services people value: comparative, absolute, or unique. Second, we assess the degree of investment that must be made to bring the dog into the production process: to simplify the analysis, we dichotomize that investment level as either high or low. We label this investment as selection and training to recognize the possible trade-offs between investment in the selection of a particular breed and individual dog and investment in training.

7.4.1 Comparative Advantage Occupations

In some occupations, the labor of dogs can be substituted for human labor or other inputs. When the substitution offers lower opportunity costs for completing the task, we consider the dog to have a comparative advantage. We classify two types of occupations as falling into the comparative advantage category. The first type is the service dog. Service dogs help the blind, the hearing impaired, and the disabled. Each of these occupations require substantial training for dogs to be able to reliably carry out their tasks. (Note that we use the service label rather than the assistance label as the encompassing term to be consistent with the terminology that U.S. federal agencies use.)[13] Service dogs usually reside with their human partners so that they can provide help at any time of day or night. The second type of occupation consists of emotional support, therapy, and guard dogs. These occupations require comparatively little training beyond that provided to juvenile pets. Both emotional support and guard dogs typically reside with their clients, while therapy dogs often do not.

High Selection and Training Costs. Guide dogs for the blind and the visually impaired have been trained as service dogs for over a century. They receive substantial training so that they can safely guide their human partner around stationary and moving obstacles. Although they normally do not have the capability to fully replace a human guide, they offer a comparative advantage with respect to simple navigation because

---

[13] For an historical overview and discussion of increasing professionalization in the training of service dogs, see Aubrey H. Fine, Alan M. Beck, and Zenithson Ng. "The State of Animal-Assisted Interventions: Addressing the Contemporary Issues That Will Shape the Future." *International Journal of Environmental Research and Public Health* 16, no. 20 (2019): 1–19.

of their relatively low "wage" and ready availability. We provide a fuller treatment of guide dogs in the next section. It includes a review of an analysis that assesses some of the costs and benefits of guide dogs that offers insight into their comparative advantage.

Hearing dogs alert their human partners with hearing loss to various important distinct sounds, such as smoke alarms, doorbells or door knocks, alarm clocks, or telephones. Hearing dogs may also be trained to alert their partners to the presence of another person, the cry of a baby or child, or a spoken name. Perhaps not surprising in view of the general responsiveness of dogs to physical signals, hearing dogs can even learn some words in American Sign Language. When they hear a relevant sound, hearing dogs are trained to paw their partners to indicate that they have heard something and then lead their partners to the source of the sound. Because of these needed physical interactions with their partners, hearing dogs tend to be smaller breeds so that they do not inadvertently cause harm in summoning and leading.

Several studies have assessed the impact of hearing dogs on their partners' wellbeing and functionality. One longitudinal study that followed hearing impaired recipients for at least a year after receiving a hearing dog found statistically significant reductions in anxiety, tension, and depression and improved social functioning and integration compared to the period during which they were waiting to receive their dogs.[14] An experimental study in the United Kingdom randomly assigned hearing dogs to people on the hearing dog waiting list and then compared those who had received them with those who did not in terms of a mental wellbeing scale and other outcomes.[15] Those who received hearing dogs experienced "significant improvements in anxiety, depression, functioning, fearfulness/social isolation, and perceived dependency" at the six-month follow-up (p. 1). Despite some reductions in use of health services by those receiving hearing dogs, the researchers nonetheless concluded that the incremental gains in quality of life of those who received dogs was not cost-effective if the National Health Service had to pay the entire

---

[14] Claire M. Guest, Glyn M. Collis, and June McNicholas. "Hearing Dogs: A Longitudinal Study of Social and Psychological Effects on Deaf and Hard-of-Hearing Recipients." *Journal of Deaf Studies and Deaf Education* 11, no. 2 (2006): 252–261.

[15] Lucy Stuttard, Philip Boyle, Caroline Fairhurst, Catherine Hewitt, Francesco Longo, Simon Walker, Helen Weatherly, Emese Mayhew, and Bryony Beresford. "Hearing Dogs for People with Severe and Profound Hearing Loss: A Wait-List Design Randomised Controlled Trial Investigating Their Effectiveness and Cost-Effectiveness." *Trials* 22, no. 1 (2021): 1–15.

cost of providing the hearing dog. As with guide dogs, hearing dogs have a comparative advantage rather than an absolute advantage.

Assistance dogs help people who have a variety of physical disabilities. They are trained to perform specific tasks relevant to their partners, such as helping them move about, open doors, retrieve dropped items, and turn lights on and off. They can also be trained to assist in many of the activities of daily living, such as dressing, bathing, grooming, eating, toileting, and oral hygiene.[16] As with guide and hearing dogs, research suggests that they also usually provide psychological benefits to their human partners while performing their basic work.[17] Assistance dogs may also contribute to greater participation in recreation and social interaction, including within organizations and with relatives.[18] The most commonly reported problems disabled people face in their partnership with assistance dogs are in performing grooming and providing veterinary care.[19]

Psychiatric assistance dogs are trained to help people with psychiatric disabilities to function more effectively. Their tasks may include helping their partners take medication on schedule, break compulsive habits, prevent them from oversleeping, and help them find people or places when they become disoriented. These dogs are increasingly being used to help veterans who have been in combat overcome post-traumatic stress disorder. These dogs are able to act as socializing agents by contributing to a feeling of safety and "detecting and intervening when the veteran is anxious, disoriented in time or space, depressed or aggressive."[20] The level of training required to perform these tasks is similar to that required for other types of service dogs. Indeed, their status as service dogs is

---

[16] Terry K. Crowe, Suzanne Perea-Burns, Jessica S. Sedillo, Ingrid C. Hendrix, Melissa Winkle, and Jean Deitz. "Effects of Partnerships between People with Mobility Challenges and Service Dogs." *American Journal of Occupational Therapy* 68, no. 2 (2014): 194–202.

[17] For reviews, see Nicola Futeran, Lynette Mackenzie, Sarah Wilkes-Gillan, and Claire Dickson. "Understanding the Participation Outcomes for Persons with Disability when Partnered with Assistance Dogs: A Scoping Review." *Australian Occupational Therapy Journal* 69, no. 4 (2022): 475–492 and Melissa Winkle, Terry K. Crowe, and Ingrid Hendrix. "Service Dogs and People with Physical Disabilities Partnerships: A Systematic Review." *Occupational Therapy International* 19, no. 1 (2012): 54–66.

[18] Sophie S. Hall, Jessica MacMichael, Amy Turner, and Daniel S. Mills. "A Survey of the Impact of Owning a Service Dog on Quality of Life for Individuals with Physical and Hearing Disability: A Pilot Study." *Health and Quality of Life Outcomes* 15, no. 1 (2017): 1–9.

[19] Melissa Winkle, Terry K. Crowe, and Ingrid Hendrix, p. 64.

[20] Geneviève Lessard, Claude Vincent, Dany H. Gagnon, Geneviève Belleville, Édouard Auger, Vicky Lavoie, Markus Besemann, Noël Champagne, Frédéric Dumont, and Elisabeth Béland. "Psychiatric Service Dogs as a Tertiary Prevention Modality for Veterans Living with Post-Traumatic Stress Disorder." *Mental Health & Prevention* 10 (2018): 42–49 at 45.

consistent with equity-oriented public policies intended to reduce dispari-
ties in the treatment of mental and physical disabilities.

Low to Moderate Selection and Training Costs. We next consider the
three comparative advantage occupations that require a lower level of training: namely, therapy, emotional support, and guard dogs. All three involve
minimal training beyond that given to pets. Indeed, all three occupations
usually involve part-time work for full-time pets! The human partners of
many therapy dogs typically make them available in settings such as hospi-
tals, nursing homes, and schools where they bring comfort to people under
stress. Dogs that are obedient and like to meet new people can qualify as
therapy dogs. A number of nonprofit organizations and commercial firms
have certified therapy teams and charge for their services. In recent years,
however, the number of for-profit organizations that certify therapy dogs
has proliferated.[21] Emotional support dogs play a somewhat similar role to
therapy dogs, but for their owners. Later in this chapter, we discuss the recent
controversy over whether airlines should be legally prohibited from charging
a "pet fee" for emotional support dogs that travel with their owners.

We also place guard dogs in this occupational category. Not too long
ago, it would have been reasonable to argue that dogs enjoyed an absolute advantage over humans in guarding. This would be based on their
acute hearing and also because they are less likely than a person to sleep
through an intrusion. However, recent advances in home security systems reduce the opportunities for dogs to provide superior guard services. Ferocious sounding dogs may still have an advantage as guards
in some situations, but in many others, an automatic call to a security
office may be more effective in providing protection. More generally,
this illustrates that the type of advantage that we use to classify canine
occupations can change with changes in technology or even norms about
how dogs should be treated.

7.4.2 Absolute Advantage Occupations

In some occupations, we think it is plausible to make the case that dogs
enjoy an absolute advantage in the sense that it is more costly to replace
their labor with human labor or other inputs. As with the relative advantage occupations, however, training costs vary across these occupations.

[21] James A. Serpell, Katherine A. Kruger, Lisa M. Freeman, James A. Griffin, and Zenithson Y. Ng. "Current Standards and Practices within the Therapy Dog Industry: Results
of a Representative Survey of United States Therapy Dog Organizations." *Frontiers in
Veterinary Science* 7 (2020): 1–12.

High Selection and Training Costs. Several canine occupations involve costly training. Search and rescue dogs use their acute sense of smell to help locate people or their remains. The bloodhound searching for an escaped criminal is a familiar example from quite a few classic movies, as are search and rescue teams searching for survivors or casualties at disaster sites. These dogs also are commonly used to search for lost people in open areas and human remains in burnt buildings. Dogs must be trained to reliably locate potential targets, to return to their handlers and communicate that potentially relevant smells have been found, and then lead their handlers to the locations where they were found. Some evidence exists suggesting both the effectiveness of search and rescue teams, as well as their contribution to covering more territory than could be covered by humans acting without search and rescue dogs.[22]

Dogs employed to detect substances rather than persons also require a substantial amount of training. The two most common specializations are sniffing for drugs and sniffing for explosives. Both tasks raise legal issues, particularly around concerns about Fourth Amendment constitutional protections. U.S. courts generally treat a positive response from a sniffing dog as establishing probable cause for a more thorough search. Like humans, however, dogs do make mistakes, falsely identifying the presence of the substance in question or falsely not identifying it when it is present. False positives are particularly important in drug detection contexts, while false negatives are of particular relevance to explosive detection. Some researchers have also raised concerns about the methodologies used in studies that purport to assess the accuracy of dogs sniffing.[23] Critics of this occupation also point to the current lack of standardized training and certification.[24] Nonetheless, we would argue that dogs in this profession currently do enjoy an absolute advantage over other detection methods that can be used for broad screening.

Most large U.S. police departments have K-9 (a homophone of canine) units that pair dogs with police officers. K-9 units typically train to deploy for crowd control and suspect apprehension duties. Although a variety of

[22] Ian Greatbatch, Rebecca J. Gosling, and Sophie Allen. "Quantifying Search Dog Effectiveness in a Terrestrial Search and Rescue Environment." *Wilderness & Environmental Medicine* 26, no. 3 (2015): 327–334.

[23] For a review of relevant studies and their methodological limitations, see Dorothea Johnen, Wolfgang Heuwieser, and Carola Fischer-Tenhagen. "An Approach to Identify Bias in Scent Detection Dog Testing." *Applied Animal Behaviour Science* 189 (2017): 1–12.

[24] Matthew Slaughter. "Supreme Court's Treatment of Drug Detection Dogs Doesn't Pass the Sniff Test." *New Criminal Law Review* 19, no. 2 (2016): 279–311.

breeds work as police service dogs, German shepherds currently dominate this occupation to such an extent that people sometimes refer to them simply as police dogs. Aside from a breed tendency for high levels of courage, loyalty, and intelligence, German shepherds have a wolf-like appearance that many people view as intimidating in potentially confrontational situations. The public's perception of police dogs as intimidating was reinforced by media coverage of their use to threaten and attack peaceful marchers during both the civil rights movement and subsequent public demonstrations. Indeed, police dogs have been described as manifesting the "beast in police."[25]

The safe use of K-9 units in suspect apprehension requires substantial training. Dogs can be trained to either "bite and hold" or "bark and hold."[26] These methods involve trade-offs in human safety. Bite-and-hold, which involves the dog gripping the suspect in a bite, can result in the serious injury or death of suspects, especially when they are seized by dogs who have outrun communication with their partners. Bark-and-hold, which involves the dog circling and barking to threaten the suspect until the dog's partner arrives, poses less danger to yielding suspects, but is perceived to put officers and dogs in greater danger if suspects do resist. However, the evidence on the relative risks is limited, though it does appear that preliminary training like that used in the Schutzhund sport makes both methods safer and more effective.[27] Controversy remains over which method is more desirable.

Low to Moderate Selection and Training Costs. Earlier in the chapter, we noted research that suggests that the predictive role of breed in canine occupations may be overestimated. Despite that, there are a number of ancient occupations involving low to moderate training costs for which breed does seem to contribute somewhat to an absolute advantage. For example, sheep and cattle farmers still employ breeds that have been selectively bred for centuries to have an enhanced herding instinct. This instinct can make herding dogs, such as the Australian shepherd, challenging pets. However, along with their mobility over all sorts of terrain, it gives them an absolute advantage in herding over humans with or without vehicles. Similarly, huskies have been bred for sled work. Although

[25] Tyler Wall. "'For the Very Existence of Civilization': The Police Dog and Racial Terror." *American Quarterly* 68, no. 4 (2016): 861–882.
[26] Jonathan K. Dorriety. "Police Service Dogs in the Use-of-Force Continuum." *Criminal Justice Policy Review* 16, no. 1 (2005): 88–98.
[27] Charlie Mesloh. "Barks or Bites? The Impact of Training on Police Canine Force Outcomes." *Police Practice and Research* 7, no. 4 (2006), 323–335.

dog sleds continue to be used by indigenous peoples in Alaska, Northern Canada, and Greenland, the best prospects for employment are now as members of sled racing teams!

Greyhounds were bred specifically for racing and still dominate that sport.[28] Beginning in the 1930s, pari-mutuel betting on dog races became popular in the United States. By the 1980s, there were about 50 greyhound racetracks in operation. Growing concerns about the treatment of greyhounds, including the common euthanasia of unpromising puppies and retired dogs as well as poor conditions during their racing careers, has resulted in the majority of states outlawing it.[29] Currently, greyhound tracks operate only in West Virginia. With a plethora of alternative betting opportunities and widespread public perception of the inhumane treatment of racing dogs, it is unlikely that this will remain a canine occupation in the United States. It might very well join dog fighting, an occupation dominated by pit bulls, that is, now banned in all states and subjects its human sponsors to felony prosecution.[30]

Participation in hunting alongside humans is among the oldest canine occupations. Dogs have played, and continue to play, a variety of distinct roles in hunting, including retrieving, pointing, and hounding. There tends to be a degree of breed specialization for these roles. Training costs can be low, but they are more likely to be moderate, and may even shift some roles into the high-cost column of Table 7.2. As is the case with herding dogs, instincts and mobility give hunting dogs an absolute advantage over humans in some hunting roles. It might very well seem to be the dream occupation for many dogs! However, the actual work is seasonal and not without its risks. For example, hounds can be used in

---

[28] For a comprehensive history of greyhound racing, from coursing in which pairs of greyhounds raced to catch live rabbits, to the invention of the mechanical rabbit that made commercial racing possible and the changes in norms and recreational opportunities that have led to its decline, see Gwyneth A. Thayer. *Going to the Dogs: Greyhound Racing, Animal Activism, and American Popular Culture* (Lawrence, KS: Kansas University Press, 2013). She notes that the great speed of greyhounds and their otherwise relaxed nature explains their nickname: "the 45 mile-per-hour couch potato."

[29] Chelsea Lenard. "Overview of Dog Racing Laws." *Animal Legal & Historical Center*, Michigan State University College of Law (2019). www.animallaw.info/article/overview-dog-racing-laws. Accessed February 28, 2023.

[30] The conviction of professional football player Michael Vick on dog fighting charges in 2007 suggests that illicit dog fighting still occurs, sometimes with prize purses in the tens of thousands of dollars. For an account of the discovery of Vick's involvement in dog fighting and the subsequent efforts to rescue his fighting dogs, see Jim Gorant. *The Lost Dogs: Michael Vick's Dogs and Their Tale of Rescue and Redemption* (New York, NY: Gotham Books, 2010).

TABLE 7.2 *Classification of canine occupations in terms of advantage and training*

	Low to moderate selection and training costs	High selection and training costs
Comparative advantage	Therapy Emotional support Guard	Guide Hearing Assistance Psychiatric
Absolute advantage	Herding Hunting Sled Racing (Fighting)	Search and rescue Substance detection Police service
Unique advantage		Diabetic alerting Cancer detection Seizure alerting

hunting black bears and wolves in Wisconsin;[31] especially chasing bears exposes hounds to depredation by wolves.[32]

7.4.3 Unique Advantage Occupations

We would go as far as to argue that in a few occupations, dogs enjoy a unique advantage in the sense that they can perform a specific task that currently could not otherwise be performed. A narrow definition of task is necessary for such a categorization to make sense. For example, cancer can be diagnosed by a variety of intrusive tests. Dogs that can detect cancer from a person's odor currently have a unique advantage in providing a nonintrusive diagnosis, but only an absolute, or perhaps just a comparative, advantage in terms of cancer diagnosis more generally. The unique advantage currently enjoyed by dogs obviously arises from their exceptional olfactory capabilities.[33] However, technological advances,

---

[31] Joseph K. Bump, Chelsea M. Murawski, Linda M. Kartano, Dean E. Beyer Jr, and Brian J. Roell. "Bear-Baiting May Exacerbate Wolf-Hunting Dog Conflict." *PLoS One* 8, no. 4 (2013): 1–7.

[32] In Wisconsin in 2022, 17 hunting dogs were killed by gray wolves. Wolf Depredation Reports in 2022. Wisconsin Department of Natural Resources. These data are available because the state pays compensation to owners of dogs killed by wolves. https://dnrx .wisconsin.gov/wdacp/public/depredation/2022. Accessed February 28, 2023.

[33] Paula Jendrny, Friederike Twele, Sebastian Meller, Albertus D. M. E. Osterhaus, Esther Schalke, and Holger A. Volk. "Canine Olfactory Detection and Its Relevance to Medical Detection." *BMC Infectious Diseases* 21, 1 (2021): 1–15.

especially in chemical detection, may eventually eliminate their unique advantage, even when we define this task narrowly.

Dogs currently have unique advantages in some types of cancer detection and possibly also in alerting diabetics to glycemia and epileptics to imminent seizures. These applications require substantial training to reduce error rates. As with all diagnostic tests, the effectiveness of dogs can be assessed in terms of "sensitivity," the probability that a test will give a positive designation when the relevant condition is present, and "specificity," the probability that a test will give a negative designation when the relevant condition is not present. A test with a high sensitivity will generate few false negative results; a test with a high specificity will generate few false positive results. There are usually trade-offs between sensitivity and specificity in selecting thresholds for designating a test result as positive one.

Cancer detection usually involves dogs sniffing urine or exhaled breath. Some studies suggest that dogs can be trained to detect cancers fairly effectively, especially using exhaled breath. Although some early studies reported very high specificities and sensitivities, especially for lung and ovarian cancer,[34] some more recent studies have failed to find effective detection, such as from urine sniffing for prostate cancer.[35] Nonetheless, a recent systematic review identified 58 studies that it considered methodologically valid and that reported a median sensitivity of 90 percent (ranging from 17 to 100 percent) and a median specificity of 96 percent (ranging from 8 to 100 percent) across the studies.[36]

Dogs assist people with epilepsy either by helping them respond to seizures or by alerting them that a seizure is imminent. Helping people respond to seizures is similar to the other service role we have discussed as representing a comparative advantage. Alerting people about an imminent seizure involves a unique advantage. Although many people with epilepsy believe that dogs trained to assist them, or even their pet dogs,

---

[34] Emily Moser and Michael McCulloch. "Canine Scent Detection of Human Cancers: A Review of Methods and Accuracy." *Journal of Veterinary Behavior* 5, no. 3 (2010): 145–152.

[35] Kevin R. Elliker, Barbara A. Sommerville, Donald M. Broom, David E. Neal, Sarah Armstrong, and Hywel C. Williams. "Key Considerations for the Experimental Training and Evaluation of Cancer Odour Detection Dogs: Lessons Learnt from a Double-blind, Controlled Trial of Prostate Cancer Detection." *BMC Urology* 14, no. 1 (2014): 1–9.

[36] Aiden E. Juge, Margaret F. Foster, and Courtney L. Daigle. "Canine Olfaction as a Disease Detection Technology: A Systematic Review." *Applied Animal Behaviour Science* 253 (2022): 1–12.

can alert them to an imminent seizure,[37] there have been no methodologically strong studies of effectiveness – seizures and their circumstances are difficult to study because of their random occurrence outside of clinic or laboratory settings. The theoretical case for the existence of a capacity of dogs to alert people to imminent seizures has been strengthened by the discovery of an odor that is specifically related to epileptic seizures.[38] Although studies directly observing seizures will continue to be difficult to implement, laboratory studies based on odor samples are more feasible and may help determine how effectively dogs are able to detect imminent seizures.

The effectiveness of glycemia alert dogs, however, has received more systematic study. For example, a study of 27 trained dogs in the United Kingdom reports median sensitivities of 83 percent and 67 percent for hypoglycemic and hyperglycemic episodes, respectively, with a specificity of 81 percent relative to the normal glycemic range.[39] Although people with type 1 diabetes generally believe that their detection dogs do provide them with early alerts, observation of dog behaviors and simultaneous blood measurements have brought into question their advantage over devices that directly measure blood glucose.[40] As devices that directly monitor glucose levels in blood become more convenient and available, it is likely that glycemia alert dogs will lose the unique advantage that we think they currently enjoy.

7.5 ASSESSING THE GUIDE DOG'S COMPARATIVE ADVANTAGE: SOME COST–BENEFIT EVIDENCE

Although there are a few references to dogs assisting the blind in antiquity, they would often have had to compete against slaves. There are

---

[37] Ana M. Martinez-Caja, Veerle De Herdt, Paul Boon, Ulrich Brandl, Hannah Cock, Jaime Parra, Emilio Perucca, Vijay Thadani, and Christel P. M. Moons. "Seizure-Alerting Behavior in Dogs Owned by People Experiencing Seizures." *Epilepsy & Behavior* 94 (2019): 104–111.

[38] Amélie Catala, Marine Grandgeorge, Jean-Luc Schaff, Hugo Cousillas, Martine Hausberger, and Jennifer Cattet. "Dogs Demonstrate the Existence of an Epileptic Seizure Odour in Humans." *Scientific Reports* 9, no. 1 (2019): 1–7.

[39] Nicola J. Rooney, Claire M. Guest, Lydia C. M. Swanson, and Steve V. Morant. "How Effective Are Trained Dogs at Alerting Their Owners to Changes in Blood Glycaemic Levels? Variations in Performance of Glycaemia Alert Dogs." *PLoS One* 14, no. 1 (2019): 1–16.

[40] Evan A. Los, Katrina L. Ramsey, Ines Guttmann-Bauman, and Andrew J. Ahmann. "Reliability of Trained Dogs to Alert to Hypoglycemia in Patients with Type 1 Diabetes." *Journal of Diabetes Science and Technology* 11, no. 3 (2017): 506–512.

numerous depictions of guide dogs in European medieval illustrations, including some touching scenes preserved in the British Library's collection. Krista Murchison suggests that many of these dogs actually performed double-duty, as they also appear to be carrying begging bowls.[41] The modern increased demand for guide dogs, and so their training, however, was prompted by the return of many thousands of veterans blinded by poison gas and shrapnel during World War I.[42] The first organized program in Germany, not surprisingly, employed German shepherds as the preferred breed for guides. Although German shepherds continue to be used to this day as guides, they are no longer the dominant guide dog breed in the United States because of people's perception of them as aggressive. The most common breeds of guide dogs are now Labrador retrievers or golden retrievers. Any of these dog breeds require extensive training to be reliable guides for the blind.

Currently, over 7 million Americans suffer from loss of vision acuity, including over 1 million who are medically and legally blind.[43] Yet, fewer than 10 thousand guide dog teams (dogs paired with blind persons) are currently working in the United States.[44] Guide dogs increase mobility and significantly counter the adverse effects of social isolation, especially for those who live alone. It surprises us that only about one out of a hundred blind Americans have guide dogs. Undoubtedly, many blind persons have comorbidities or living situations that make teaming up with a guide dog impractical or considerably more costly. However, those for whom a guide dog is a feasible option still face substantial upfront costs if they hope to secure an appropriately trained dog. Because of the financial and organizational constraints, many nonprofit organizations now provide financial assistance to help defray the upfront costs

---

[41] Kristina A. Murchison. "Guide Dogs in Medieval Art and Writing." Blog at https://kristamurchison.com/medieval-guide-dogs/. Accessed February 23, 2023.

[42] For an overview, see Mark Ostermeier. "History of Guide Dog Use by Veterans." *Military Medicine* 175, no. 8 (2010): 587–593.

[43] Abraham D. Flaxman, John S. Wittenborn, Toshana Robalik, Rohit Gulia, Robert B. Gerzoff, Elizabeth A. Lundeen, Jinan Saaddine et al. "Prevalence of Visual Acuity Loss or Blindness in the US: A Bayesian Meta-analysis." *JAMA Ophthalmology* 139, no. 7 (2021): 717–723.

[44] Assistance Dogs International, an organization of nonprofits that promote the use of guide dogs by the blind, reports that its member organizations in the United States and Canada supported about 7 thousand teams. www.assistancedogsinternational.org/members/member-program-statistics/. Accessed February 16, 2023. The International Guide Dog Federation, which includes commercial as well as nonprofit guide dog suppliers, reports that its members worldwide facilitated about 23 thousand guide dog teams. www.igdf.org.uk/about-us/facts-and-figures/. Accessed February 16, 2023.

of guide dogs; these costs represent real opportunity costs, that is, costs that must be borne by someone in society. The ability of nonprofits to provide financial assistance and subsidization is not the only benefit that these organizations provide. Even putatively nonprofit dog markets present a risk of misrepresentation and fraud. Established organizations with good reputations offer some protection against scams because they have a strong incentive to preserve and enhance their reputations by advancing the interests of their clients.

From the perspective of economic efficiency, we focus on the net social costs of a proposed or existing policy or program. Offsetting upfront costs, one of the potential benefits is actually an avoided cost: lower costs of care from humans that would otherwise be required. How should we think about this trade-off from an economic perspective? We could ask whether a guide dog is as valuable to the visually impaired as an empathetic, full-time companion or, maintaining our working orientation, a team of paid employees that are available 24/7. If the visually impaired person and society were prepared to totally ignore the costs, many, perhaps most, would prefer human employees to provide 24/7 coverage. (We know, we know, some would still take the guide dog!) However, round-the-clock care is prohibitively expensive, so the blind typically must rely on quite limited amounts of paid human assistance. A guide dog may not be as valuable as having a full-time employee, but however costly the training, it is likely less costly than the human alternative. We hope we have lured you into considering whether guide dogs may offer a comparative advantage rather than absolute advantage over human assistance in some situations. What are the relative costs and benefits of substituting canine for human labor for a typical blind person?

Kathleen Wirth and David Rein assess some of the economic costs and benefits of guide dogs for the blind.[45] Because they do not assess all costs and benefits, it could also be considered a cost-effective analysis. Their analysis does provide some important insights into why more blind people do not team up with guide dogs. Fortunately for our purposes, it also offers an opportunity to illustrate four important considerations in using cost–benefit analysis to assess economic efficiency. First, in most social and health policy applications, like the provision of guide dogs, the most important benefits of proposals are often avoided costs. Second, predicting all the relevant impacts and appropriately monetizing them

---

[45] Kathleen E. Wirth and David B. Rein. "The Economic Costs and Benefits of Dog Guides for the Blind." *Ophthalmic Epidemiology* 15, no. 2 (2008): 92–98.

is challenging and almost always requires piecing together information from a variety of sources. Third, impacts are often realized over time so that discounting future costs and benefits is required. Fourth, in social policy arenas, equity is usually as important as efficiency. As disability policy explicitly addresses equity in access to social, economic, and political lives, assessing programs to expand the use of guide and other service dogs should not be conducted in terms of only efficiency. The following description of the Wirth and Rein analysis reports their estimates relevant to efficiency, updated to 2022 dollars.[46]

Guide teams require dogs. Prior to training teams as a unit, dogs with the appropriate temperaments must be raised from puppies and trained to be obedient. The U.S. industry consists primarily of nonprofit schools that rely on donations and also on fostering that is often provided by volunteers.[47] The schools generally breed their own puppies using females that typically live with foster families when not breeding. Larger schools have their own nurseries for whelping and weaning puppies, but smaller schools often also rely on foster homes for the initial care of puppies. Once puppies have been weaned, they live with foster families that socialize them according to an established routine and are encouraged to expose them to a wide range of everyday experiences. The next level of training usually begins at 15 months, sometimes with the dog continuing to live in the foster home. About half of puppies make it through the process to eventually train as a team with a blind person. The family of one of your authors has fostered three candidate guide dogs, as well as working with two females (Eileen and Tazzy), used in breeding, and several of their broods. Two of the three guide candidates eventually became guides, but the third dog, Zephyr, had too much self-concern, especially about food, to make it to the next step of guide training. Zephyr, the ham thief mentioned in Chapter 2, was adopted by a widow whose spouse had recently died. He went on to live a very happy, normal dog's life without an occupation.

Wirth and Rein estimated the expenses related to breeding, veterinary care, and food, as well as the paid time of staff trainers required to prepare a dog for joining a team to be about $48,600. They did not impute

[46] Wirth and Rein report their estimates of costs and benefits in 2006 dollars. We update them to 2022 dollars using the consumer price index factor of 1.39 to account for general inflation based on the Bureau of Labor Statistics CPI Calculator. www.bls.gov/data/inflation_calculator.htm. Accessed February 16, 2023.

[47] For example, the nonprofit Guide Dogs for the Blind has been training guide dogs in the United States since 1942. www.guidedogs.com/. Accessed February 23, 2023.

a cost to volunteer time, which implicitly assumes that these costs were offset by the value of the experience to the volunteers.[48] Taking account of the fraction of the blind that are employed, they estimated the average lost wages per participant during team training to be about $800. Therefore, they estimated the total direct economic cost of fielding a team to be $49,400.

The cost of fielding a team is an upfront investment that will involve maintenance costs and produce benefits each year over the working life of the dog, which Wirth and Rein assumed would be 8 years. The maintenance costs were assumed to be $970 per year. The annual benefits were assumed to result from a reduction in the average annual cost of paid assistance, $4,300, and unpaid assistance, $1,600.[49] The guide dog was assumed to reduce paid assistance and informal care by 48 percent and 40 percent in the first year, respectively, and by 76 percent and 67 percent in each of the remaining 7 years, respectively.[50] The net benefit that they estimated accrued in each of the 8 years following the fielding of the team was the difference between the reductions in paid assistance and informal care (the benefits) and the maintenance cost.

The timing of the costs and benefits of a guide team has the usual pattern of a classic investment project: high upfront costs that subsequently produce positive net benefits in each of a number of subsequent years. Assessing the economic efficiency of an investment project must take account of the lower value that people, and therefore society, place on future relative to current costs and benefits. From the perspective of consumption, would you rather have an additional $100

[48] Appropriately valuing volunteer time is complicated. On the one hand, it has an opportunity cost. On the other hand, in most situations volunteering really is voluntary, implying that the volunteer is receiving offsetting benefit. See Aidan R. Vining and David L. Weimer. "An Assessment of Important Issues Concerning the Application of Benefit-Cost Analysis to Social Policy." *Journal of Benefit–Cost Analysis* 1, no.1 (2010): 1–38. If an opportunity cost is assigned to volunteer time, it most likely would be valued in terms of the value of lost leisure. John Posnett and Stephen Jan. "Indirect Cost in Economic Evaluation: The Opportunity Cost of Unpaid Inputs." *Health Economics* 5, no. 1 (1996): 13–23.

[49] Kevin D. Frick, Emily W. Gower, John H. Kempen, and Jennifer L. Wolff. "Economic Impact of Visual Impairment and Blindness in the United States." *Archives of Ophthalmology* 125, no. 4 (2007): 544–550.

[50] Unfortunately, estimates of these reductions were not available for guide dogs. Instead, Wirth and Rein had to rely on a study that assessed reductions for other service dogs. Karen Allen and Jim Blascovich. "The Value of Service Dogs for People with Severe Ambulatory Disabilities: A Randomized Controlled Trial." *JAMA* 275, no. 13 (1996): 1001–1006.

today or $100 a year from now? Most people prefer immediate consumption that could be financed by the additional money rather than the consumption that could be financed with it a year from now. From the perspective of investment, if there were a preference for greater consumption a year from now, then putting the $100 in a bank for a year and then spending it with the accumulated interest would provide more consumption that waiting a year to receive the $100. Note that this preference for consumption sooner rather than latter does not depend on inflation. Indeed, in cost–benefit analysis costs and benefits are normally projected in real dollars that have the same purchasing power over time. Wirth and Rein predicted future costs and benefits in real dollars by using the then current prices in projecting costs and benefits over the 8 years of service.

Cost–benefit analysis takes account of this time preference by discounting costs and benefits that accrue in the future in order to calculate the present value of a project. The present value can be thought of as the amount of current consumption that could be obtained by borrowing against all future net benefits. To calculate a present value, costs or benefits that accrues T years in the future are discounted by $1 / (1 + d)^T$ where d is the real discount rate.[51] For projects with mostly upfront costs, like guide teams, a higher discount rate reduces the present value. Wirth and Rein used a reasonable real discount rate of 3 percent that resulted in a net present value of negative $26,400. That is, in terms of the costs and benefits that they monetized, a guide team would incur an excess of costs over benefits of this amount.[52] They divide this amount by eight to obtain a net annual cost of $3,300. A more appropriate annualization, introduced in Chapter 5, divides the net present value by an annuity factor based on the discount rate and project length of 8 years, yields an annualized cost of $3,800.

---

[51] The choice of the social discount rate is one of the most controversial issues in cost–benefit analysis because it can dramatically change the net present values of projects with long time horizons. See Mark A. Moore, Anthony E. Boardman, Aidan R. Vining, David L. Weimer, and David H. Greenberg. "'Just Give Me a Number!' Practical Values for the Social Discount Rate." *Journal of Policy Analysis and Management* 23, no. 4 (2004): 789–812.

[52] Wirth and Rein used the common practice of discounting annual amounts as if they accrued at the end of the year. For costs or benefits that accrue over the course of the year, it is more appropriate to discount mid-year. For example, instead of discounting the net benefits for year three by $1 / (1 + d)^3$, it would be more appropriate to discount the year three net benefits by $1 / (1 + d)^{2.5}$. Such mid-year discounting would reduce the net present value of costs by about $300.

If we consider only those costs and benefits included in the analysis, the cost–benefit analysis indicates that guide teams are not an economically efficient investment! Also, if the blind participant has to pay the full up-front costs, then the analysis predicts that he or she would not want to be part of a guide team because it would involve significant net costs over the 8 years. However, with a subsidy of about 55 percent of the upfront costs, the blind participant would financially break even. As most of the nonprofit suppliers of guide dogs offer donation-supported subsidies to cover all or most of the upfront costs, it is not surprising that there generally are waiting lists for dogs.

Even if we adopt a strictly economic efficiency perspective, Wirth and Rein may have underestimated the value of the reduction in formal care costs resulting from having a guide dog. The average wage of home care aides provides a good starting point for a *shadow price* to monetize hours saved. However, there are also costs associated with arranging for that care, which would be avoided by those for whom the guide dog eliminated the need for formal care. They selected the average wage of home care aides as the shadow price for informal care as well. A more common shadow pricing would be to use the mean wage and fringe benefits for the given population. Using such a shadow price would more than double their estimate of the benefits of the avoided costs of informal care.

The validity of any assessment of economic efficiency using a cost–benefit analysis requires that all the relevant impacts be monetized and included in the calculation of net benefits. As Wirth and Rein acknowledged, their analysis leaves out one very important potential impact: an improved quality of life for the blind member of the team. Surveys generally support the expectation of positive quality-of-life impacts from guide dogs. Particularly informative are two studies from the United Kingdom that directly addressed the quality-of-life impacts of guide dogs. The first study compared cohorts of visually impaired with and without guide dogs and reported quality-of-life benefits including greater independence and confidence, improved social interaction, and increased mobility for those in guide teams.[53] However, this study also found that almost a third of respondents currently in guide teams saw the responsibility of caring for their dogs as a drawback. A second study is a longitudinal study that compares those who stayed on the waiting list to join guide teams, those who did join teams, and those who continued to be in teams at a baseline

[53] Lorraine Whitmarsh. "The Benefits of Guide Dog Ownership." *Visual Impairment Research* 7, no. 1 (2005): 27–42.

and six months later. This study did find an increase in reported independence for those who joined a team.[54] Overall, both studies suggest there are net positive impacts for most of the blind that are part of guide teams.

We are currently unable to find any studies that attempt to monetize these impacts. One approach would be to use the value of dog life-year laid out in Chapter 5. If one used that value, it would offset about two-thirds of the annual net cost that Wirth and Rein estimated. This value, however, derives from dogs that function as pets rather than as guides. Therefore, it almost certainly underestimates the net value of the impacts that guide teams provide. Indeed, a study from Sweden estimates that physical service and diabetes-alert dogs offer both financial and quality-of-life gains over companion dogs.[55]

What would be the best way to attempt to monetize any expected quality of life gains in a more comprehensive cost–benefit analysis of guide dogs? A more comprehensive analysis might well use the quality-adjusted life year (QALY) concept that we introduced in the last chapter. The QALY is a utility scale that assigns a value of 0 to death and a value of 1 to perfect health. Various levels of imperfect health fall along a spectrum between the two end values. We would estimate the annual impact as the difference in the QALY with and without a guide dog. Finally, we would monetize this change by multiplying it by a value of an appropriate statistical life year (VSLY) for a blind person.

How would we get some credible numbers? Surveys of appropriate samples of individuals elicit QALY utilities through risk and time trade-offs.[56] In the application at hand, the appropriate sample would be people who are blind. An appropriate sample depends on whether the impact results in a healthy person moving to the less than fully healthy state or someone in the less than healthy state moving to perfect health. Those being asked to consider moving from perfect health to a lower health state generally place a lower utility on the health state than those who are moving from that health state to the perfect health state. One possible

---

[54] Sara McIver, Sophie Hall, and Daniel S. Mills. "The Impact of Owning a Guide Dog on Owners' Quality of Life: A Longitudinal Study." *Anthrozoös* 33, no. 1 (2020): 103–117.

[55] Martina Lundqvist, Jenny Alwin, and Lars-Åke Levin. "Certified Service Dogs – A Cost-Effectiveness Analysis Appraisal." *PLoS One* 14, no. 9 (2019): 1–13 and Martina Lundqvist, Lars-Åke Levin, Kerstin Roback, and Jenny Alwin. "The Impact of Service and Hearing Dogs on Health-Related Quality of Life and Activity Level: A Swedish Longitudinal Intervention Study." *BMC Health Services Research* 18 (2018): 1–9.

[56] For an overview, see Anthony E. Boardman, David H. Greenberg, Aidan R. Vining, and David L. Weimer. *Cost-Benefit Analysis: Concepts and Practice*, 5th ed. (New York, NY: Cambridge University Press, 2018), Chapter 18.

explanation is that those living in any (imperfect) health state learn to adjust to it. An alternative explanation is that it is a manifestation of the endowment effect. This bias is quite common: many people place greater weight on losses than gains.

The risk-based approach for finding utilities to create QALYs is the standard gamble (SG) method, which asks respondents to compare a specified health state to a lottery with two "prizes." One prize is perfect health and the other prize is death! (It does remind one of Monty Python's grim reaper.) A utility is then assigned to the health state equal to the probability of perfect health, that makes a respondent indifferent to the health condition or the lottery.

The time-based approach, the time trade-off (TTO) method, asks respondents to indicate how many years of perfect health would make them indifferent to some longer number of years of life with the health state being valued. A utility is assigned to the health state equal to the ratio of the number of years of perfect health to the longer number of years in the health status. When done well, these methods tend to produce similar utilities for health states.[57] Unfortunately, doing the SG or TTO method well is very costly. As a shortcut, utilities from these studies are usually statistically related to a variety of health dimensions, such as cognition, ambulation, vision, hearing, speech, dexterity, and emotion. The weights for these dimensions can sometimes provide a reasonable estimate of the change in utility from changes along these dimensions.[58]

The medical literature provides a number of estimates of the disutility of blindness.[59] These estimates, on average, are around 0.70.[60] That is, a QALY for living one year with blindness is only about 70 percent of the value of living a year in perfect health. As only a low percentage of the blind are in guide dog teams, we could take this estimate as representing a plausible estimate of their QALY. If joining a guide team does represent

[57] For example, see Bernt Kartman, Gudrun Gatz, and Magnus Johannesson, "Health State Utilities in Gastroesophageal Reflux Disease Patients with Heartburn: A Study in Germany and Sweden." *Medical Decision Making* 24, no. 1 (2004): 40–50.

[58] The comparisons provided by Kartman et al. suggest that this method tends to provide lower utilities for health states than the SG and TTO methods.

[59] Edith Poku, John Brazier, Jill Carlton, and Alberto Ferreira. "Health State Utilities in Patients with Diabetic Retinopathy, Diabetic Macular Oedema and Age-related Macular Degeneration: A Systematic Review." *BMC Ophthalmology* 13 (2013): 1–13.

[60] For example, a recent study assumed a value of 0.69 for the utility of blindness. Sandeep Vijan, Timothy P. Hofer, and Rodney A. Hayward. "Cost-Utility Analysis of Screening Intervals for Diabetic Retinopathy in Patients with Type 2 Diabetes Mellitus." *JAMA* 283, no. 7 (2000): 889–896.

a net positive impact on the quality of life of the blind person, then an increase in their QALY would result from teaming, so that each year over the working life of the dog there would be a quality of life gain equal to the QALY difference.

The most common approach to monetizing the QALY gain is to multiply it by the value of a statistical life-year (VSLY), which, as discussed in Chapter 5, is related to the value of statistical life (VSL) for the selected population. The Food and Drug Administration currently uses an estimate of approximately $400 thousand for someone from the general population, implicitly with the U.S. median income.[61] However, because blind persons tend to have lower incomes than the general population, $400 thousand is almost certainly too large a value for the economic shadow price based on people's own willingness to pay to reduce mortality risk. A rough adjustment that would produce a conservative estimate of the VSLY for blind person would adjust the population estimate based on a median U.S. individual income in 2022 of $54,132 and a minimum income for blind individuals of $27,120 in that year from the federal SSI program. Doing so using an income elasticity of 0.6 for willingness to pay for risk reduction yields an estimate of about $265 thousand for the VSLY estimate for a blind person.[62] (We fully understand an initial rejection of the idea that an additional life year for one person should be valued differently than for another person. Yet we remind readers that this adjustment is consistent with valuations people implicitly make in their own trade-offs between mortality risk and money. Nonetheless, we agree that there are usually relevant values in addition to economic efficiency, usually related to equity or fairness, that should also be considered.)

Without an estimate of the QALY increase from being in a guide team, we cannot directly apply the VSLY. Instead, we can ask how large a gain would be needed to offset the annualized loss of $3,800? This answer can be calculated as the ratio of $3,800 to the VSLY, which is about 0.014. Thus, a very plausible increase in the QALY from 0.70 to 0.72 would more than offset the annualized loss, so that net benefits would be positive. Further, the blind member of the team may also get a companionship benefit beyond the direct quality of life gains. As estimated in Chapter 5, this VDLY would be on the order of $2,400, which would

---

[61] W. Kip Viscusi. *Pricing Lives: Guideposts for a Safer Society* (Princeton, NJ: Princeton University Press, 2018), 106.

[62] James K. Hammitt and Lisa A. Robinson. "The Income Elasticity of the Value per Statistical Life: Transferring Estimates between High and Low Income Populations." *Journal of Benefit-Cost Analysis* 2, no. 1 (2011): 1–27.

reduce the annualized loss so that an even smaller QALY gain would be needed. Thus, monetizing quality of life would very likely result in positive net benefits, so that we would conclude that investment in guide dogs is economically efficient.

As we have noted, any application of cost–benefit analysis to guide dogs involves many uncertainties. Good practice requires that the reported estimate of net benefits take account of these uncertainties. Worth and Rein provided traditional sensitivity analysis, where they reported net benefits using a number of alternative assumptions. Monte Carlo simulation, which we believe to be a preferable approach, would specify distributions for uncertain values and repeat the analysis many times with randomly drawn values from them to predict a distribution of net benefits.[63]

7.6 REGULATING EMOTIONAL SUPPORT ANIMAL ACCESS TO FREE AIR TRAVEL

The Air Carrier Access Act of 1986 (P.L. 99–435) prohibits airlines that operate within the United States from engaging in discrimination against persons with disabilities. The rules that the Department of Transportation (DOT) issued to implement its provisions required airlines to make "reasonable accommodations" for service animals that assist passengers with disabilities. Although airlines can and do require passengers to pay a fee for accompanying pets, they cannot charge a fee for service animals. This price difference creates an incentive for passengers to claim that pets are actually service animals. Prior to 2020, emotional support animals (ESAs) qualified as service animals. Not surprisingly, the number of ESAs on flights ballooned over the last decade, prompting calls from the airlines and some advocacy groups representing the disabled for a clearer definition of service animals. In December 2020, the DOT finalized major changes to its rules that defined more narrowly the service animals that must be accommodated by airlines.[64]

The guidance that the DOT provided for airlines in 2003 set the stage for widespread claims by passengers that their accompanying pets were ESAs.[65] That guidance listed animals that are trained to respond to

[63] Boardman et al., Chapter 11.
[64] Department of Transportation. "Final Rule: Travelling by Air with Service Animals." *Federal Register* 85, no. 238 (2020): 79742–79766.
[65] Department of Transportation. "Guidance Concerning Service Animals in Air Transportation." *Federal Register* 68, no. 90 (2003): 24874–24878.

panic attacks and extreme social anxiety as counting as legitimate service animals. However, the guidance did not require any documentation to support the claim that an animal was trained to provide a service to a disabled person. Instead, the guidance indicated to airlines that they should rely on statements by passengers, which could be supported by the presence of physical indicators, such as "harnesses, vests, capes, or backpacks," that are often used by service animals (p. 24876). Internet vendors quickly began to offer these items with no questions asked. This obviously enabled airline passengers to use them to bolster their claims that their pets were emotional support animals. In response to growing concerns that pets were being misclassified as ESAs, in 2008 the DOT issued enforcement guidance clarifying that airlines could request documentation of medical conditions requiring ESAs or psychiatric service animals (PSAs). Airlines could request this documentation as much as 48 hours in advance of flights.[66] However, the airlines had difficulty implementing this provision; it was especially difficult for them to assess the validity of the documentation of the need for ESAs, which became increasingly available from online providers. Advocates for psychiatric service dogs, which receive training that is more comparable to that of other service dogs in intensity, objected to them being put in the same regulatory category as ESAs.

The variety of animal species that advocates claim are able to provide emotional support has also increased over the last decade. By far the most common emotional support animal claims are for dogs, but passengers have also claimed cats, miniature horses, and capuchin monkeys, among other species, to be ESAs. Media reports of more exotic animals that were claimed to be emotional support animals gained public attention and stoked concern that an epidemic of fake service animals was emerging.[67] For example, one flight was substantially delayed when passengers had to deplane while the crew dealt with an emotional support squirrel.[68] Airlines were given explicit authority in the 2003 guidance to exclude snakes, reptiles, ferrets, rodents, and spiders from ESA designation; they

---

[66] Department of Transportation. "Guidance Concerning Service Animals." *Federal Register* 73, no. 93 (2008): 27614–27687.

[67] News reports of a few exceptional cases may have created the public impression that emotional support animals posed a more serious problem than was actually the case. John Sorenson and Atsuko Matsuoka. "Moral Panic over Fake Service Animals." *Social Sciences* 11, no. 10 (2022): 439–458.

[68] Lindsey Bever. "A Woman Brought Her 'Emotional Support' Squirrel on a Plane. Frontier Wouldn't Let It Fly." *Washington Post*, October 10 (2018).

could exclude other exotic animals on a case-by-case basis if the airlines believed they pose either a significant threat of disruption of service or a direct threat to health or safety.

Airlines and disability groups were also concerned that some passengers were being accompanied by poorly trained dogs that were serving as ESAs. There were media reports of passengers, including children and flight attendants, being bitten by ESA dogs, both in flight and in airport terminals.[69] Flight attendants sometimes had to clean up after dogs that urinated or defecated during flights. The service dogs of disabled persons have sometimes been attacked in terminals and during flights by ESA dogs. Unlike the case with more exotic ESAs, airlines found it virtually impossible to determine through verbal communication with potential passengers if their dogs would be likely to cause problems. Consequently, they were unable to identify "bad dogs" (well, bad ESAs) to exclude under the 2003 guidance, especially as fraudulent ESA claims were supported by documentation that had been obtained from online vendors for effectively just a fee.

7.6.1 DOT Rulemaking

In response to these concerns, in 2018, the DOT published an advanced notice of proposed rulemaking to solicit comments on possible approaches to addressing the various concerns about service animals traveling on flights.[70] The notice summarized the recommendations that the ACCESS Advisory Committee had submitted. This committee consisted of a group of stakeholders and experts that DOT convened in 2016 to provide advice about service animals.[71] DOT also reported on comments it had received from various other stakeholders on a number of

---

[69] Kristine Phillips. "A Little Girl Saw an Emotional-Support Dog on a Plane. It Went for Her Face." *Washington Post*, February 22 (2018).

[70] Department of Transportation. "Advanced Notice of Proposed Rulemaking: Traveling by Air with Service Animals." *Federal Register* 83, no. 100 (2018): 23832–23842.

[71] The ACCESS Advisory Committee was an attempt by DOT to engage stakeholders formally in the development of the content of rules governing the use of service animals on airlines. It was an attempt to use a process called negotiated rulemaking that seeks agreement among stakeholders on rule content to avoid subsequent legal challenges. As the committee did not reach consensus, the DOT resorted to the standard notice and comment procedure in which it develops the content of the rules. On negotiated rulemaking, see Laura I. Langbein and Cornelius M. Kerwin. "Regulatory Negotiation versus Conventional Rule Making: Claims, Counter Claims, and Empirical Evidence." *Journal of Public Administration Research and Theory* 10, no. 3 (2000): 599–632.

topics, including the status of ESAs and PSAs, service animal documentation, and allowed species. It requested comments on these topics as well as on several other topics, including the number of service animals per passenger that should be permitted, whether there should be size limits for service animals, and whether airlines can require passengers to provide veterinary forms attesting that their service animals are healthy and capable of appropriate behavior.

The DOT received over 4,500 responses to its request for comments. At the same time, Congress was also receiving comments from airlines and disability advocates about the need for greater clarity in the rules governing the use of service animals on flights. As a result, the FAA Reauthorization Act of 2018 (P.L. 115–254) directed the DOT to issue revised rules that define service animals and prevent passengers from claiming service animal status for pets. In response, the DOT proposed amended rules in February 2020.[72]

Among the proposed provisions, there are three that are most relevant to service dogs. First, dogs got the job! The DOT proposed that dogs would be the only species of service animal that airlines were required to accommodate without charge. Further, airlines could not exclude a dog from service animal designation solely on the basis of breed. Several organizations that represented airlines strongly advocated for a unique recognition of the dog's capabilities: "dogs in particular can hold their elimination functions for extended amounts of time, have the correct temperament to serve as service animals, and can be trained to behave appropriately in public and around large groups of people" (p. 6453). Miniature horses were excluded because of their relatively large size and inflexibility, which makes it difficult to seat them near their disabled owners. Although capuchin monkeys can be very effective in assisting the disabled in the tasks of daily living, they can transmit disease and unexpectedly exhibit aggressive behavior. Cats and rabbits were excluded because of the limited extent to which they can (or will!) be trained.

Second, the DOT proposed "to define a service animal as a dog that is individually trained to do work or perform tasks for the benefit of a qualified individual with a disability" (p. 6458). This definition excludes ESAs from being included in the service animal category. This restriction was a high priority for the airlines, which had expressed concerns about both fraud and harm (negative externalities) from poorly trained dogs.

---

[72] Department of Transportation. "Notice of Proposed Rulemaking: Traveling by Air with Service Animals." *Federal Register* 85, no. 24 (2020): 6448–6476.

The revised classification would, however, include PSAs, and so would remove the separate requirements that they shared with ESAs. As we discuss below, the exclusion of ESAs from service animal status was the focus of the economic analysis supporting the rule.

Third, DOT proposed to standardize the documentation that airlines could request. Airlines could "require individuals traveling with a service animal to provide to the airlines standardized documentation of the service animal's behavior, training, and health. Also, if the service animal would be on a flight segment that is longer than 8 hours, the Department is proposing to allow a standard form attesting that the animal will not need to relieve itself or can relieve itself in a way that does not create a health or sanitation risk" (p. 6464). The standardized forms would impose additional costs on passengers with service animals. However, standardization would reduce the burden on passengers and airlines somewhat. Additionally, the form required the following attestation: "I am signing an official document of the U.S. Department of Transportation. My answers are true to the best of my knowledge. I understand that if I knowingly make false statements on this document, I can be subject to fines and other penalties (p. 6466)." This attestation requirement was expected to significantly reduce fraud.

The proposed rule received about 14,600 comments from individuals as well as 70 comments from stakeholder organizations.[73] About two-thirds of the comments from individuals concerned ESAs, with a majority opposing the exclusion of ESAs from the service animal definition. However, the airline industry and associations representing airline employees expressed strong support for the exclusion. Disability advocacy organizations were divided and lined up on both sides. Organizations whose members relied on guide and hearing dogs generally supported the exclusion, while organizations representing veterans and people with autism generally opposed it. The final rule kept the ESA exclusion as well as the provisions that recognized dogs' exclusive role and allowed airlines to request documentation through standardized forms.

7.6.2 Economic Analysis of DOT Rules

As we discuss in Chapter 5, federal agencies must justify major rules with regulatory impact analyses that include estimates of costs, benefits, and transfers. The proposed service animal rules would potentially have

---

[73] Department of Transportation. "Final Rule: Traveling by Air With Service Animals."

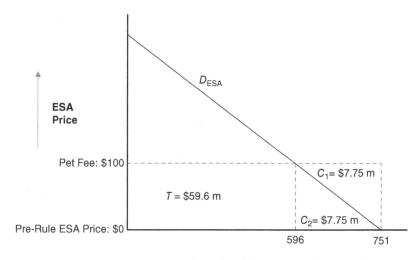

FIGURE 7.2 Annual costs and benefits of ESA exclusion
Source: Based on information provided by the Office of General Counsel,
Department of Transportation. "Traveling by Air with Service Animals
Regulatory Impact Analysis RIN 2105-AE63." November (2020).

impacts that qualified them as a major rulemaking. Consequently, the
DOT's Office of the General Counsel prepared a cost–benefit analysis to
support their issuance.[74]

The DOT analysis focused on the costs and benefits in the market
for ESA travel. Figure 7.2 summarizes the most important factors. The
demand schedule for ESAs is shown as D_{ESA}. Each point on D_{ESA} indicates the number of ESA flights demanded annually at each price. As passengers did not have to pay to travel with their ESAs prior to the service
animal rule, the quantity demanded occurs where the demand schedule
intersects the horizontal axis, indicating the zero price. The analysis fixed
this point using data from 2017 at 751 thousand flights per year. (By
comparison, in 2017, there were only 281 thousand flights made with
service animals and 784 thousand flights made with pets.)

The next step in the analysis was to predict the quantity of ESAs
that would be demanded if passengers had to pay the pet fee to travel
with them. Based on a review of existing pet fees, for the purposes of

---

[74] Office of General Counsel, Department of Transportation. "Traveling by Air with Service Animals Regulatory Impact Analysis RIN 2105-AE63." November (2020).

the analysis, it was assumed that the fee would be $100 per ESA flight. Determining the quantity of ESA flights demanded at this price requires an assumption about the slope of the demand schedule. Ideally, a price elasticity of demand for traveling with either pets or ESAs would be available in the empirical economic literature. Unfortunately, there were no elasticity estimates available. As an expedient substitute, the analysis assumed that the price elasticity of demand for traveling with pets could be reasonably approximated based on the price elasticity of demand for a similar good or service. In this case, the analysis assumed that reasonable approximations would be the price elasticities of demand for medical services, including mental health and substance abuse treatment. These elasticities broadly fall in the range of –0.26 to –0.39. As a reminder, the –0.26 elasticity indicates that for each 1-percent increase in price, the quantity demanded will fall by 0.26 percent.

The analysis assumed a linear demand schedule. Because the price elasticity of demand is different at each point on the linear demand schedule, the analysis had to specify at which point on the demand schedule the elasticity applied. It assumed that the elasticity applied to the point on the demand schedule that corresponds to the pet fee of $100. Figure 7.2 shows the predicted quantity demanded of 596 thousand for the price elasticity of demand of –0.26. (The price elasticity of demand of –0.39 produces a prediction of 540 thousand.)

To estimate costs, benefits, and *transfers* from treating ESAs just like pets, the analysis assumed that the $100 pet fee represents the real resources that an airline has to expend to accommodate a pet. That is, the analysis assumes a constant marginal cost of $100. Reducing the quantity of ESA flights demanded from 751 thousand flights to 596 thousand flights is a benefit as it represents avoided costs. This benefit is shown in Figure 7.2 as the area of $C_1 + C_2$, which equals $15.5 million per year. However, consumers lose value (consumer surplus) from this reduction in the number of ESA flights, as shown by the area under the demand schedule from 596 thousand to 751 thousand flights, or the area of C_2, which equals $7.75 million per year. Netting these out results in a net social gain in this market of C_1, or, again, $7.75 million per year. A similar analysis instead using the –0.39 elasticity produced a net social gain of $13.3 million per year. The overall analysis included an additional paperwork cost of $1.3 million, yielding rounded positive net benefits of between $3.7 million and $12.5 million annually. Thus, the analysis suggests that the proposed ESA rules would be economically efficient.

These estimated costs and benefits, however, would be dwarfed by the magnitude of the annual transfer from ESA travelers to airlines. This is shown as the area of rectangle T in Figure 7.2 and is equal to $59.6 million. This amount is a transfer and not relevant to an assessment of economic efficiency because, although it captures the shift in costs from airlines to travelers, it does not change the magnitude of the cost to society of supplying the inframarginal ESA flights, those that continue to be supplied after the implementation of the rule.[75]

The analysis also discussed several possibly excluded costs and benefits. Of most relevance, the analysis pointed out that there may be costs of ESA travel borne by other passengers, including the disabled with service dogs, beyond the costs borne directly by airlines. Thus, there may be a negative externality in this market. It would be represented by a social marginal cost curve that lies about the pet fee line. Of course, there may also be positive externalities realized by those who are fond of dogs and relish observing and interacting with them in the terminal, if not in the plane cabin. In any event, the analysis did not attempt to estimate these externalities or their net impact.

7.6.3 Postscript: ESA Issues on the Homefront

The DOT definition of service animals addressed the problem of fliers avoiding paying pet fees by claiming that their pets are ESAs. A similar issue is currently being played out with respect to housing. Under Department of Housing and Urban Development rules, landlords cannot exclude or charge fees for an ESA, as long as the tenant documents the need for the animal. This creates an incentive for tenants to obtain ESA documentation for pets, which is available from the same sources that provided it fraudulently to airline passengers. A number of states are attempting to cut down on questionable ESA claims. For example, California now requires that mental health practitioners who prescribe ESAs must have at least a 30-day relationship with the client and makes it clear that ESAs are not service dogs and therefore can be banned from restaurants and stores.[76]

---

[75] Recognizing that efficiency is usually measured in triangles and transfers are usually measured in rectangles, the political economy quip for why we often fail to adopt policies that are economically efficient is that rectangles tend to be larger than triangles!

[76] Elaine S. Povich. "States Struggle to Curb Fake Emotional Support Animals." *PEW Stateline*, November 4 (2022). www.pewtrusts.org/en/research-and-analysis/blogs/stateline/2022/11/04/states-struggle-to-curb-fake-emotional-support-animals. Accessed February 22, 2023.

7.7 THE WORKERS' PERSPECTIVE

Although we might imagine that some dogs reject recruitment into an occupation by displaying incompatible traits during selection or failing to progress through training, they really do not choose occupations. Rather, people recruit them into occupations, many of which severely restrict their agency relative to being pets. How does this loss of agency affect the welfare of working dogs?

Ethicists have sought to answer this question by considering how working impacts dogs in five domains: nutrition, environment, behavioral interaction, physical health, and mental state.[77] Concerns can be raised about the adverse effects of employment in each of these domains. For example, low-income people who team with service dogs may have difficulty providing adequate nutrition and veterinary care relevant to their dogs' physical health.[78] People with psychological disabilities may not be able to provide consistent care of their dogs. Dogs working in outdoor environments can suffer from heat exhaustion if not properly hydrated and rested. Across most occupations, working dogs have little control over when they can rest, eat, and relieve themselves, as well as the permissible interactions with other dogs and people. These losses of control that can result in stress that negatively affects their mental state.[79] Dogs whose mental state is positively affected by their work and attachment to their human partners likely suffer loss when they become unemployed because of their age or the death or institutionalization of their partners.

These ethical concerns about the wellbeing of working dogs deserve attention in their own right. Although economics does not directly take account of animal welfare, it does so indirectly through the willingness of people to pay for improvements in animal welfare. We currently see a willingness of people to donate time and money to provide service dogs for those who need them. As societal norms about appropriate treatment of animals change, so too might be the willingness to invest more in

---

[77] David J. Mellor, Ngaio J. Beausoleil, Katherine E. Littlewood, Andrew N. McLean, Paul D. McGreevy, Bidda Jones, and Cristina Wilkins. "The 2020 Five Domains Model: Including Human–Animal Interactions in Assessments of Animal Welfare." *Animals (Basel)* 10, no. 10 (2020): 1–24.

[78] Amanda Salmon, Carlie Driscoll, Mandy B. A. Paterson, Paul Harpur, and Nancy A. Pachana. "Issues Regarding the Welfare of Assistance Dogs." *Animals (Basel)* 12, no. 23 (2022): 1–10.

[79] Mia L. Cobb, Cynthia M. Otto, and Aubrey H. Fine. "The Animal Welfare Science of Working Dogs: Current Perspectives on Recent Advances and Future Directions." *Frontiers in Veterinary Science* 8 (2021): 1–13.

improving the wellbeing of working dogs while they are employed and after they retire.[80] Public policies, such as the bans on dog racing adopted by a majority of states, also affect canine labor and will undoubtedly change in response to changes in social norms.

7.8 CONCLUSION

Dogs can enrich our lives as companions. They can also provide valuable services through a variety of occupations. In this chapter, we provided a classification of canine occupations based on the relative advantage of canine compared to human labor and the investment needed to make dogs reliable workers. These occupations include some that arose early in the human relationship with dogs. They also include some that are relatively recent in human history. Although changes in technology will likely continue to affect the economic viability of canine occupations, the patience of dogs in service to humans and their superior olfactory capabilities will likely keep them employed for years to come.

---

[80] Michael J. Kranzler. "Don't Let Slip the Dogs of War: An Argument for Reclassifying Military Working Dogs as Canine Members of the Armed Forces." *National Security & Armed Conflict Law Review* 4 (2013): 268–294.

8

Dogonomics

Past, Present, and Future

Our purpose in the preceding chapters has been to offer economic perspectives on some of the important questions concerning the relationship between people and dogs. We hope those who share our fondness for dogs but have not thought about dogonomics found it to be an interesting and novel perspective. Beyond that, we hope you have found it to be a thought-provoking perspective when it comes to thinking about canine-related public policy issues that we can all influence as citizens. We also hope that we have persuaded you that economic concepts can help us better understand the explicitly economic decisions that we all face on a daily basis, but also in our social interactions. We look forward to more professional economists joining with veterinary researchers, biologists, anthropologists, archaeologists, and sociologists who are continuously expanding our knowledge about dogs and how they affect our lives and we theirs. We look forward to seeing economists embrace dogonomics as worthy of study.

Rather than presenting economic concepts as complete explanations of social phenomena, our approach has been to use them to help us think more clearly about important aspects of people's relationships with dogs. The statistician George Box famously reminded us that "All models are wrong; some models are useful."[1] We hope we have convinced you that neoclassical economics can be useful in helping us understand the incentives our ancestors faced to continue domestication through artificial selection once it began, whether initiated by people or dogs. We also

---

[1] The "all models are wrong" part of the aphorism first appears in his 1976 tribute to R. A. Fischer and George E. P. Box. "Science and Statistics." *Journal of the American Statistical Association* 71, no. 356 (1976): 791–799.

hope our brief excursion into game theory, although not providing a true representation of interactions between humans and wolves, nonetheless offered some insight into how the domestication process got started.

It should have been relatively easy to convince you that neoclassical economics is useful for understanding the supply of, and demand for, dogs. Relatively straightforward concepts from neoclassical economics are useful for understanding the supply side of the market for dogs and its potential inefficiencies. Concepts from neoclassical economics, along with some from the rapidly growing field of behavioral economics, we argued, help us better understand the demand side.

Beyond supply and demand, assessing the value of economic concepts gets trickier. Existing economic models of the family can be stretched to treat dogs as family members who can be substitutes or complements for children. Theories of property rights offer a framework for thinking more systematically about our responsibilities toward dogs, if not necessarily about why dogs are regarded as regulated commodities in most legal regimes. Despite that status, dogs are sometimes either effectively treated as simple commodities by puppy mills or as quasi-persons by people who make extraordinary efforts to extend the lives of their ill or elderly dogs. It also does not help us understand why dogs have a somewhat different status than cats and why they both differ in status from the animals (some) people eat.

We believe economic perspectives, broadly conceived, are relevant to a number of public policies affecting dogs. Most generally, the estimate of the value of statistical dog life we present in Chapter 5 provides a systematic way for federal and state regulatory agencies to place a value on avoided dog mortality. It does so within the anthropomorphic framework of conventional economics. In other words, policy analysts can monetize the value of reducing mortality risk for dogs solely based on people's willingness to pay for those reductions. Most obviously, this value is useful in formulating rules concerning products, such as food marketed to pet owners for their dogs, that affect canine mortality risk. The value is also germane to laws and regulations affecting the environment we share with dogs, travel with dogs, and medical research using dogs.

Economic perspectives have direct relevance to public policies that affect the supply of dogs. Preventing the inhumane treatment of dogs in puppy mills provides an ethical rationale for regulating them more stringently. As we argue in Chapter 4, however, there are also strong economic rationales for more stringent regulation: information asymmetries and negative externalities make the market for puppies economically inefficient. Unlike many other public policy arenas that involve trade-offs between economic efficiency and other values, preventing abuse by puppy mills potentially offers economic benefits as well as moral value beyond the efficient use of resources.

In Chapter 2, we present an initial economic framing of dogs as jointly consumption goods and productive resources in societies in which they had roles in economic activities like herding or hunting. We return to the working dog in Chapter 7. As society has evolved, so too have canine occupations, especially the services dogs provide to people who are sight- or hearing-impaired or physically or mentally disabled. In some of these occupations, dogs enjoy an absolute or unique advantage over humans, with or without machines. However, drawing on the theory of comparative advantage, we considered how dogs can provide economically useful labor even in some roles that could also be filled by people.

While pet dogs contribute relatively less nowadays to these activities, they help produce another good of value to families: positive (for the most part) social interaction. Walking dogs often facilitates interaction with neighbors in a world where the auto and now the e-bike have reduced interaction. If the focus of the interaction consists of persistent barking, of course, then the interaction will be negative. Yet more often than not, it involves positive encounters largely prompted by the presence of the dog (although we have observed some people walking their cats!). Dog owners typically do share interests around dogs; even nonowners may find the paraded dog attractive, interesting, or even funny in appearance or behavior, and interact with the owner, who is recognized as "Fido's mommy" or "Fido's daddy" – they are no longer just strangers. With about half of U.S. households now possessing dogs, the potential for dogs contributing to positive social interaction is large. Thus, dogs may help ameliorate the social isolation bemoaned by many observers of contemporary society. It may thus be good public policy for local governments to facilitate interaction through conveniently located dog parks and dog-friendly services for the homeless.

In this final chapter, we allow ourselves to contemplate the future of the relationship between people and dogs in the coming decades. Although we retain our economic orientation, we now try to place the relationship within a broader sociopolitical context. To do so, we consider some of the important forces that we think will influence social and, particularly, public policy in the coming decades. In our view, several of these forces are inextricably linked to each other. In this final chapter, we focus on the four we see as most important, although others will also shape the future.

First, and most importantly, we think the continuing evolution of property rights with respect to dogs, has the potential for cumulatively changing expectations about the duties people owe to dogs. Second, and relatedly, flowing from changes in property rights, we expect changes in how governments regulate the relationship between people and dogs at all levels in the United States as well as in many other countries around the world. Put another way: as property rights change, so will the purpose and content of regulation. Third, we expect the continuing growth of dog ownership to encourage the emergence of more active interest group politics around dogs. Fourth, we expect the emergence of canine genetic sequencing and knowledge of specific phenotypic behavior to drive society further toward boutique selection, a step beyond the artificial selection that has driven the evolution of breeds.

8.1 WHAT ARE OUR DUTIES TO DOGS?
EVOLVING PROPERTY RIGHTS

Property rights underlie economic relationships. De jure property rights specify the claims people have to things and the duties others have to respect these claims. De facto property rights supplement or override these formal rights, so that some combination of laws and norms determines the system of property rights that actually shapes the behavior of economic actors. In the United States and most other Western countries, dogs currently have the status of regulated property. Dogs have not always been regulated property, and it is quite possible that they will be endowed by law or norms with some other status in the future.

Our primary focus on dogs in contemporary American society allows us to paint a very positive picture of dogs, consistent with our fondness for them. Some people certainly do not share our fondness, but the public overwhelmingly does, as evidenced by the many households that welcome dogs as if they are family members. Yet it would be misguided to think that this status is immutable. Our Western culture has not always shared the view of dogs as benign beings. Cerberus was a rather unpleasant canine guarding the underworld. During the Middle Ages, dogs were often considered "witch familiars" who were manifestations of the devil or participated in spells.[2] Indeed, consistent with German folklore, the

---

[2] Boria Sax. "The Magic of Animals: English Witch Trials in the Perspective of Folklore." *Anthrozoös* 22, no. 4 (2009): 317–332.

devil took the form of a black poodle in his initial encounter with Faust.[3] We do not know if the fear of demonic dogs faded with the Enlightenment or earlier, but it was only in the nineteenth century that formal property rights began to change to give dogs protection from cruelty.

The property rights of people have certainly changed dramatically over the last two centuries. The abomination of slavery was eliminated, women gained the right to own property and vote, and workers gained protections from extreme exploitation. In view of these dramatic changes in the property rights of people, would it be surprising if property rights affecting dogs changed in the future? We have already seen the shift from dogs being a commodity that owners could dispose of as they see fit to dogs being a regulated commodity that restricts how they can be disposed of by owners. Changing norms often precede de jure changes in property rights. If the status of dogs as family members continues to strengthen, then we might very well see further changes in the de jure property rights relevant to dogs, perhaps even to the point of giving them the status of quasi-personhood. However, changing property rights favoring dogs will also raise a question about what might be called dog exceptionalism: why should dogs be treated differently than other animals?

8.2 LEGAL AND REGULATORY PROTECTION WITH TEETH?

Changing laws and regulations in the United States over the last few decades have largely made de jure property rights more favorable to dogs. However, de facto rights depend on how these changes are implemented. We share Jerry Mitchell's view that the administrative processes relevant to our relationship with animals deserve much more scholarly attention.[4] The future of dogs will be shaped by federal and state laws, rulemaking that gives them content, administrative resources that enforce the rules, and judicial decisions that shape them.

Major changes to public policy through legislation occur infrequently in the United States by design: bicameralism, supermajorities to overcome Senate filibusters, and executive vetoes make lawmaking difficult.[5]

---

[3] Barbara Allen Woods. "The Devil in Dog Form." *Western Folklore* 13, no. 4 (1954): 229–235.
[4] Jerry Mitchell. "Animals in the Study of Public Administration." *Public Administration Review* 82, no. 6 (2022): 1179–1185.
[5] William H. Riker. *Liberalism against Populism* (San Francisco, CA: Freeman, 1982).

Extreme partisanship further impedes legislating, though it is likely that improving the welfare of dogs is truly a bipartisan issue! Major changes in law through legislation generally occur only when exogenous events have opened a "policy window" that focuses both the public and therefore public officials on an issue.[6] The melamine disaster that killed many pet dogs and cats opened a policy window for legislation that empowered the Food and Drug Administration to regulate pet food, essentially giving dog owners, and therefore their dogs, the property right to unadulterated food that had previously been given to people. Unfortunately, major changes in federal laws relevant to the welfare of dogs are unlikely without some disaster that opens another policy window.

Significant policy changes affecting dogs are much more likely at the state level. Although U.S. states also have checks and balances that make legislating difficult, their smaller scale often offers greater access to interests seeking change. Some states have strengthened their laws aimed at preventing the worst abuses of puppy mills, and others have adopted laws promoting the welfare of dogs that have been subjects in medical experiments. Policies adopted by one state often provide a model that diffuses more widely.[7] Although state laws that exercise policy powers preempt local ordinances, including those governing dogs, states often delegate this authority to municipalities or counties.[8] Local governments can sometimes achieve policy change through their adoption of ordinances, and these changes can promote change at the state level. For example, many California municipalities adopted ordinances prohibiting the sale of puppies in pet stores before a ban was adopted at the state level. Although we know of no study that considered the diffusion of dog ordinances among municipalities, studies of other local policies suggest that they can diffuse widely.[9] Consequently, focusing on changing municipal ordinances may sometimes be an effective strategy for those seeking to improve the welfare of dogs.

Laws almost always require government agencies to add substantive content through rulemaking. We examine several examples, including the FDA rules on pet food (in Chapter 5), the Department of Agriculture

---

[6] See John W. Kingdon. *Agendas, Alternatives, and Public Polices* (Boston, MA: Little, Brown, 1984).

[7] For an overview, see Andrew Karch. "Emerging Issues and Future Directions in State Policy Diffusion Research." *State Politics & Policy Quarterly* 7, no. 1 (2007): 54–80.

[8] Michael P. Fix and Joshua L. Mitchell. "Examining the Policy Learning Dynamics of Atypical Policies with an Application to State Preemption of Local Dog Laws." *Statistics, Politics and Policy* 8, no. 2 (2017): 223–247.

[9] Charles R. Shipan and Craig Volden. "The Mechanisms of Policy Diffusion." *American Journal of Political Science* 52, no. 4 (2008): 840–857.

rules on sources and treatment of animals used in research (in Chapter 6), and the Department of Transportation Rules on traveling with emotional support animals (in Chapter 7). Our focus on the economic analysis and implications of these rules should not distract from their inherently political nature.[10] Those seeking to change the property rights relevant to dogs should anticipate the importance of rulemaking after legislative victories, and the possibility of more favorable rulemaking under existing law following legislative defeats.

To be effective, rules must be enforceable. Lax enforcement by the U.S. Department of Agriculture and, in most states, by state departments of agriculture have not eliminated puppy mills that violate federal or state rules. For most of these agencies, the lack of sufficient resources plays a role in lax enforcement by discouraging the frequent and thorough inspections required to find and document violations of rules. There may also be a mismatch between state agency organizational norms and the effective protection of dogs: agricultural departments are typically oriented more to producers and their production than to animal welfare.[11] The more laws and rules give implicit rights to dogs, the more important it will be to question whether departments of agriculture make the best enforcers.

Where statutory law and implementing rules are silent, Anglo-Saxon common law does have the capacity to create property rights relevant to dogs. Some courts have done so by considering the best interests of pets, especially dogs, in determining custody in divorce cases. Precedents influence other courts and sometimes prompt statutory changes.[12] Chapter 5 suggests the possibility that some courts will eventually reject the market value standard in favor of an estimate like the statistical value of dog life in awarding damages in cases involving the wrongful death of pet dogs.

8.3 CHANGING NORMS AND POLITICAL ECONOMY

Norms about how we should treat dogs have evolved over decades and, indeed, centuries and will likely continue to do so. Views that dogs

---

[10] For an overview, see Susan W. Yackee. "The Politics of Rulemaking in the United States." *Annual Review of Political Science* 22 (2019): 37–55.

[11] Kailey A. Burger. "Solving the Problem of Puppy Mills: Why the Animal Welfare Movement's Bark Is Stronger than Its Bite." *Washington University Journal of Law & Policy* 43 (2013): 259–284.

[12] Several states have joined Alaska in requiring judges to consider the best interest of pets in divorce cases. See Carolina Abdullah, April Pacis, and Lisa F. Grumet. "New Family Law Statutes in 2021: Selected State Legislation." *Family Law Quarterly* 55, no. 4 (2021): 475–512.

deserve treatment more akin to family members have grown in recent decades, along with the prevalence of dogs in American homes. This dog exceptionalism is occurring against a backdrop of increasing numbers of people who challenge the exploitation of other species more generally, both in their personal lives by becoming vegetarians or vegans and in their political lives by supporting advocacy groups for animal welfare. How will changing norms affect the political economy of public policies toward dogs?

One of the central concepts of political economy is the recognition of the advantage that *concentrated interests* enjoy over *diffuse interests* in obtaining favorable public policy from representative governments.[13] Concentrated interests, such as industries, have an incentive to bear the costs of lobbying because they anticipate larger individual gains. In contrast, nonorganized individuals that share a diffuse interest, such as consumers, do not have a strong economic incentive to bear the costs of lobbying and monitoring their representatives because, even though the gains from doing so may be very large in aggregate, they are small for any one individual. In terms of market failures, when interests are diffuse, lobbying has the characteristics of a public good that will be undersupplied by voluntary action. Thus, for example, there may be a widespread norm that puppies should not be treated as agricultural commodities, but the commercial puppy breeders have a strong incentive to organize and lobby to maintain the status quo while opposing individuals do not. Or consider the use of dogs in medical research: pharmaceutical companies have a strong economic incentive to lobby to avoid new restrictions, while individuals with no economic interest who believe in greater oversight of this research do not.

It is important to recognize that the political environment and those incentives can sometimes tip the balance in favor of diffuse interests. There are two primary mechanisms. One way is through the development of organizations of people that share an interest – around, for example, animal welfare – who coalesce to overcome diffuseness. These organizations, from the anti-vivisectionist organizations of Victorian England to contemporary humane societies, may be able to use some of the dues collected to provide the public good of lobbying to promote the interests of their members. Another way is through the actions of political entrepreneurs who take advantage of high-salience public events to

---

[13] Mancur Olson. *The Logic of Collective Action* (Cambridge, MA: Harvard University Press, 1973).

mobilize, if however briefly, diffuse interests to express demand for policy change, thereby opening a policy window; for example, the melamine poisoning of pet food promoted public calls for federal action.

We usually think of concentrated interests as using their advantage to make economic gains that on net are bad for society. Indeed, political economists have a term for this political behavior: *rent seeking*.[14] However, the majoritarian success of mobilized diffuse interests can also result in inefficient and undesirable policies when relevant trade-offs are not considered. For example, stringent hunting bans may have adverse ecological effects, and blunt restrictions on the use of animals in medical research may prevent or delay the development of valuable medical treatments. At its best, economic analysis helps identify and, ideally, monetize trade-offs that might otherwise be ignored by either concentrated or diffuse interests.

8.4 RISE OF THE DESIGNER DOG(S)

Genetic analysis, especially phenotypic analysis that links observable characteristics to genes, is increasingly playing an important role in assessing individual behavioral traits within dog breeds. This research is just beginning to have an impact on the selection and training of working dogs. Chapter 7 cites important recent evidence based on large dog samples indicating that selection based on breed currently provides some useful information on behavior, but not that much. However, we expect that the continual development of phylogenetic knowledge about dogs to increasingly affect both the selection of, and training costs for, working dogs. In aggregate, we expect that expanded canine genetic knowledge will raise the cost of selection (because phenotypic research and analysis is expensive), but lower training costs as better selection reduces training costs. We also note that the distribution of these costs may well change as well. Most of the costs of genetic research are borne by universities, research institutes, and pharmaceutical companies rather than by dog owners. Most of the benefits of reduced training costs will probably accrue to public and nonprofit organizations that train future working dogs. Whatever the distributional consequences, however, any net changes represent real changes in social opportunity costs. We expect that phylogenetic knowledge that enables the more fine-grained creation of designer dogs will also continue to grow rapidly over the next decade.

---

[14] Anne O. Krueger. "The Political Economy of the Rent-Seeking Society." *American Economic Review* 64, no. 3 (1974): 291–303.

We further expect three additional types of designer dogs to increase in number and importance. First, we expect more dogs to be selected for home companionship based on pure breed hybridization, the popular cultural meaning of designer dog. Hybrid dog types and numbers have increased over the last decade. These hybrids are mostly the offspring of two purebreds and are becoming increasingly popular as household pets. These hybrids, such as goldendoodles and cockapoos, are widely perceived as possessing desirable characteristics, particularly superior hypoallergenic coats. It is certainly clear that hybridization within a species can increase heterozygosity and reduce some disease-causing alleles that are disproportionally present in the original breeds.[15] This kind of increased genetic diversity is intrinsically valuable, especially in the presence of small or isolated purebred parental populations. Describing and categorizing these dogs, however, is somewhat problematic because breed accreditation organizations do not recognize such hybrids (this does not seem to concern the dogs themselves, of course). However, some of the other advantages commonly attributed to these hybrids currently do not appear to be based on demonstrable scientific evidence.[16]

The second additional type of designer dog derives from the increasing recognition that dogs are superior "model species" as human homologues for genetically focused medical research. Dogs are generally superior human homologues to other species and even in some circumstances, to human samples.[17] As a species, dogs offer the unique benefit of genetic homogeneity within breeds and genetic heterogeneity across breeds that results from the presence of small initial founding breed populations (when breeds were created by artificial selection) and the subsequent selective breeding of dogs within the breed.[18] Minimal genetic diversity within breed, a so-called bottleneck, can usefully be used to study diseases related to human bottlenecks, especially the out-of-Africa genetic bottleneck that has resulted in less genetic variation for Eurasian than

---

[15] Lindsay L. Farrell, Jeffrey J. Schoenebeck, Pamela Wiener, Dylan N. Clements, and Kim M. Summers. "The Challenges of Pedigree Dog Health: Approaches to Combating Inherited Disease." *Canine Genetics and Epidemiology* 2, no. 1 (2015): 1–14.

[16] Bridget Hladky-Krage and Christy L. Hoffman. "Expectations versus Reality of Designer Dog Ownership in the United States." *Animals (Basel)* 12, no. 23 (2022): 1–13.

[17] Abigail L. Shearin and Elaine A. Ostrander. "Leading the Way: Canine Models of Genomics and Disease." *Disease Models & Mechanisms* 3, no. 1–2 (2010): 27–34.

[18] Canine genetics offers the prospect for efficient phenotypic analysis. See Nathan B. Sutter, Michael A. Eberle, Heidi G. Parker, Barbara J. Pullar, Ewen F. Kirkness, Leonid Kruglyak, and Elaine A. Ostrander. "Extensive and Breed-Specific Linkage Disequilibrium in *Canis Familiaris*." *Genome Research* 14, no. 12 (2004): 2388–2396.

African populations.[19] Further, research on the canine genome has facilitated the detailed mapping of almost 200 Mendelian traits and various disorders;[20] these factors allow the use of smaller sample sizes than are currently required in human disease associative studies. Interestingly, this kind of useful medical information is now being derived not only from standard genetic testing of dog samples, but also from canine breeding "natural experiments." A recent study of the so-called Chernobyl dogs shows they can provide valuable, indeed unique, information about the genetic effects of radiation over multiple generations.[21]

Some may disagree with our use of designer terminology for this purpose because it represents historical design, or selection, for very different purposes. We think it is appropriate and useful, even though it represents new wine in old bottles. We think it is important to highlight the emerging role of dogs for a number of reasons. For example, it will almost certainly result in some dogs living in institutional settings for much of their lives. It also raises ethical questions: Should the welfare of dogs serving as medical models be the same as for working dogs? Is the creation of these medical models humane?

The third additional type of designer dog we expect to increase in number is the cloned dog. In 1998, the birth of Dolly the sheep drew public attention to cloning. Since then, dog cloning has become both common and controversial. By 2022, over 1,500 dogs and approximately 20 percent of American Kennel Club breeds had been cloned.[22] Canine cloning is complex, and any deleterious impacts are likely to be subtle and probably multigenerational. However, cloners claim that the birth survival rates and longevities of cloned dogs are comparable to dogs resulting from sexual reproduction.[23] We can approach canine cloning

[19] Ning Yu, Feng-Chi Chen, Satoshi Ota, Lynn B. Jorde, Pekka Pamilo, Laszlo Patthy, Michele Ramsay, Trefor Jenkins, Song-Kun Shyue, and Wen-Hsiung Li. "Larger Genetic Differences within Africans than between Africans and Eurasians." *Genetics* 161, no. 1 (2002): 269–274.

[20] Jessica J. Hayward, Marta G. Castelhano, Kyle C. Oliveira, Elizabeth Corey, Cheryl Balkman, Tara L. Baxter, Margret L. Casal et al. "Complex Disease and Phenotype Mapping in the Domestic Dog." *Nature Communications* 7, no. 1 (2016): 1–11.

[21] Gabriella J. Spatola, Reuben M. Buckley, Megan Dillon, Emily V. Dutrow, Jennifer A. Betz, Małgorzata Pilot, Heidi G. Parker et al. "The Dogs of Chernobyl: Demographic Insights into Populations Inhabiting the Nuclear Exclusion Zone." *Science Advances* 9, no. 9 (2023): 1–16.

[22] P. Olof Olsson, Yeon W. Jeong, Yeonik Jeong, Mina Kang, Gang B. Park, Eunji Choi, Sun Kim, Mohammed S. Hossein, Young-Bum Son, and Woo S. Hwang. "Insights from One Thousand Cloned Dogs." *Scientific Reports* 12, no. 1 (2022): 1–10.

[23] Ibid.

adopting either a consequentialist or deontological ethical perspective.[24] As the economic perspective is inherently consequentialist, as is the neo-Darwinian interpretation of evolution, it is natural to consider the long-term consequences of dog cloning for the fitness of the species and whether cloning involves a negative externality.

At least at the current scale of cloning, there does not appear to be evidence that it is harmful to the fitness of the cloned dogs. However, the evolutionary dominance of sexual over asexual reproduction suggests caution. Sexual reproduction is generally more costly to species than asexual reproduction: the necessity of keeping males around at the population level and the need for devoting energy to germ cells at the individual level.[25] Indeed, John Maynard Smith, whom we encounter in Chapter 2 as a pioneer of evolutionary game theory, saw the dominance of sexual reproduction as a puzzle.[26] One possible answer, the so-called Red Queen hypothesis, is that coevolving parasites of a species act to select against asexual genotypes because sexual reproduction and the mutations it produces speed up the production of new genotypes that are more resistant to parasites. This running in place (as Alice was forced to do in Wonderland when she was with the Red Queen) allows a species to escape parasites that are only adapted to the prior generations of that species.[27]

As asexual reproduction, cloning forgoes the benefits of the genetic variation produced through sexual reproduction. The loss of genetic variation potentially poses a risk to cloned lineages of dogs. Therefore, if cloning becomes widespread, it could put the species at risk. Because those providing the cloning do not bear the full costs of these risks, cloning may involve a negative externality.

Will the cloning of dogs become widespread? Currently, its high costs deter all but the wealthiest. However, as price falls from improving technology and economies of scale, breeders may be tempted to use cloning

---

[24] Autumn Fiester. "Ethical Issues in Animal Cloning." *Perspectives in Biology and Medicine* 48, no. 3 (2005): 328–343.

[25] Amanda K. Gibson, Lynda F. Delph, and Curtis M. Lively. "The Two-Fold Cost of Sex: Experimental Evidence from a Natural System." *Evolution Letters* 1, no. 1 (2017): 6–15.

[26] J. Maynard Smith. *The Evolution of Sex* (New York, NY: Cambridge University Press, 1978).

[27] The Red Queen hypothesis is only one potentially relevant explanation. For an overview of possible explanations, see Tim F. Cooper, Richard E. Lenski, and Santiago F. Elena. "Parasites and Mutational Load: An Experimental Test of a Pluralistic Theory for the Evolution of Sex." *Proceedings of the Royal Society B: Biological Sciences* 272, no. 1560 (2005): 311–317.

to produce breed-exemplary dogs: the economic incentives to cater to fads could thus result in the rapid growth in the percentage of cloned dogs in the dog population. Further, many dog lovers will undoubtedly be tempted to replicate their departed pets with genetically identical puppies. Indeed, as people generally have greater longevity than dogs, one can imagine a family having a series of genetically identical pets over the years, each receiving improved socialization and training based on experience with earlier versions! This cloning would provide an opportunity to redo the parenting of dogs, which is not available for children. Thus, cloning poses a long-term risk through the incentives for its use on both the supply and demand sides of the market.

8.5 CONCLUSION

We began this book with the musings of Angus Lordie about why people bring dogs into their lives. Like the best fictional characters, he asked an interesting and meaningful question. We have enjoyed analyzing the extent to which economic concepts can help answer his question as well as better understand the various decisions people make that shape their relationships with dogs. We hope that those who read this book primarily because "Dog" is in the title found enough substance – we have certainly learned a lot more about dogs in writing it, and we have done our best to convey the most interesting and important things we have learned about them. We also hope that those who read the book primarily because "Economics" is in the title appreciate our applications of economic concepts. We will also be pleased if readers from other disciplines who are new to economics see its value as at least providing a somewhat useful lens for making sense of human behavior in contexts with some economic, writ broadly, content.

Glossary of Economic Terms

Absolute advantage: the capacity of one entity for producing a good at a lower cost than another entity.

Adverse selection: the purchasing of insurance by those who have greater risks than the average risk of the pool of potential purchasers at the offered price. It results from *hidden information*. For example, insurers may set premiums for pet insurance based on observable characteristics of dogs, but through familiarity with their dogs, owners may be able to make a better prediction of the risk of loss than the insurer. Owners who expect veterinary expenses greater than the insurer are more likely to find the purchase attractive than those who expect the average expenses predicted by the insurer.

Agency loss: the monetary value of the difference between the actions taken by agents and those that would best promote the interests of their principals. For example, veterinarians may recommend expensive treatments that do not promote the owners' preferences over the suffering and longevity of their dogs.

Allocative efficiency: an allocation of goods such that it would not be possible to identify an alternative allocation that would make at least one person better off without making anyone else worse off. In practical application to markets, an allocation is efficient if it maximizes *social surplus.*

Altruism: regard by one person for another person's wellbeing. Economists often model altruism as the consumption, income, or *utility* of one person appearing in the utility function of another. Families generally display reciprocal altruism among their members, perhaps effectively extending personhood to their dogs so that their wellbeing affects the utility of the human family members.

Behavioral economics: the branch of economics that seeks to integrate psychology and economics in order to understand the consumption choices that people make. It focuses especially on choices that apparently deviate from the rationality of constrained optimization. The empirical branch tests whether, and to what degree, choices appear irrational. For example, people may ignore, or grossly underestimate, the known health risks of a particular breed in choosing their dogs.

Coherent Preferences: preferences are coherent for a set of alternatives if the individual has a transitive ordering over all the relevant alternatives. Transitive simply means that if the person prefers alternative A to alternative B and alternative B to alternative C, then that person prefers alternative A over alternative C. Neoclassical models often impose stronger restrictions on preferences to guarantee solutions. For example, models often assume that consumers prefer more of a good to less of it, but that the value they place on incremental units goes down as they consume more of the good. That is, there is declining marginal utility.

Comparative advantage: a theory that explains the possibility for mutual gains from trade between two entities even when one entity has an *absolute advantage* in the production of all the traded goods. The underlying mechanism is *opportunity cost*: if the two entities have different opportunity costs in terms of how many units of one good they must give up to get an additional unit of another good, then there is the possibility of mutually beneficial trade by the entities based on specialization to exploit the lower opportunity cost of one of the entities.

Comparative statics: the differences in equilibrium prices and quantities that result from an exogenous change to a market. The concept can be extended to non-market models with equilibria.

Complements: goods that tend to be consumed together. If the price of a good increases, then less of it and its complement are demanded. Children and dogs are complements for a family if having children shifts the *demand schedule* for dogs upward.

Concentrated interest: situations in which one or a small number of economic actors can potentially obtain large benefits or avoid large costs from political activity. The concentration of the costs or benefits in a small group increases the chances that its members can successfully cooperate to gain favorable public policies.

Consumer durables: commodities that are intended to provide services multiple times. For example, unlike a dog treat that is consumed once, a dog leash will be used multiple times, perhaps over multiple years. The rational assessment of the value of consumer durables thus requires potential purchasers to take account of the stream of future services they are likely to provide.

Consumer surplus: in a market, the difference between the value of consumption of good and the expenditure consumers must make to obtain it.

Demand schedule: the quantity of a good demanded at each price. It is also a *marginal valuation schedule*.

Diffuse interests: a situation in which a large number of economic actors bear the costs or benefits of public policies: costs or benefits may be large in aggregate but small for any individual. Favorable policies for a diffuse interest have the characteristics of a *public good* and therefore are likely to be undersupplied.

Elasticity: the percentage change in one quantity that results from a one percent change in another. For example, the price elasticity of demand is the percentage change in the quantity demanded for a one percent change in price.

Endowment effect: in the absence of learning new information about the quality of the good during ownership, a higher valuation of an owned good than the same good before it is owned.

Evolutionary stable strategy (ESS): in an evolutionary game, a phenotype (specification of what an individual will do in any choice situation), such that if all members of the population adopt it, no mutant phenotype can successfully invade the population through natural selection. It could be a *pure strategy* as would be the case if the game had the structure of the Prisoner's Dilemma. It would be a *mixed strategy* as in the Hawk–Dove Game when fighting costs exceed the value of the resource. Note that the mixed strategy ESS, which allows both phenotypes to exist in the population in a specific proportion, requires the assumption of pairwise random interaction among the population members.

Experience good: a good (or service) whose quality can only be fully assessed after consumption. For example, new owners of puppies may only discover behavioral problems once they bring them home.

Exponential discounting: the current (present) value of a cost or benefit that accrues in a future time period such that the fractional reduction from one period to the next is constant. If δ is the fractional reduction per period, then the current value of a cost of C accruing N periods in the future is $\delta^N C$. Exponential discounting is employed in cost–benefit analysis with $\delta = 1/(1+d)$, where d is the social discount rate.

Hidden action: actions taken by agents in principal–agent relationships that cannot be fully observed by their principals. It underlies *moral hazard* in insurance markets. It enables agent behavior that can increase *agency cost*.

Hidden information: informational asymmetry in principal–agent relationships that favors the agents. It underlies *adverse selection* in insurance markets. It enables agent behavior that can increase *agency cost*.

Incomplete contracts: agreements between parties that do not fully specify rights and duties under all possible contingencies. The more complex and the longer the time horizon of contracts, the more likely that an unspecified contingency will arise.

Indifference curve: the set of the consumption bundles that provide the same level of *utility* to an individual, so that the individual is indifferent about which bundle he or she receives. For example, a person may be indifferent between on one hand a dog with simple furniture and on the other hand no dog and fancy furniture.

Information asymmetry: a market failure that occurs when one party to an exchange has information that, if provided to the other party, would change that party's participation in the exchange. For example, the sellers of puppies generally have more information about the care that the puppies received prior to sale than do the buyers. Information asymmetry is most economically relevant if having the information would have resulted in a buyer not purchasing the puppy.

Institutional economics: the branch of economics that considers how the evolution and content of institutions affect economic behavior. Institutions in this context are fairly stable sets of formal and informal rules that coordinate or constrain the behaviors of individuals in social, political, and economic interactions.

Marginal cost schedule: at each level of supply of a good, the marginal cost of producing an additional unit of the good. The marginal cost schedule is the *supply schedule*.

Marginal valuation schedule: at each level of consumption of a good, the marginal value of consuming an additional unit of the good. The marginal value schedule is the *demand schedule*.

Market failures: those situations in which the equilibrium price and quantity in a market result in an inefficient allocation of goods or resources.

It occurs when a reallocation of goods or resources would provide greater total benefit to those who gain from the reallocation than total costs to those who lose from it. A market failure, like *information asymmetry*, results in a failure of the market to maximize *social surplus*.

Mixed strategy: a strategy in a game that involves randomizing over *pure strategies*. For example, a mixed strategy in the Hawk–Dove Game would involve playing Hawk with some probability p and playing Dove with probability $1-p$.

Moral hazard: the reduced incentive of insurees to prevent compensable losses. For example, dog owners with pet insurance may be less vigorous in assessing the necessity of veterinary care than they would be if they did not have insurance.

Nash equilibrium: a set of strategies for the players such that no player could unilaterally increase his or her payoff by changing strategy. For example, always defecting is a Nash equilibrium in the Prisoner's Dilemma Game. Games may have multiple Nash equilibria. For example, the Hawk–Dove Game has two *pure strategy* equilibria and one *mixed-strategy* equilibrium.

Negative externality: a negative impact resulting from any action that affects someone who did not fully consent to it through participation in a voluntary exchange. These can occur in production, such as when dogs used for breeding by puppy mills end up in shelters, or in consumption, such as when owners keep dogs in their yards whose barking disturbs neighbors.

Neoclassical economics: the dominant branch of economics that seeks to explain behavior in terms of constrained optimization. It assumes consumers have, or act as if they have, utility functions that allow them to rank the desirability of alternative bundles of goods they could consume. They are assumed to choose the bundles providing the highest levels of utility subject to satisfying any constraints they face, such as their disposable income and available time. Producers seek to maximize profits by choosing inputs and products that maximize their profits. Equilibria result from the interaction of consumers and producers in markets.

Opportunity cost: the value of a resource in its next best alternative use. For example, the opportunity cost of time spent caring for a sick dog is the forgone value of that time in either work or leisure.

Optimism bias: overestimating the probability of positive outcomes and underestimating the probability of negative outcomes. For example, potential dog owners may be aware of the objective health risk associated with a particular breed of dog, but they may subjectively assess the breed risks that they face to be lower.

Pareto efficiency: an allocation is Pareto efficient if it is impossible to make someone better off without making anyone else worse off. A Pareto improvement does make someone better off without making anyone else worse off. A potential Pareto improvement would create sufficient gains so that someone could be made better off without making anyone else worse off if the benefits to those who gain are sufficiently large so that, if those who lose could be fully compensated, the result would be a Pareto improvement.

Post-experience good: a good (or service) whose quality cannot be fully assessed even after consumption. For example, a specific dog food may have an ingredient that increases the risk of canine cancer but only several years after consumption. If the supplier of the dog food either knew of the risk or should have known about it through best practice, then the post-experience good represents a particularly wicked *information asymmetry*.

Producer surplus: in a market, the difference between the revenue that suppliers receive for a good and the cost of supplying it.

Property rights: the relations among people concerning the use of things. Formal (de jure) property rights specify who has legal rights of use and who has legal duties to respect those rights. De facto property rights are the uses for which duties can be enforced.

Public good: a pure public good is one that is nonrivalrous and nonexcludable. Nonrivalrous means that everyone consumes the good being provided; nonexcludable means that no one can be prevented from consuming it. The classic example is national defense: everyone consumes the same level of defense provided without reducing the consumption of anyone else and no one can be prevented from consuming it.

Pure strategy: playing one of the possible strategies with certainty. For example, in the Hawk–Dove Game playing Hawk with certainty is a pure strategy; playing Dove with certainty is an alternative pure strategy. In contrast, randomizing over these strategies is a *mixed strategy*.

Rent seeking: the activity of *concentrated interests* aimed at securing public policies that restrict competition to create economic profits, or rents. The restrictions result in economic inefficiency. Competition among concentrated interests may add to inefficiency by dissipating the rents. A classic example is competition among nobles for a royal monopoly on production of salt.

Repeated game: the repetition of a *stage game* either a fixed or random number of times. Cooperative equilibria may be possible even when they are not in the stage game. For example, in the Hunting Game, *the Nash equilibrium* in the stage game is mutual hoarding, but if the probability of playing another round is sufficiently high, then mutual sharing can be a Nash equilibrium.

Revealed preference method: estimation of economic values of interest from observed choices people actually make when engaging in economic activity. For example, a demand schedule for cigarettes might be estimated by comparing consumption rates in states with different cigarette taxes. Because most observed behaviors are influenced by many factors, sophisticated statistical analyses are usually required to make valid, or at least convincing, inferences about the economic values.

Search good: a good whose quality can be fully assessed prior to purchase. Although consumers may have to spend resources searching for a desirable combination of price and quality, search goods usually do not involve serious *information asymmetry*.

Shadow price: an imputed unit value of a good that is not traded in a market. Rather than price being revealed in the "light" of the market, it must be found indirectly in the shadows. Economists can sometime develop shadow prices by observing behaviors related to the non-traded good (revealed preference methods) but must sometimes turn to survey methods to ask respondents about their valuations of goods (stated preference methods).

Social surplus: in a market, the difference between the value of the good supplied and its cost of supply. It is the sum of *consumer surplus* and *producer surplus*.

Stage game: the structure of a game for one round of play.

Stated preference method: estimation of economic values from responses people make to questions in survey experiments that randomize some variable to assess its causal relationship to some other value. The most common stated preference method is contingent valuation, which environmental economists developed to value changes in environmental amenities. For example, to estimate a population's willingness to pay for some environmental amenity, such as cleaner air in a national park, a sample of the population is asked about support for the policy if it would raise their taxes by an amount randomly assigned to individuals by the experiment.

Substitutes: goods that provide alternative ways of gaining some consumption value. If the price of one of these goods increases, then the *demand schedule* for the other good shifts upward, resulting in an increase in its consumption. For example, if children and dogs are substitutes, then if the price of raising children increases so fewer children are added to the family, the demand for dogs increases.

Supply schedule: the quantity of a good supplied to a market at each price. It is also the *marginal cost schedule.*

Transaction costs: the sum of the resource costs required to create and enforce property rights and the resulting *agency loss.* Economically efficient contracts minimize transaction costs.

Transfers: increased costs borne by one party that are exactly offset by benefits to another party. For example, a per unit excise tax on a good reduced the quantity supplied and demanded, an economic efficiency effect, but also a transfer of money from consumers and producers to the government from the revenue collected on the inframarginal units of the good than continue to be supplied and demanded.

Unique advantage: the capacity for producing a good that cannot otherwise be produced. In the context in which firms have unique advantages, such as location, it would be called a firm-specific advantage. In the advertising literature, it would be called a differential advantage.

Utility: an index of satisfaction derived from some bundle of consumed goods. It assigns higher scores to more preferred bundles of goods through a utility function. In neoclassical consumer theory, an individual chooses the bundle of goods (including leisure) that maximize his or her utility.

Value of statistical dog life (VSDL): a shadow price for changes in premature dog deaths. It can be imputed from the average of the implicit values the members of a population put on their dogs' lives in making decisions about tradeoffs between small changes in the dogs' mortality risk and other things of value. For example, the VSDL can be estimated from people's willingness to pay for a vaccine that will reduce the risk of their dogs dying from a disease.

Value of statistical life (VSL): a shadow price for changes in premature human deaths. It can be imputed from the average of the implicit values that the members of a population put on their own lives in making decisions about tradeoffs between small changes in mortality risk and other things of value. For example, the VSL can be estimated from the differences in wages paid for otherwise identical jobs except for different levels of mortality risk.

Index

Printed in the United States
by Baker & Taylor Publisher Services